CW00537588

BOURDIEU, LANGUAGE-BASED ETHNOGRAPHIES AND REFLEXIVITY

Offering a unique and original perspective on Bourdieu, language-based ethnographies and reflexivity, this volume provides a nuanced, in-depth discussion of the complex relationship between these interconnected topics and their impact in real-world contexts. Part I opens the book with an overview of the historical background and development of language-based ethnographic research and Bourdieu's work in this space. Part II presents a series of case studies that highlight a Bourdieusian perspective and demonstrate how reflexivity impacts on language-based ethnography. In each study, Bourdieu's conceptual framework of reflexively-informed objectivity examines the ways in which the studies themselves were constructed and understood. Building on Parts I and II, the concluding set of chapters in Part III unpack the messiness of the theory and practice of language-based ethnography, and provides insights into what reflexivity means for Bourdieu in practical contexts. Arguing for a greater reflexive understanding in research practice, this volume sets an agenda for future literacy and language research.

Michael Grenfell is Emeritus Professor at the Southampton Education School at University of Southampton, UK.

Kate Pahl is Professor of Arts and Literacy at Manchester Metropolitan University, UK.

BOURDIEU, LANGUAGE-BASED ETHNOGRAPHIES AND REFLEXIVITY

Putting Theory into Practice

Michael Grenfell and Kate Pahl

WITH CONTRIBUTIONS FROM
CHERYL McLEAN, CATHERINE COMPTON-LILLY
AND LISYA SELONI

Routledge
Taylor & Francis Group

NEW YORK AND LONDON

First published 2019
by Routledge
711 Third Avenue, New York, NY 10017

and by Routledge
2 Park Square, Milton Park, Abingdon, Oxon, OX14 4RN

Routledge is an imprint of the Taylor & Francis Group, an informa business

© 2019 Taylor & Francis

The right of Michael Grenfell and Kate Pahl to be identified as authors of this work has been asserted by them in accordance with sections 77 and 78 of the Copyright, Designs and Patents Act 1988.

All rights reserved. No part of this book may be reprinted or reproduced or utilised in any form or by any electronic, mechanical, or other means, now known or hereafter invented, including photocopying and recording, or in any information storage or retrieval system, without permission in writing from the publishers.

Trademark notice: Product or corporate names may be trademarks or registered trademarks, and are used only for identification and explanation without intent to infringe.

Library of Congress Cataloging-in-Publication Data
Names: Grenfell, Michael, 1953– author. | Pahl, Kate, author.
Title: Bourdieu, language-based ethnographies and reflexivity : putting theory into practice / Michael Grenfell and Kate Pahl ; with contributions from Cheryl McClean, Catherine Compton-Lilly and Lisya Seloni.
Description: New York, NY : Routledge, 2019. |
Includes bibliographical references and index. |
Description based on print version record and CIP data provided by publisher; resource not viewed.
Identifiers: LCCN 2018027977 (print) | LCCN 2018043511 (ebook) |
ISBN 9781315205151 (ebook) | ISBN 9781351793162 (ebook) |
ISBN 9781351793179 (ebook) | ISBN 9781351793155 (ebook) |
ISBN 9781138645271 (hardback) | ISBN 9781138652262 (pbk.) |
ISBN 9781315205151 (ebook)
Subjects: LCSH: Language and culture. | Literacy—Social aspects. |
Sociolinguistics. | Bourdieu, Pierre, 1930–2002.
Classification: LCC P35 (ebook) | LCC P35 .G74 2019 (print) |
DDC 306.44—dc23
LC record available at https://lccn.loc.gov/2018027977

ISBN: 978-1-138-64527-1 (hbk)
ISBN: 978-1-138-65226-2 (pbk)
ISBN: 978-1-315-20515-1 (ebk)

Typeset in Bembo
by Florence Production Ltd, Stoodleigh, Devon, UK

CONTENTS

INTRODUCTION

Each of the main themes contained in the title of this book represent significant areas in the research and academic literature. Such is true if we were to take them individually; it is even more so if we consider them together - as inextricably linked. And, yet, the linkages between them are often allowed to exist implicitly within an overall scholarly discussion, or remain half-articulated. It is just such a relative oversight that this book seeks to address. It does so by taking as its topic the *relationship* between Bourdieu's theory of practice as developed in language-based ethnographies with a special focus on the workings of reflexivity within such research endeavours. Over the course of the book, we go from theory – in each area – to practice and back to theory again, with a scoping arch that creates a kind of iterative reflexive narrative leading us to a point of greater practical and theoretical understanding in terms of its interconnecting strands.

Of course, Pierre Bourdieu is now considered the leading intellectual in his generation; one that contained many other prominent thinkers who shaped much of our understandings of the world from the second half of the twentieth century – for example, Foucault, Derrida, Barthes, Althusser, Lacan, Deleuze, Lyotard, etc. This group shared quite a wide spread of disciplinary specialisms, including history, philosophy and psychology. Bourdieu own orientation can be considered as *social philosophy*. In fact, his original academic training was in philosophy; but this was somewhat displaced when he was thrust into the very real violent experience of colonial war in Algeria in the 1950s during his military service. He turned towards ethnography and anthropology somewhat as an escape mechanism: to make sense of the world and what was going on around him. Here, he saw issues of identity and cultural practice, the old and the new, the disruptions of social structures and the way such played out in contemporary politics. In a sense, he understood all this in terms of a practical application of the philosophy disciplines in which he had been trained. No wonder the resultant method was presented as a theory *of* practice. At is heart was a methodological approach and a series of conceptual tools used to explicate social phenomena. As well as voluminous accounts of Algeria at a point of transformation, he took the same approach to other areas of French life: peasant farmers, education, culture, etc. In each area, he was able to elucidate the grounding structures of the field as well as their generating principles. What he found was commonalities of cause and effect, even if they were played out in vastly different arenas.

In this book, we at one point describe these studies as making up "an anthropology of modern France". Of course, anthropology is hardly a "new" discipline area, and men and women have studied each other's cultures for millennia. However, such activities became more formally expressed and institutionalised in the nineteenth and early twentieth centuries, as the world opened up through commercial travel, and indeed colonialisation (Algeria was colonised by the French in 1832). Discovering different, often exotic cultures, only encouraged scholars and philanthropic missionaries to record the worlds which surrounded them. Such an expanse of the field led to a still greater formalisation of method and form, and there are now "classic" texts based on early anthropological studies. What happened as a significant development in the second half of the twentieth century is the way that anthropology became an influential source of method for a much larger range of research activities in the social sciences. So, for example, researchers began to appreciate that the same cultural approach to enquiry could be taken to all sorts of others areas of human endeavour: for example, the professions, education, art, politics, social class, race, etc. Often, such an approach was termed "ethnography" or "ethnology", which clearly connect with their anthropological antecedents. We shall explore the fine differences between these terms in the proceeding chapters. Their research practice then clearly drew on an extensive selection of philosophical sources in elucidating methodological rationale, including writers mentioned in the previous paragraph. Such writers often took "language" as their starting point, since it had become a grounding issue in twentieth century intellectual discourse. Questions such as what was language? and what were its potentialities and limits? became central to philosophical enquiry, as was the analogy between the structure of language and the structure of the human world. Little surprise, therefore, that many ethnographers took language as being their key research focus in investigations when going out "in the field". They would concentrate on differences in the speech patterns and linguistics habits between social classes and sub-groups, regions, educational institutions and professions – to name but a view. The "speech event" became a significant social analytical unit in studying the way human interaction was shaped by and reflected in language. Again, "classic" language-based ethnographies appeared and these will be set out later in the book.

Ethnography has been described as a "culture studying culture", and it was not long before researchers themselves realised that their own research background should also be considered as a cultural field, and indeed including its own ways of doing things, with words and otherwise. All the more need, therefore, to take the researcher and the research as its own topic of objectification, as a way of understanding how its activity was structured as well as the language used to express its findings. These preoccupations formed the bases of a "reflexive" attitude to the research; where the researcher made explicit their own cultural dispositions and presumptions in articulating their scholarly stance. Indeed, pushed to an extreme, some writers concluded that any interpretation of ethnographic data should even be seen as an adulteration of cultural authenticity leading invariably to a kind of symbolic act of violence on the researched. Others attempted to get around these arguments by reverting to literary forms in expressing their findings as "poetics", or indeed, taking a robust political stance over the researcher and the researched. Such are some of the elements of reflexivity similarly addressed in later chapters of the book.

In taking *Bourdieu, Language-based Ethnographies and Reflexivity* as our main themes, we as the book's authors clearly believe that there is a significant connection between them, which we aim to build on over its chapters. It is divided into three parts.

Part I really lays the foundational bases for the rest of the book; so, each of its chapters is in turn dedicated to Language-based ethnographies, reflexivity and Bourdieu. The first chapter lays out a discussion of the chronological development of ethnography as a salient methodological approach to the study of language behaviours in social situ. We see the way language featured in such ethnographies and the special focus given to literary practice. Classic studies are referred to. We also see development in principles of enquiries over time, including the post-modern, multimodal and digital. In short, the chapter presents the language-based ethnographic research field in itself. As noted above, reflexivity is inherent in ethnographic enquiry. Chapter 2 then deals with this topic. Again, a somewhat historical overview is taken in tracing back and through time the antecedents of reflexivity in philosophical and social science research since the Enlightenment project of the seventeenth, eighteenth and nineteenth centuries. Critical to this development is, as noted, language and its role both in human activity and under-standing. What it is, or can be, to reflect is highlighted and from a range of theoretical perspectives. These include both the instrumental and the most abstract, the utilitarian and post-modern. We see these as "possibilities" and "potentials". The chapter leads to a consideration of the way reflexivity may operate in a language-ethnography, and indeed offers an example from the relatively new field of *Linguistic Ethnography*. This exemplar provides us with food for thought over what can be and what might yet be. The third chapter in Part I formally presents Bourdieu, his theory of practice and the centrality of reflexivity to it. We begin with some biographical information, which sets a basis for understanding his intellectual trajectory. We consider his theory of practice, its underlying rationale and define its key concepts. Much of this discussion deals with issues of epistemology, and we again focus on language and its operation within research activity. We consider the principal anthropologies he carried out and the perspective findings they gave rise to. Finally, the chapter offers an introduction to what Bourdieu understand by reflexivity – what he referred to as "participant objectivation" – and how it may be operationised in practice.

This final part of Chapter 3 acts as a kind of springboard to Part II. In this part we present four sets of researchers working on language-based ethnographies. Each of them has their own special arena of activity, and indeed motive and understanding. Their approach varies, as does their way of articulating both their method and findings. However, as well as being language ethnographers, our contributors in Part II chapters all share a common interest and intent to use a Bourdieusian perspective and method in their research, and are committed in particular to operating according to his principles of reflexivity. Again, interpretation and application vary, but we see that as a positive advantage in highlighting various dimensions to what reflexivity can be in the research field as carried out though individual projects. Diversity and commonality are therefore key themes in reading the Part II chapters.

Part III takes these chapters as its *point de départ*. So, in the first chapter in Part III we consider Part II in overview: what did each of the chapter highlight?; what did our contributors share and differ over?; how did they use Bourdieu and to what extent?; what did his method mean for them within a reflexive medium?; indeed, what were strengths and shortcomings in the approach? Both Part II and the first chapter of Part III present the reality of language-based ethnographical research practice in all its messiness, and the way sense emerges from it. In a way, Chapter 8 can be seen a "reflection on a reflection". This theme is taken one stage further in our final full chapter of the book which returns us to the theory we began with. Chapter 9 is consequently a theoretical reflection of a practical reflection on a practical reflection. In it, we try to distill out further principled and methodological points from a theory *about* and *of* practice. We re-assert what reflexivity is for Bourdieu and what it can mean in this practical context. At the same time, we build on Bourdieu's own writings and, in the light of Parts I and II of the book, we develop areas and dimensions of reflexive practice as a way of suggesting to future researchers what this might be and how to set about doing it.

The book then concludes with some final comments by way of over view of the journey we have taken in it.

In a sense, it is a journey that every reader can define for themselves and, to this extent, there are accordingly various ways of reading this book. For example, it may be read chronologically from Part I through to Parts II and III, taking in the theoretical outset, the practical exemplification and the distillation and synthesis of these in Part III to a greater understanding of what reflexivity can be in language-based ethnographic practice. Some might begin with the practical chapters in Part II before reading backwards to the theoretical underpinnings to the activities set out in these research accounts and then forward to the "advanced" forms of reflexivity suggested by them. Still others might begin at this endpoint and then dip into previous chapters as and when is necessary according to individual perspectives and the groundings they provide. Whatever way the reader selects, we are sure to have provided an exegetic text here, one that will equally inform and stimulate both interest in and indeed readiness for developing a greater reflexive understanding in research practice in these and other areas.

Finally, we see reflexivity as a notion that is both ubiquitous in a range of research literature and activity, yet curiously underused in terms of developing our comprehension of language as both subject and object of study. Wherever that leads, it is our intent to steer towards it.

PART I

Theoretical Perspectives

Language-based Ethnographies, Reflexivity and Bourdieu

Introduction

In this first part of the book, we dedicate a chapter to each of our main themes: Language-based ethnographies, Reflexivity and Bourdieu.

In the first chapter, we set out the range of issues, which have shaped the research field of language ethnographies over the decades. A chronological approach is taken as we see the way that interests in language behaviours grew out of traditional anthropological and ethnographic research. We consider the "classic" language-focused ethnographies and both what they set out to do and what they did in fact discover. However, this retrospective account is also framed by contemporary concerns including the multimodal and the digital. The whole provides a context for the practical chapters in Part II.

The second chapter addresses our theme of reflexivity. This account is set within a historical context as a way of showing how issues of knowledge developed in philosophy and how such concerns shaped research practice. We consider the relationship between knowledge and the knower, as well as the significant role that language plays in it. This discussion then looks at language per se and the kind of twentieth century developments, which shaped our understanding of it, and the impact such had on our knowledge fields; all this as a prelude to considering reflexivity and the place of language in its operation. Various approaches to reflexivity are considered including the positivist and the post-modern. Finally, we look at Linguistic Ethnography as a way of highlighting how a research field *does* reflexivity, and what are its limits.

The third chapter deals with Bourdieu. After a brief biographical account of his intellectual trajectory, we consider his methodology in terms of the theory of practice according to which he worked and the main conceptual tools he used.

These tools are also examined in terms of their own underlying epistemological rationale – how significant are they? The chapter discusses a range of Bourdieu's own ethnographic research; in the Béarn, Algeria, Education and Culture. We see something of his ethnographic field theory in practice. Central to his project was reflexivity. An introduction to this is given in terms of the relationship between the research subject and object, and the biases that this necessarily entails. The chapter concludes with some introductory remarks concerning "participant objectivation", which was Bourdieu's main method for operationalising reflexivity in practice. We see what it is and how to do it.

All these chapters are seen as providing the main foundational bases: first, for the chapters in Part II, which are practically orientated towards actual empirical projects and the way researchers saw reflexivity within them; and second, Part III, where we both draw out the salient issues of reflexivity as demonstrated by the Part II accounts, and then take up and extend our discussion of what reflexivity is and can be from a Bourdieusian point of view.

1

LANGUAGE-BASED ETHNOGRAPHIES

Kate Pahl

Introduction

This chapter provides a chronological discussion of a history of language and literacy ethnographies as they have emerged in North America and the UK in recent decades. It does not pretend to be exhaustive; rather here the work in this book is situated within a historical context. This approach brings some specific aspects of the field to the reader's attention, in preparation for the chapters to come. Particular aspects of the disciplinary area are highlighted that are important throughout the book. These include the changing way that the word "literacy" has been used and the developing emphasis on everyday models of literacy and language. With these has come a slow collapse of the certainties concerning literacy studies due to the development of post-modern epistemological positions. In this discussion, the definition of the word "literacy" moves from being something anchored in writing and skills, to a more nuanced idea from the New Literacy Studies of literacy as a social practice, to a further understanding that some of what we might call "literacy" has features that cannot always be representational and are not tied to written forms. In this way, we see how the study of language within an ethnographic framework is itself represented and contested. In other words, by discussing the field of language-based ethnographies, the field itself becomes subject to discussion.

Our *point de départ* is that the study of language and literacy practices in schools and communities has drawn principally on ethnography as a methodology. Indeed, the focus has been on naturalistic modes of inquiry that privilege the local, and particular, with an attention to unfolding events captured through detailed naturalistic methodologies (see Hymes, 1996; Maybin, 2006; Rampton, 2007a). It is a field that has developed and grown over the years, with a number of linked traditions and methodological genealogies, including those of social anthropology and ethnography. It has diversified, however, in response to new challenges. These include considerations of what literacy and language practices are in practice and how they can be described (see Baynham and Prinsloo, 2009; Parkin, 2016; Rowsell and Pahl, 2015). In fact, not only has the field shifted in terms of epistemological ways of knowing in order to encompass far wider practices than just writing, it has shifted substantially in terms of what and how as researchers we come to know and what can be known. These shifts have particularly been located in modes of enquiry that can be seen to have "de-centred" linguistic paradigms as central. Indeed, scholarship has subsequently focused more on the multimodal (Kress, 1997), the sensory and embodied (Leander and Boldt, 2013) and the post-human and new materialism (Braidotti, 2013; Kuby, Gutshall Rucker, and Kirchhofer, 2015). There has, therefore, been a shift away from modernist conceptualisations of language and literacy to less certain post-modern understandings of what has been understood to be important within the field of literacy and language ethnographies. Moreover, post-human and new materialist positions, as exemplified by a number of recent journal special issues (for example, Kuby and Rowsell, 2017), have appeared alongside other shifts. The work of Karen Barad (2007), for example, enables a re-thinking of the ways that the relationship between humans and objects could be conceived of. Literacy researchers have also begun to incorporate "more-than human ontologies" into their theoretical understandings of literacy and language (Kuby et al., 2015). These new positions are discussed more fully in Chapter 8.

The chapter addresses such histories of language ethnographies. The complex and shifting world of the New Literacy Studies, and its diversifications across contexts, will be delineated. In the rest of the book, and after the four contextually rich chapters that follow in Part II, the thread of this discussion will be taken up once more in reflecting on how the new field of language-based ethnography is emerging. We shall trace the ways in which literacy and language ethnographies have changed and adapted to new contexts. This contextual information will both situate the data chapters, but bring a rich argument to bear on the potential of Bourdieu's reflexivity as described by Grenfell in this volume.

It is important to emphasise again the way that ethnographies of language and literacy grew from a concern that there was an insufficient understanding of the everyday, as opposed to largely prescriptive, psychological or cognitive models of literacy. Initially (from the early 1980s to the early 2000s), language and literacy practices were understood within language ethnographies as being "situated" and located within "practice"; studies were rooted in everyday settings and drew on naturalistic data (see for example, Heath, 1983; Street, 1993; Barton and Hamilton, 1998; Barton, Hamilton and Ivanic, 2000). These lenses enabled richer understandings of what people did with literacy to come to the surface. Studying literacy and language closely revealed practices that lay outside of the education context to be rich and contextually different. This insight implied a shift in ways of knowing and conceptualising literacy with a renewed focus on the nature of the contexts for literacy and language research (see Duranti and Goodwin, 1992).

These shifts in approach led to a more pluralistic understanding of the relationship between methods and methodologies, and opened up epistemological as well as ontological uncertainties. While epistemologies might be about knowing, ontological understandings included a more physically grounded "state of being" in literacy. As Parkin (2016: 81) suggested, "the ontological is about being and presence, and, as such is commonly expressed through the body or body parts". These new understandings of literacy led to a shift in perspective within the study of literacy and language ethnographies. The field then became even more diverse as digital, multimodal and maker perspectives informed theory on the "situated" nature of literacies and language (Rowsell et al., 2016). The beginnings of the "New Literacy Studies" and the *turn* to the social had derived from an interest in language and literacy practices in everyday and within situated language contexts. As suggested above, part of the reason for the "turn" to the social was that the field previously had focused on reified accounts of language that did not recognise the shifting, everyday nature of language practice. A ground-breaking response to autonomous models of language was Halliday's *Language as Social Semiotic* (1978), which acknowledged the situated nature of linguistic interactions. This developed partly as a response to ways in which language had been traditionally reified or codified into systems that could be named or aspired to. However, what people *did* with literacy and language was less commonly understood. The concept of "situated literacy practices" recognised what was going on with literacy and language in the everyday (see for example, Street, 1984). The "turn" in research that concentrated on understanding what people do with literacy and language had diversified, and was then extended to include multimodal, visual, affective and digital literacy practices (see Rowsell and Pahl, 2015). New understandings of digital, material, (im)material, multilingual and post-human perspectives were developed, producing a more pluralistic and complex space (see Burnett et al,. 2014; Leander and Boldt, 2013; Enriquez et al., 2016). The research field is therefore very different in recent times from where is began. So, it has changed from the early days of "Situated Literacies" (Barton, Hamilton and Ivani, 2000). The central argument is that everyday literacies come from somewhere. We locate this "somewhere" within the histories of literacy and language ethnographies. We address these issues with a particular eye on the US and the UK traditions of linguistic ethnography (UK) and linguistic anthropology (US).

Threaded through the chapter are also the voices of research participants (Lem in "Ways with Words" 1982), researchers thinking about writing (Hymes, 1996) about analysis (Rampton, 2007a) about revisiting (Sefton-Green and Rowsell, 2015) and about group analysis (Copland and Creese et al., 2015). We draw attention to those voices as part of the history of the field, and an analysis of their language to trace that history. So, we re-read the field, reflexively and also, personally. Who creates the canon?

One aspect of this work is concerned with who gets named and who does not; with women's scholarship being sometimes absent from a settled trail of citations (see Ahmed, 2017). Presenting a "citation trail" in itself constructs a history and a story of voices from a field. Writing about it means making sense of it anew. Reflexivity can provide a layer of thinking from which to reflect on what has been created, what it has made, and what it could be. Locating moments within this field is a choice that is itself political, located in discursive choices and stances. Citation trails then can be seen as themselves traces of practice and provide genealogies that, analysed reflexively, shape and construct the field. Telling this story is itself a form of academic literacy and a literacy practice (see Seloni, this volume).

Epistemological positions are, therefore, important. As noted, research in the field of language and literacy research initially focused more on texts, practices, scripts and discourses (Candlin and Hyland, 1999). The written was more salient as a category and the oral was still in a more indeterminate space; although Ruth Finnegan's work was challenging the boundaries of the relationship between oral and written texts (Finnegan, 2007). The work of Gunther Kress on multimodality, particularly in his seminal "Before Writing" (1997), enabled "writing-plus-other-stuff" to be seen as communicative practice in its own right. The demands of digital literacies then unsettled the relationship between speech, writing and the visual so profoundly that literacy in the "new media age" could be conceptualised in new ways that challenged conventional binaries of speech, writing and the visual (Kress, 2003).

The chapter begins by outlining the salient features of the study of literacy and language ethnographies and the salient scholars in the field. It then addresses the nature of ethnography itself and the significance of the New Literacy Studies movement. This account leads to an exploration of new "re-imaginings" of language-based ethnography before we consider themes coming from Bourdieu's own theory of practice with respect to method and reflexivity in the other two chapters of this part of the book.

Where did Language Ethnography Begin?

There are many different threads and themes that have developed the field known as "New Literacy Studies". These intersect with another field known as "Linguistic Ethnography". These two traditions have links and intersections, and some authors cross over and conduct linguistic ethnography but draw on a New Literacy Studies perspective (for example, Tusting, 2000; Maybin, 2006; Rampton, 2007a). However, in some cases it is possible to perceive distinct boundaries between them.

The "New Literacy Studies" or "NLS" movement as it is commonly called, can be traced through the initial work of Street (1984, 1993) in describing the idea of models of literacy that can be identified with the word "autonomous" and "ideological". "Ideological literacies", is a model of literacy that understands literacy to be embedded within discourses of power and located in cultural and ideologically positioned contexts. The work of Barton and Hamilton (1998) in their book "Local Literacies" further delineated the ways in which literacy practices were used in everyday life, using ethnographic methodologies. In a series of ethnographic studies, Gregory and Williams (2000) drew on similar methods to map the literacies of the city in their work in Bethnal Green in East London in their book, "City Literacies". Bringing in multilingualism to New Literacy Studies, and seeing the situated nature of multilingual literacy practices was a key contribution of work by Martin-Jones and Jones (2000), which considered the ways in which multilingual literacies were situated in everyday contexts.

The field of "Linguistic Ethnography" can also be traced, particularly in the UK through the work of Tusting (2000), Maybin (2006) and Rampton (2007a) in combining fine-grained ethnographic work on language and interaction with an understanding of context. This was the core methodology for a large-scale team ethnography of supplementary schools in the UK led by Angela Creese and Adrian Blackledge (Blackledge and Creese 2010; Copland and Creese et al., 2015). Of equal interest in North America is the field of "linguistic anthropology", as exemplified by the work of Anna De Fina (2009). Anna De Fina (2009) explored ways in which spatialised understandings of narrative could produce different conceptual framings of border narratives that located these narratives more precisely in particular spatial configurations. There are differences between these two fields: the one, linguistic anthropology drawing on the heritage of Gumperz (1982) and resulting in work by scholars such as Monica Heller (2011); the other developed by scholars such as Ben Rampton (2007a), Janet Maybin (2006) and Karin Tusting (2000), who began to map out the implications of a detailed linguistic analyses of oral speech together with writing in naturalistic settings together with ethnographic contextual work to make sense of that field. While these two traditions have much in common, they do have different antecedents and genealogies.

At the heart of much of this work is a focus on power, on recognising the "ways with words" of people in everyday settings and acknowledging that theory building about language has to come from those everyday intersections (Heath, 1983). The initial and pioneering work on language came from the research of ethnographers such as Del Hymes (1996) as well as John Gumperz (1982). Followers of Gumperz such as Monica Heller (2011) and others worked to challenge and disrupt language ideologies through linguistic ethnographic studies of how these ideologies work within institutional and community settings. Ethnography as a way of knowing, of collaboratively "coming to know", is hence a mode of engagement with that process; a respectful and careful understanding of what is going on here, and what matters (see also Lassiter, 2005; Campbell and

Lassiter, 2015). Collaborative and situated understandings of discourse practices across contexts brought to light new and evolving insights into how literacy practices evolved on sites and across sites (see, for example, Kell, 2006). I now look at some classic studies in the field of literacy and language ethnographies.

Ways with Words

Where language ethnographies began is often linked to the work of Shirley Brice Heath in "Ways with Words" (1983). Her book delineated the literacy and language practices of three communities in the Carolinas in the US. Her ethnographic approach, which closely described linguistic practices in the everyday, was informed by the ethnography of communication as developed by Del Hymes and others at the University of Pennsylvania (Hymes, 1996). This work was framed in the context of an analysis of language and literacy practices that recognised diversity. Speech and language were not a standardised set of rules but a locally variable set of situated practices. In "Ways with Words" Heath describes, drawing on detailed language ethnographies, the literacy and language practices of three communities in the Carolinas: Trackton, a mainly African-American community; Roadville, a predominately white working-class community; and Maintown, a more urban middle-class community which included teachers. Locating and providing a language of description for their respective literacy and language practices yielded ground-breaking data on the ways in which different communities understood language and literacy, and the consequent disconnect of the Trackton and Roadville communities from mainstream schooling. Only the Maintown children were able to recognise and perform literacy practices in school that were congruent to their everyday lived experience of literacy and language. Heath gives a vivid description of the linguistic practices of Trackton child, Lem, aged 3, sitting on a porch in the 1970s showed an appreciation of everyday speech but also a recognition of the poetic cadences of his language:

> Way
> Far
> Now
> It a church bell
> Ringing'
> Dey singing'
> Ringing'
> You hear it?
> I hear it
> Far
> Now

(Heath, 1982: 67)

This lyric demonstrated the "textual architecture" of the narrative and poetic traditions of the African American community of which Lem was a part. Working against "deficit discourses", and an abiding concern with a lack of recognition of the lived reality of language and literacy practices of marginalised groups, was key for these researchers.

This repositioning work had echoes in later studies that minutely traced the ways in which communities spoke and interacted, often collaboratively and with a focus on combating institutional racism and deficit models of language and literacy in communities. For example, Morrell (2008) worked with youth to critically examine discourses of power and resistance with a focus on collaborative literacies in community contexts. Kinloch (2010) followed and worked with a group of students who were combating increased "gentrification" in Harlem, and through the literacies of place, explored their own narratives. As Khaleeq, one of the young men in her study observed, "We belong, our identities wrapped up in our place" (p. 91). Focusing on the lived literacies of place through young narrators from Harlem, New York City telling stories of identity, her work engaged with the lived realities of gentrification through literacy. These studies continue to wrestle with the nexus of identities, place, lived experience and the literacies of activism in new ways.

Life as a Source of Narrative

Everyday life, Hymes argued, was the generator of narratives within communities. Hymes worked within the tradition of "ethnography as an approach, linguistics as a field and narrative as a human accomplishment" (1996: x). He brought together different ways of knowing and understanding from deeply lived community contexts into one field. His work was particularly located with personal narrative. As part of his ethnographic lens he invites the reader to take part in the "Warm Springs Interlude" (p. 117) in which he and his wife, with his friend, Hazel Suppah, walked around a place they knew well, and Hymes, listening, observed that, "one often saw a bit of experience becoming an event to be told, being told and being retold until it took shape as a narrative, one that might become a narrative told by others" (p. 119). He later observed that, "Ethnography is the way in which one can find out and know this aspect of a way of life" (p. 118).

One of the key aspects of Hymes' work is a "situating quality", which is: "embodied in the rhythm of continuing life and observation and reflection of life. One has to go around and be around to come to see how the world is a world closely observed" (p. 119). In the "Warm Springs Interlude", this is about being with old friends, sharing, listening, chewing the cud, witnessing the world together. Being together in a space, in a more genuine and shared space than one demarcated by the word "research" is critical to this commitment. This way of working is integral to a situated language ethnographic approach with its focus on people's everyday lived experience, and shared conceptual framings of culture (see also Campbell and Lassiter, 2015).

The contribution of Hymes and then Gumperz (1982), Gee (1996), Street (1984, 1993, 2000), Barton and Hamilton (1998) and many others, was to draw attention to, probe and celebrate the ways in which language and literacy practices flourished within the everyday, under the noses of possibly un-seeing educationalists and traditional linguists. While "schooled literacy practices" (Street and Street, 1991) were associated with particular forms of language and literacy, such as regularity of spelling, performance-based language practices, standard English and other genres that comprise academic literacies, many of these scholars were able to show how the non-standard and the hybrid as forms of everyday interaction were valuable and important. Snell (2013) drew on linguistic ethnography to investigate the ways in which linguistics could surface discussion of dialect and standard English. Maybin (2013) argued that sociolinguistics could also no longer ignore the visual, further developing the field.

This focus on the everyday and on the uses of literacy and language practices in communities was partly achieved through an attention to ethnographic methods and modes of description, but was also because of an ideological resistance to the codification of language that in reality privileged white middle-class, Western understandings of what literacy and language was. The ideological constructs of "language" and "literacy" were in fact already under contestation from anthropologists who could see more complex forms emerging from such phenomena as performance-based narration and everyday interaction (Finnegan, 2015). These challenges to the boundaries of what can be recognised as literacy and language practices continue to this day, as ways of describing language and literacy practices shift and change as usage evolve, and understandings move with the times. The concept of "trans-languaging", for example, has shifted understandings of everyday language in use (see Blackledge and Creese, 2010; Arnaut et al., 2016). Parkin (2016) offers a nuanced conceptual framework for looking at how language can be creatively mixed to produce new configurations for semiotic resources to be deployed. This created what might be considered as an ontologically adept framework for recognising new stylistic practices as they emerge.

Ethnography

Ethnography is the situating discipline that underpins New Literacy Studies and Linguistic Ethnography. Ethnography, as a way of "making the familiar strange" (Agar, 1996) and as a "thick description" (Geertz, 1993), has its histories in modes of inquiry that were situated, language based and reflexive. While many initial ethnographies in the past tended to document in painstaking detail the ways with words of "other" cultures – extensively documented in, for example, "Writing Culture" by Clifford and Marcus (1986) – a "turn" to a much more reflective and reflexive mode of "doing ethnography" that did not "other" communities was strong from the 1980s onwards. Ethnographers such as Paul Rabinow (1977) also wrote about their own failure to account for certain aspects of their fieldwork, for the "gaps" and "lapses" of the gaze they brought onto the field. Ethnography and reflexivity have always been closely linked with each other. For example, Annette Lareau in Lareau and Schultz (1996) emphasised her own positionality as a mother and as a parent within her field research. Within team ethnography, issues of voice, reflexivity and uncertainty come even more to the fore (Copland and Creese et al., 2015) within collaborative ethnography, where the representation of communities as equal partners in the research process has also been critical (see Campbell and Lassiter, 2010). The settled determinism of the ethnographer (all too often white, male) who comes to "the field", has also been overturned by a move to a greater understanding of how reflexivity itself questions the stance of the researcher; this is what we explore in the rest of the book in case example chapters and further theoretical discussion.

New Literacy Studies, Linguistic Ethnography, Multi-modality

As we have seen, understandings of literacy in everyday life have been developed through a number of ethnographic studies carried out in the 1970s, 1980s and 1990s with an interest in linking particular literacy practices, observed over time, and noticing literacy events within them. Initially, these studies focused on literacy as script, and written text, but increasingly the lens widened to include visual and multimodal texts (Flewitt, 2008). Many of these studies focused on practices within the everyday (for example, Richardson, 2006). Janet Maybin (2000) described how this theoretical work, "enables researchers to more clearly conceptualise the pivotal role of literacy practices in articulating the links between individual people's everyday experience, and wider social institutions and structures" (Maybin 2000: 197). The location of literacy practices within space and time also provided an anchoring framework for New Literacy Studies:

> Literacy events are located in time and space. Reading and writing are things which people do, either alone or with other people, but always in a social context – always in a place and at a time. To make sense of people's literacy practices we need to situate them within this context.
>
> (Barton and Hamilton, 1998: 23)

In this opening section of a chapter of "Local Literacies" with a focus on a history of Lancaster, David Barton and Mary Hamilton together articulated a shared commitment to the spatial and historical location of their study. Re-reading it now some twenty years later, the study seems quaintly old fashioned – before mobile phones, the internet, digital media and multimodality. Their work focused closely on the literacy practices of a community – included a large dataset involving 20 student interviews, a door-to-door survey of 65 households, together with

12 in-depth studies of people and collaborative interviews along with visual evidence and observation. Nevertheless, their resulting book provided a richly layered account of the literacy practices that people used in their daily lives, including notes of allotment meetings, shopping lists, minutes of council meetings, letters, diaries, school homework and books including war stories, the Ladybird books and Kays catalogue. In the study, literacy became something that people "did", but also was manifested in material terms, as a physical, embodied and textual form. One of the key insights of the book was that literacy practices could be understood in relation to "domains of practice"; that is, home, school and workplace. As the field developed, the idea of literacy "domains" became a heuristic from which to look at literacy practices across sites.

The "Situated Literacies" collection edited by Barton, Hamilton and Ivanic (2000) expanded the concept of "literacy practices" being linked to sites and spaces, locating literacy "in time, space and discourse" (p. 1). Immanent within this theorising was the idea of literacy as a heuristic to exploring "issues of power, through examining the relationship between micro- and macro-level contexts" (Maybin, 2000: 197). Seeing literacy as relational, and shaped within social practices and discourse, opened up spaces for further studies to take place that both located literacies in contexts (e.g. "City Literacies" by Gregory and Williams, 2000) and created new and emergent contexts that could then operate as further heuristics for literacy research – see, for example Richardson's "Hip-hop Literacies" (2006) and Blommaert's "Grassroots Literacy" (2008). This has been an expansionist time for NLS, in which literacies were everywhere, threaded through song and imbued with visual material and oral qualities. "Artifactual Literacies" by Pahl and Rowsell (2010) continued this theme with a focus on objects, stories and the literacies of material culture in homes and communities to provide as an understanding of literacy as materially situated within the everyday.

An important and burgeoning area in this field of literacy studies was studies of multilingualism. A key text was Marilyn Martin-Jones and Kathryn Jones' edited volume, "Multilingual Literacies: Reading and Writing Different Worlds" (2000). Brian Street, in an introduction to this volume, looked more closely at ways in which literacy practices and events were conceptualised, and described the methodological and empirical basis for these insights. Street referred to Maybin's insight, in the, "Situated Literacies" volume, that the NLS lens, ". . . enables the researchers to more clearly conceptualise the pivotal role of literacy practices in articulating the links between individual people's everyday experience and wider social institutions and structures" (2000: 197).

It is the relational nature of literacy practices that is brought out through an ethnographic lens, which characterised these studies. Immanent within these studies was an assumption that practices were there, and literacy practices were something that could be traced; surfacing within events, these then sedimented into practices (Rowsell and Pahl, 2007).

New Literacy Studies, then, situates itself within ethnography because ethnography provides the empirical understanding and grounding for the ways in which literacy practices are conceptualised. This perspective contextualises what happens when people do things with literacy within time and space, and it makes sense of people's motivations to use literacy and describes the webs that surround a set of literacy practices (Brandt and Clinton, 2002). What is less visible within the NLS studies that emerged between the 1990s and in the first half of the 21st century, was an emphasis on aesthetic, embodied, felt material and multi-modal literacies, particularly with the advent of digital media. This need was articulated in a new edited collection by Baynham and Prinsloo called "The Future of Literacy Studies" (2009), signalling the development in the field of dimensions of multimodality from the work of Gunther Kress and Carey Jewitt (see Jewitt and Kress, 2003), with their focus on digital literacies and new literacies (Kress, 2003).

Bringing multimodality together with ethnography was, however, a more complex task. Multimodality was focused on texts, while ethnography was more focused on practices emerging in contexts. However, scholarly work began to gather these two approaches together (see Dicks et al., 2011). Situated, ethnographic studies of multimodal and digital literacy practices, located within time and space, but also acknowledging the material and embodied quality of literacy practices, emerged during the period from about 2002 onwards and took shape as researchers engaged with young people's digital, material and multimodal literacies, and also with their embodied and "felt" literacies (Rowsell and Pahl, 2015; Enriquez et al., 2016). We will return to some of these themes in Chapter 8.

Ethnography as a mode of doing research and in opening up the "what is going on here" question has, therefore, been used to look at everyday language in context, with a focus on cultural practices. Piecing together the ways in which people make sense of the world through language has involved collecting spoken data through interviews, or collected naturalistically, together with surrounding texts, practices and other ephemera, but with a very clear concern with the "lived texture of situated experience" (Rampton, 2007a: 15). Here, the attention is on the ways in which social relations both produce and are produced within and by linguistic interaction. Methodologically and conceptually, linguistic ethnographers have sought to connect language interactions within the context from which they were produced; problematising context, as Duranti and Goodwin (1992) pointed out, is part of this process. In his book, "Language in Late Modernity" (2007a) Ben Rampton described the process of developing ways of describing the words he collected, with painstaking honesty and frankness:

> I tried to work with a rule that I would never put pen to paper about a conceptual link between one fragment and other, or incorporate an extract into a prose commentary or argument, until I had spent at least one hour

on it. Almost invariably, the hour turned into two or four and sometimes days not hours and even though I sometimes found myself sitting for ten minutes wondering what on earth else I could say to fill up the time, when I did eventually finish on a sequence, the propositions I had started out with usually looked either crude or just plain wrong.

(p. 396)

Bringing linguistic understandings of context drawing on ethnographic field-work to everyday language practices was key to recognising how discourses were constructed and powerfully assembled. The process of "making sense" of ethno-graphically informed linguistic data is here described by Rampton as being a process of conceptualisation. This also gave the process its rigour as the relationship between linguistic practices and context was described as problematic at best.

As sociolinguistics as a disciplinary field continued to diversify and change, multimodality also engaged strongly with literacy studies and this then surfaced multiple understandings of texts that themselves were visual, gestural and situated. What this led to was an emphasis on tracing "modal choices" within textual pathways, and providing fine-grained analytic tools to do that work (see Rowsell, 2013). Ethnographic understandings of multimodal texts were produced by scholars such as Stein (2003) and Kell (2006) in tracing how such texts were transformed across contexts, and were mixed and re-mixed in the process across modes, creating new configurations and modal pathways, in creating and unexpected ways. What did all this amount to for new directions for research practice in language ethnography?

Revisiting and Re-imagining Language Ethnographies

The description above was devised with respect to Linguistic Ethnography and New Literacy Studies as fields. However, other new developments continued to arrive. As literacy and language ethnographies expanded and developed in response to the contexts in which research was carried out, a number of features emerged:

- *The importance of collaborative and team ethnographies* (see Campbell and Lassiter, 2015). Research interactions with literacy and language began to be problematised, as team ethnographies were articulated and the process of analysis was surfaced more reflexively within the writing of these ethnographies (see for example, Copland and Creese et al., 2015).
- *A focus on reflexivity and voice* as the concept of revisiting developed new and emerging lenses for understanding "data" again and in new ways (see for example Heath, 2012; Sefton-Green and Rowsell, 2015).
- *Settled modes of enquiry became replaced by more visual, phenomenological and embodied forms of enquiry* that were situated within affect, and the concept of

non-representational literacies began to emerge from this (for example, Enriquez et al., 2016; Ehret, Hollett and Jocius, 2016).

I would like to explore these ideas in more detail and, in doing so, highlight how such modes of enquiry have identified new dilemmas in the field of language and literacy ethnographies. These themes will also be explored later in this book. Indeed, they are connected to concerns about the shifting terrain of the field of study, the nature of a collaborative enquiry and the role of reflexivity in that process. Further challenges to the conceptual frameworks used to describe literacy and language practices have also been articulated by approaches that draw more on theory that looks at affect and postmodern ways of knowing (see for example MacLure, 2011).

Collaborative and Team Ethnographies

Increasingly, literacy research is not done alone, and rather than hide the intensely collaborative nature of analytic encounters, ethnographers are recognising the importance of "reciprocal analysis" (Campbell and Lassiter, 2010) and the need to recognise the knowledge production practices within communities as key to interpretative understandings (Campbell and Lassiter, 2015). This means a more open transparency about the analytic process:

> The analysis of interactions in team meetings showed researchers adhering to positions, disagreeing with others, shifting their arguments, changing their minds, offering compromises and building consensus. Credentials of bilingualism, community engagement, advocacy and scholarship saw us debate what we would write about, how we should write it and for whom we should write.
>
> (Creese, 2015: 69)

Here, the writers explicitly bring the writing process into view while describing their studies. A reflexive account of writing practices is something that is increasingly visible within language ethnographies (see also Pahl, 2017). This has also led to a focus on revisiting as a process of engagement with the field.

A Focus on Reflexivity and Voice

In the last few years, a few scholars have revisited their earlier studies, notably Shirley Brice Heath in "Ways with Words" (2012) and Mary Hamilton in "Local Literacies" (2015). These "revisiting" studies identified key issues about how literacy had changed and how livelihoods have changed. In the Carolinas, people had experienced recession, young people had, in many cases, gone away to university and the nature of literacy had changed to being more collaborative, digitally mediated and multimodal (Heath, 2012: 143). Likewise, Mary Hamilton in her revisit of "Local Literacies" noted that, "the most striking change has been in communication practices themselves" (2015:99). These practices included digital, virtual, multimodal communicative practices that themselves were transformed and transforming constantly. One of the issues that these studies raised was whose voice surfaces in these ways with words?

In an epilogue to her revisiting study, "Words at Work and Play", where she went back to the families she visited in Trackton and Roadville, and followed second and third generations' language and literacy practices, Heath (2012) also recognised that:

> When I wrote the book in the early 1980s, I took the objective stance that was then the norm of social-science reporting [however] the unusual nature of the current work and of my long-term association with the families and children whose stories are told here seems now to call for some autobiographical explanation.
>
> (p. 177)

Heath then tells us her own story in which she learned to challenge and make sense of segregation in the Carolinas through her growing up and her studies. This story resonates across "Ways with Words" and the sequel and the impetus behind the studies comes alive:

> I grew up on my grandmother's small farm in rural south-eastern Virginia. Our farm located sixty miles from the nearest town with as many as 10,000 residents, was surrounded by tobacco farms, most of which were owned by black families. Our nearest neighbours were black and the black church was across the road from my grandmother's house.
>
> (p. 177)

Heath then traces back her own history and describes her studies at Columbia with the anthropologist Margaret Mead, and subsequently her studies with Del Hymes on the ethnography of communication. What emerges from this revisiting process is a much more engaged notion of scholarship as in process, in dialogue with the self and with the studies.

Revisiting is a methodological as well as a personal journey. The question Mary Hamilton asks when she revisits "Local Literacies" is, what would she have done differently? Her conclusion was that:

> Much remained to be explored about how to work, both methodologically and conceptually, with the relationships between the everyday and faraway, the local and the global, without returning to old ideas about literacy as an autonomous set of universal skills.
>
> (p. 111)

New conceptual frameworks, such as Actor Network Theory, would have enabled a more nuanced understanding of the relationship between the individual participants and the "threads of their lives" (p. 113). Hamilton concludes:

> However, it is the threads that connect this life to other lives, times, events and issues – the web of meanings and relationships from which Shirley's stories are assembled – that now seem of most value to me in understanding literacies.
>
> (p. 113).

The kinds of knowledge that Hamilton was most interested in when she revisited – that is connectivities, networks and relationships – were less focused on in the earlier study. In "Local Literacies", the focus was more on the "ruling passions" of the participants and their located literacy lives. Now, she admits, it was the relational and connected nature of literacy practices that she realised was worthy of further research.

Visual, Embodied and Felt Forms of Literacy

As people's lives are shifting, contexts for literacy research also shift. Currently, research is articulating the importance of "activist literacies" (Blackburn and Clark, 2007; Rogers, 2018; Rogers et al., 2009) and a posthuman new materialist turn to literacy methodologies (Kuby et al., 2015). Tracing these shifts in literacy and language ethnographies is an important part of that process. Feelings within literacy events and the importance of affect are being identified within ethnographic studies of literacy and language (Ehret, Hollett and Jocius, 2016). This creates a new landscape of literacy and language research, resting on postmodern assumptions that trace trajectories but acknowledge the limitations of representational practice.

In Summary

In the field of language ethnographies, whose words count and why? The insights that Street had that literacy practices are always ideological and the autonomous model is in itself ideological resonate still (Street, 1993). There is, nevertheless, a utopian quality to Street's work that he himself acknowledged here:

> But "progressive" educators have their own fears and desires, built into the process of learning and studying themselves. The desire to privilege the dialogic, contestable and social nature of language and literacy, to live with diversity, still entails its own struggle: it is the struggle of all Utopian movements, with the order and constraint within which freedom and

variation are possible. Utopian desires too are tempered by the reality that social life, including language and literacy practices, is patterned and persistent even amidst its rich diversity.

(1997: 52)

Street here recognised that the New Literacy Studies, with its acknowledgement that literacies are ideological and framed by power relations, is itself a utopian project. By understanding that all literacies are valuable, the pedagogical space of teaching opens out. This insight has become a tool for thinking with and a way of recognising and valuing literacies within communities in ways that are surprising and generative. Language ethnographies are generative spaces – they produce words and thoughts and ideas that can often run counter to schooled and classed literacy and language practices. In this way, the enterprise can also be seen to be peculiarly Bourdieusian: and, as an ideological project, it has run far longer than many projects and has resonated within many different fields of study. Naming the field is also a counter narrative to what is, and what could be in a world dominated by functional, skills-focused, "autonomous" models of literacy in schools. The field in this chapter is yet incomplete – it is a story that is waiting to be finished. What gets said and what gets unsaid is both the subject and object of this chapter. In this history, a particular story has been told. In the rest of this book we explore the relationship of this field of literacy and language ethnographies to the experience of the researcher, and understand this in relation to Bourdieu's theoretical contributions to the concept of reflexivity and fieldwork.

2

REFLEXIVITY

Michael Grenfell

Introduction

This chapter addresses the second of our major themes: Reflexivity. We are dealing with these themes one by one in order to present the discrete elements of the book before extending and integrating them in Parts II and III. Reflexivity is, in many ways, quite a problematic word. Similar words such as "reflex" and "reflexive" are closely associated to it; but, then, so are "reflection", "reflective" and "reflect". Everyday dictionary definitions of these latter see in reflection a sense of casting back, or returning to source. At the same time, and closely associated with this, to be *reflective* is in some ways to act in a way that is thoughtful, meditative or even deliberate. *Reflexive*, on the other hand, is used linguistically to pertain to the way someone doing an action is also the recipient of it. It therefore implies a certain relationship between cause and effect, subject and object and self-reference. *Reflexivity* by extension becomes the way that a person's thoughts or ideas – including the values they carry – become embedded in what they do and know. Clearly, there are several nuances and dimensions to this notion of reflexivity, some of which we shall attempt to unravel in the proceeding chapter. What we can already see from these definitions is that they raise issues of what it is and how it is to know, how that knowledge is acquired, and how is it expressed. These questions are central to our concerns since they connect with theory and practice, and the language with which research activity is conveyed. This chapter goes into detail on these topics in the light of what we previously set out on Language-based ethnographies.

Reflecting Knowledge and Knowing

It is impossible to understand the significance of reflexivity, and just what it is and how it might operate, without setting it within an intellectual tradition of knowledge and knowing – basically, science. Explaining these, of course, would take us back millennia. However, for convenience and brevity's sake, we can pitch the beginning of our discussion from the eighteenth and nineteenth century. Before these times, of course, there was a mix of knowledge fields – astronomy, anatomy, theology. However, many of these included but a little of the "scientific" aspects as we would understand them in contemporary times – objective theory and evidence; although they did embrace more "moral" aspects of human knowledge, which even bordered on the religious. Newton, one of the greatest physicist the world has ever known, and who gave us much of our present day understanding of gravity, was also an alchemist; that is, with a fascination for the transmutation of matter (often into gold) and finding a universal elixir. What is significant about the period about which we write is that at this point, the two aspects – physics and alchemy – became increasingly divided and separate. So, the "natural sciences" developed as separate disciplines – chemistry, biology, physics, etc. with little concern for the moral aspects of knowledge, whilst the "human sciences" pursued more metaphysical questions of philosophy and beliefs. The word "meta" means "beyond", so that "metaphysics" can be understood as "beyond physics"; in other words, beyond the physical world as we know it. Metaphysical speculation opened the door on any form of mental speculation. Yet, "hard science", in the purely physical plain, is just as prone to speculation as the metaphysical; for example, whether what we observe really exists in the world as real objects. We can see immediately that these questions are still very pertinent to the issues of our discussion: does what we see in ethnography actual exist, or is it our own self recreating itself? does language actually convey what it describes?; what is reflexivity anyway – a higher form of objectivity or subjectivity?

For Kant (1724–1804), it was indeed the human mind that creates the structure of human experience. He makes a distinction between the *noumenal* – things in themselves, which we cannot know – and the *phenomenal* – that is what is conveyed by our senses. However, the latter, is not merely speculative but, indeed, the basis of reason and morality themselves. Natural and human scientists have walked the tightrope of these issues ever since and, if the former have struggled to establish objectivity for their theories, the latter have followed in their wake searching for the holy grail of evidence for their metaphysical explorations. No surprise, therefore, to find the recognised father of modern sociology – Auguste Comte (1798–1857) – attempting to establish it as a positivist science on a par with any natural science. The founder of modern language studies – Ferdinand de Saussure (1857–1913) – similarly sought to found linguistics as a "science" comparable to any other. Anthropology too has often looked for the "objective" structures of cultures, even if these are being expressed in socio-cultural or even biological terms.

These tendencies can be traced through to twentieth century social scientists. So, for example, writers such as Talcott Parsons (1902–1979) and Robert Merton (1910–2003), working in the structural functionalist tradition of sociology, focused on predictable forms of social action set within overarching and "mid-range" theories of how society worked. In some ways, this might seem to stand opposed to the type of socio-cultural thinking that was required in anthropology, but a leading exponent at a similar time – Claude Lévi-Strauss (1908–2009) – was just as concerned to discover the underlying "rules" and "objective structures" of myth in traditional societies. However, from the 1950s onwards, and with the explosion in communications and all things cultural – a more reflexive, interpretative paradigm began to take over. Educational research is an excellent example of this change. Up until the 1950s, what research that did take place was predicated on a "hard science" view, which assumed emergent theory based on "fact" with the power of predictability (see O'Connor, 1958). Much of such research was, therefore, psychological in nature since this discipline came closest to providing the necessary predictive results. So, in the natural sciences, theories are developed through hypotheses formed in analysing data, which are interconnected and verified through observation. Theories tell us the way the world is and can be tested through replication and exemplification. So, if we conclude that water boils at 100 degrees C, we can test this theory by boiling water and measuring the temperature – highly predictive. However, as the British philosopher Paul Hirst pointed out (1966), if we judge educational theory by this standard, it comes off badly, and rarely has such a power of description or prediction. "Facts" are harder to establish in social contexts; situations are in flux and outcomes unpredictable. Hirst consequently argues that educational theory might better be seen, therefore, as providing a *rationale* for educational practice – its values and modus operandi – rather than predictable theory. Central to this argument, of course, is just what we mean by theory anyway?

Actually, the word "theory" from its origins means little more than "observing something". More generally, however, it is seen as offering somewhat of a rationale-based "generalisation" with statements that can be tested against future data. *En passant*, we probably could name all sorts of theory: mathematical, Marxist, political, astrological, medical. From the list, it is possible to see how most of these conform to our "rationale"/"generalisation" criteria, but we might suspect that some are more worthy of our trust than others. The problem is that a theory works as long as it works – there can always be the exception that disproves it, possibly in a critical context; "the exception that proves the rule" is a common aphorism. This problem led the philosopher Karl Popper to turn it on its head (see Popper, 1967). For him, the issue was less about having to prove a theory to be right but the possibility to prove it wrong. For Popper, *strong* theoretical statements could be "falsified", that is liable to be proved wrong; for example, "all swans are white". Whilst *weak* theoretical statements could not; for example, capitalism is leading to a revolution. A moment's reflection will show how this approach works. In the first example, all one has to do is find a single exception – a black swan – to disprove the theory, which makes it strong; in the second, even if it has not happened yet, it may still do, so is non-falsifiable – so weak. Several axioms and implications follow on from this position. First, if a theory is always falsified, it might be a "strong theory" but it is not always of much use. Second, if a theory is never falsified, then it is not a theory, it is a statement of reality. Third, some theories are easily falsified – for example, all cats are black – which again makes them strong but of little use. By now, we can see that there are tensions between strong and weak theories and their respective usefulness. Fourth, all theories are expressed in language, which raises the whole question of the exactitude of linguistic description in description, conjecture and falsification. Fifth, both types of data – natural and human – used to measure theory and their robustness are clearly key factors in the actual verification/ falsification process.

We have already named certain theories by way of exemplification; to which we might add Bourdieu's theory of practice, about which, more in the next chapter, and a range of other associated theories. Certainly, in terms of the disciplines we have already mentioned – for example, sociology and anthropology – what we see in the development of these research fields is the extemporisation of theory in consideration of observed fact and interpretation. With sociology, Comte, Durkheim, Weber, Marx and Parsons would all have different theories about society; in anthropology, the same would be true for Lévi-Strauss, Malinowski, Geertz, Mead, etc. So, what of theory and the language that expresses it, and what of the place of reflexivity in it?

Language and Knowledge

So far, we have seen something of knowledge and knowing, and hinted at the place that reflexivity might play in "scientific research". Clearly, what is at stake is how we know the things we know and how sure we can be of this knowledge – reflexivity suggests there may be cause to question this surety. What we do know is that a lot of pre-twentieth century knowledge proceeded from deductive enquiry – that is intellectual pursuit by reasoned thought. Popperian philosophy was presented as an antidote to what might lead to phantasy and imagination, as it required, at least in theory, an element of evidence – potentially, at least. For Popper, we might see science as consequently engaging with three worlds: World 1 being the world of physical objects; World 2 being the world of mental objects and events; and World 3 being "Objective Knowledge". In the process of developing this latter, theories are refined by forming hypotheses, which can then be tested against evidence. The end point is "objective" since it is "knowledge without a knowing subject". In other words, even if the entire population of the planet disappeared, such objective facts would still be true – for example, the boiling point of water.

Such a position certainly has clarity and definition. However, there are issues, which suggest that it might not be quite so robust as it apparently claims to be. For a start, there is reason to question whether anything – even in a physical space – is ever absolutely true; everything still is a product of the questions we ask. Moreover, once we venture beyond the physical sciences, a degree of relativism opens up in as much that what passes within socio-cultural spaces is highly prone to the influences of contextual elements. Social trends, individual actions, are rarely objectively predictable, which is not so to say they are not dispositionally orientated. The dichotomy between "hard fact" and "extreme relativism" is ably demonstrated in modern linguistics. As noted above, the founder of modern day linguistics was Ferdinand de Saussure, and his intent was to offer a "science of language". Ironically, whilst certainly doing this, he also opened the door on its total collapse into meaning relativity. First, he posited that we should acknowledge a distinction between *langue* and *parole*. If the latter could be seen as individual speech utterances, the former – language – was the internal language systems as developed by a particular social group. Later, Noam Chomsky (1928–) was to make a similar distinction, this time between *competence* and *performance* in arguing for language as an "innate biological" characteristic of the brain; further insisting that linguistics should be concerned with "an ideal speech-listener, in a completely homogeneous speech community, which knows a language perfectly and is unaffected by such grammatically irrelevant conditions as memory limitations, distractions, shifts of attention, and errors" (Chomsky, 1965: 3). In other words, linguistics questions can be answered by looking at the nature of language itself, unencumbered by socio-cultural factors. Can this be? And, if it can, how useful are the results? The same questions might be applied to Popperian science in that, even if it is possible, it is questionable as to the extent to which the product of proceeding in this manner is useful in understanding the actuality of real social phenomena.

To this doubt, we need to add a second Saussurian derived problem. Saussure proposed a second fundamental feature of language when he distinguished between "things" and the "words" used to designate their meaning: what he called "the signified" and the "signifier"; in other words, the actual cat and the word "cat". However, so far, so good, but he also saw that there was a dis-association between the signified and the signifier. For example, any word might do and, furthermore, whatever it is, it only signifies a general category, not the individual manifestation. For Saussure, therefore, the "signifier" was *arbitrary* to the "signified". This may seem an innocent observation but, in effect, it bears the seed of the collapse of Western rationality, since it soon becomes clear that meaning itself is both arbitrary and relative. Even to make statements susceptible to Popperian type falsification is to employ language which, as we have seen, we have grounds to doubt. Language might literally mean anything.

This "trope" entered Western knowledge field somewhat like a computer virus, internally clearing away once well respected and accepted narratives. Indeed, the very modernist project emerging from the Enlightenment itself was undermined by the realisation that its basic tenets were often *signifiers* in search of something to *signify*. What was cut dead in the water – even if seemingly slowly – was the commitment to the progress towards "truth" – the modernist/humanist project; that through science, mankind was moving forward to a better version of our understanding of the world in theory and practice. This commitment continued well beyond the mid-point of the twentieth century before the "linguistic turn" caught up with it. For example, Alvin Gouldner (1971) argued, in *The Coming Crisis in Western Sociology*, that "objective truth" was not possible in modern sociology, which should be much more concerned with the subjective nature of understanding within the context in which it is formed: "sociologists must surrender the human but elitist assumption that others behave out of need whereas they believe because of the dictates of logic and reason" (p. 26). This argument about sociology is following a similar direction as the one taken by Hirst in philosophy above, and indeed expresses some of the reflexivity of language-based ethnographers referred to in Chapter 1. Of course, neither Hirst nor Gouldner were the first to question the limits of knowledge as defined by Aristotelian logic (see, for example the *Negative Dialectics* of Theodor Adorno, 1990/1966). And, even stating such would seem to begin to point in the direction of a "sociology of sociology" in order to "transform the sociologist, to penetrate deeply into his daily life and work, enriching them with new sensitivities, to raise the sociologist's self-awareness" (Gouldner, 1971: 489). This statement itself might be seen as a call for reflexivity and, although not being the first, was symptomatic of a point in time – itself highly conditioned by the socio-cultural communications revolutions of the 1960s – where the significance of the linguistic turn began to really bite into traditional scholarly discourses. There were many significant consequences, of which:

First, a fragmentation of academic disciplines. It is not unusual for principal disciplines to have a series of "sub-disciplines", but these only expanded and increased in the last third of the twentieth century: so, in human language sciences, for example, linguistics, applied linguistics, second language acquisition, social psycholinguistics, psycholinguistics, sociolinguistics, linguistics ethnography; sociology, symbolic interactionism, ethnomethodology, rational action theory, social ethnography; anthropology, sociocultural anthropology, biological anthropology, linguistic anthropology, archaeological anthropology. Furthermore, whilst it would be untrue to state all these were committed to "naturalistic" modes of enquiry, it would nonetheless be the case that many grew in direct response to the "linguistic turn" outlined above with its implications for the human sciences.

Second, would be the place of language in each of the discipline. In keeping with the new hyper-sensitivity to language, many developed their own specialised language, which was then used to define themselves and what they did. Linguistic terms such as "discourse" were adopted as metaphors to describe social systems as an analogy between them and language. Some might even have seen *society* and *individual behaviour* as basically the same as *langue* and *parole*. Indeed, in the twentieth century, the philosophy of (wo)man became the philosophy of language.

Third, and somewhat connected to the previous two, is the issue concerning the identification of just what one is doing anyway. This is not just a "sociology of sociology" but an awareness of the "knowledge community" to which one belongs and what it suggests in terms of activity and the relationship to the social world that it implicates. In 1962, Thomas Kuhn had published *The Structure of Scientific Revolutions* (1970/1962) where he argued that growth in understanding and knowledge proceeded as a series of "revolutions" when one current field of scholarly activity became incommensurate with developing knowledge and evidence. This itself implied a "critical community", which Popper had also argued for, to act as a locale for public verification of truth claims by peer review. In other words, progress occurred when a past way of thinking was abandoned to the new; not as a series of slow incremental steps but a genuine "revolution" in thinking. Indeed, the "linguistic turn" itself was one such revolution. Again, Kuhn makes the point that such a shift is often accompanied by the development of a "new" vocabulary, or language, to represent the new *paradigm*. Furthermore, Habermas, argues for overarching epistemological orientations which disclose substantive *interests* in undertaking the research in the first place. In Habermasian epistemology, three epistemological *modes* are therefore presented – *nomothetic*, *hermeneutic* and *critical* – pertaining to the *interests* of law-giving, interpretive and emancipatory (Habermas, 1987a). Such modes do not simply represent discrete, implicit epistemological interests – ways of knowing – but are defined and expressed in terms of whole social relations to the world, which have practical, ultimately political, consequences.

Method and the Reflexive Turn

In the last sections, we have set out the background to reflexivity in terms of historical developments in philosophy, which have highlighted dichotomies between theory and practice, knowledge and knowers, human and natural sciences, language and the world, subject and object, etc. All of these are antecedents to implicate reflexivity, which became a major theme in research methodology from the 1970s. However, reflexivity as a concept had certainly existed long before that, as well as its effects. William Thomas (1863–1947) in the so-called Thomas Theorem (1928) argued that, "the situations that men define as true, become true to them". Various implications follow from this observation.

First, the interpretation of an event can be subjective, and therefore prone to bias and prejudice. Second, this also applies when any one occupies an "objective" mode; in other words, even "scientific" paradigms are biased in favour of their own terms. Third, both of these will have consequences: for example, in what is and is not seen; or, further creating a self-fulfilling prophesy (that things happen because they are predicted to happen); or, forming the conditions for other things to occur. At its extreme, things happen because of a certain definition of the situation. This might seem akin to the way that in physics if we look at electrons as a wave, then they are a wave, if we look at them as flow, they are a flow. In other words, the observer has an effect on the thing they observe. As Thomas noted, "If men define situations as real, they are real in their consequences". In a sense, there is the implication that we all do this to a greater or lesser extent – in our *empirical* state. Clearly, the issue concerns what is the outcome when the same thing applies in *scientific* states.

This realisation has, and had, a major consequence for the human sciences in that it is tantamount to seeing that the researcher – whether in their empirical or scientific state – "creates" the research. In other words, they are researching themselves. Above we saw the struggle to conceive of the human sciences with the same rigor as the physical sciences, and with it a search to discover "hard" scientific facts about the world. We also saw the problems of realising such in the light of the linguistic turn. Gouldner's text was only part of a realisation that what we took as "real" could be challenged, and what we were doing may in some ways be a kind of scholastic fantasy. Hence, the eagerness with which more naturalistic approaches to research were developed – ones which returned us to the reality of data and were suspicious of theory as such. For example, Symbolic Interactionism (SI).

SI actually goes back to the earlier parts of the twentieth century and the work of George Herbert Mead (1863–1931). Mead is known as one of the leading American pragmatists of the period, and his "applied" brand of disciplinary discourse can be seen as an integration of sociology, philosophy and psychology – what would later be termed "social psychology". As such, the focus is on individuals and their behaviour: what they symbolically value in interaction with each other; for example, how doctors might behave in the world and why. In a way, this approach is not dissimilar to Vygotskyan psychology, which sees individuals enacting control over the world of self, object and others. It is just that the symbolic source and nature of that control is more accented in SI. Bourdieu also sees the world as essentially symbolic.

SI certainly grew in popularity as the century proceeded, especially as it seemed to combine methodological approach with a degree of epistemological coherence. Interpretative ethnography can be understood as a form of SI. First, it returns the research to the "real world" of data in themselves, about which plausible interpretations can be made; interpretations based on common sensical observations and explanations rather than extraneous theories. Grounded Theory

(GT) is a slightly more robust version of the same. The starting point for GT is once again authentic data. However, in this case, middle-way theories of what is to be found in them are developed in an inductive (note rather than deductive) manner. This is achieved through the systematic sorting of data from which trends are first coded. The Codes are then collected together to form Concepts out of which Categories and Theories are finally formulated. Its systematic nature and the fact that "theories" of sorts are its end point appeal as a way again into a more robust scientific realm than simple qualitative description.

Both interpretative ethnography and symbolic interactionism can be seen as part of the twists and manoeuvres instantiated by the reflexive and linguistic turns and the doubts they cast on the ability of the human sciences to mirror the physical sciences. Both make legitimacy claims, which are distinct from, but still shadow, the world of hard science and the surety under which it operates. Yet, coincidentally, reflexivity as such is still overlooked in such methodologies. If we take educational research as an example, one writer adopting an ethnographic approach noted the paucity of reflexivity on the part of researchers: "Despite the influence of interactionism on ethnography, ethnographers have not generally taken the principle of reflexivity to heart in their research practice" (Hammersley and Atkinson, 1983: 4). Whilst the editor of a collection of "accounts of accounts" also wrote of a general lack of "first-hand accounts . . . which focus on the researcher and the research process" (Burgess, 1984: vii). He quotes C. Wright-Mills approvingly that "it is better to have a personal account than codifications" (p. 4) and Bell and Newby that "you should if possible write yourself into your account" (p. 6). That being said, reflexivity was then to be given a major boost; this coming from two directions: one practical and the other philosophical.

The practical boost was generated by the publication of the book, *The Reflective Practitioner* by Donald Schön (1983). The first thing to note, of course, is that reflective is not quite the same as *reflexive*. Nevertheless, the two are close enough to discuss together in the present context. His case is not dissimilar to the one outlined earlier that juxtaposed scientific theory and educational theory. Again, Schön takes exception with a view of research that is too dedicated to cause and effect, means and outcomes. For him, such is too technicist and underrepresents a more holistic approach to practice. The world for Schön is far more "fuzzy" and imprecise, where there is little linearity between social phenomena. The professional researcher, therefore, develops more an "artistry" of practice where situations are framed in such a way that means/ends, cause/effect and theory/practice can be held together at one and the same time. The resultant understanding is then similarly holistic in that it is expressed as a series of relationships rather than uniform causality. Knowledge – some of which is conscious and some tacit – is called upon "in action" whereby new situations are made sense of through the identification of the familiar with the less familiar, which then gives rise to further new knowledge. In a way, such reflective practitioner behaviour might even be seen as a very fast, automatic form of interpretative ethnography, or grounded theory, but this time operated in an internal and practical manner. Reflection might similarly be "on action" and "in action". In a way, any action requires a degree of reflection – an interpretation and judgement of intent and experience – but, here, time is critical in that the space for reflection in action is quite limited; what exists therefore is mostly tacit. However, separated from the immediacy of experience, there is scope for "reflection-on-action"; that would be, with hindsight.

The "reflective practitioner" is a rich metaphor, and it is possible to see it manifested in everyday life and as part of a research practice. It certainly puts the emphasis on an "epistemology of practice", and stresses the way that reflection – reflexivity – raises questions about time, experience and balance between explicit and tacit understanding. It also again links with issues with respect to language: how much of reflection is tacit and unconscious, and how much of it is conscious and intentional. This in itself raises further questions about the articulatability of reflection and reflexivity, as well as the precise language used to express it. In other words, such underlines the conceptual framework used and the degree to which this is employed reflexively.

Not unconnected with these final points is the other major boost, this time philosophical, to greater adoption of reflexive methods: post-modernism.

Reflexivity, Postmodernism and Anthropology

In this section, we want to consider the way that reflexivity impacted in anthropology. However, first, and very much in the light of the above, we need to say a few words about postmodernism: first, because it is something which impacted heavily on anthropology and ethnography; and second, because it is a socio-philosophical approach against which Bourdieu very much opposed his own.

There are many names associated with postmodernism – Lyotard, Rorty, Derrida, Foucault, Baudrillard, Jameson, for example – and it is not possible to go into all of these and the various contributions they offered. However, we would make the following key points:

First, they all arise from the linguistic turn outlined above and the extensions where the stability of meaning in language – the link between the signifier and the signified – collapsed and, with it, humanist and spiritualist narratives coming out of the eighteenth-century Enlightenment. Jean-François Lyotard – who in fact coined the phrase "the post-modern condition" (1979) – argued that such humanist principles had been constructed around a series of *metanarratives*, which disguised values and motives that were other than "enlightened", and in fact were created to service the needs of their creators. In other words, their legitimacy and justification needed to be questioned. In effect, this more or less undermined the whole modernist project with its commitment to liberty and progress through emancipation.

Second, and as a result, post-modern discourse put intense focus on language itself in an effort to uncover the hidden interests they conveyed. Even the natural sciences, with their allegiance to representation and objectivity, became suspect because of its reliance on the declared autonomy between knowers and knowledge, observer and observed, subject and object. In other words, things were not as they *seemed* but how they were *seen*. This realisation further intensified preoccupations with such narratives, their constructive nature, and the search for a more authentic knowledge base – both in and for itself.

If we transpose these sorts of arguments to the study of anthropology and ethnography, we begin to see the kind of effects such a position can have. By the second half of the twentieth century, through the work of such writers as Claude Lévi Strauss and Thomas Geertz (1926–2006) (see 1993/73), there already existed attempts to move anthropologists away from the authority of their singular voice, and to reconstitute the discipline as a more objective science; for example, by identifying universal rules of myth and the symbols by which they were constituted. For Geertz, who also worked with Talcot Parsons, this was achieved first through *thick descriptions* of socio-cultural systems. However, if such approaches shifted anthropologists from asserting their own objectivity and acknowledging instead a degree of cultural relativism, and despite recognising the nature and production of knowledge, their ambition remained positivistic; that is, to come up with stable, transferable rules about the workings of cultures. This was changing.

At one point, Bourdieu writes how it took him ten years to see the world as an Algerian peasant would, and this is an apposite issue: we see as we are, which implies *our* relationship to the object of study. Many anthropologists began to recognise this; that the discipline itself was partly a legacy of colonialisation and the relationship – view – that such creates and endows. Tyler (1986: 127f.) sketches the course of this evolution. In the eighteenth century, he argues, ethnography was treated as allegory centering on the utopian myth of the "noble savage" (Rousseau), who evolved into a kind of "living fossil" or "primordial primitive" in nineteenth century anthropology. In terms of twentieth century structuralist and semiotic approaches, traditional societies then became pure data sources for their theorising. Later still, as part of what Marcus and Fischer refer to as "the experimental moment" (1986) in the human sciences, "the savage" is allowed to speak for themselves, albeit in edited extracts chosen by the ethnographer. Tyler refers to this a form of ethnography as "ethnopoetry", an alienating undertaken itself reflecting an alienated ethnographer. Tyler sums up:

> Like Derrida, they have missed the true import of "discourse", which is "the other as us", for the point of discourse is *not how to make a better representation, but how to avoid representation.* In their textualization of pseudo-discourse they have accomplished a terrorist alienation more complete

than that of the positivists. It may be that all textualization is alienation, but it is certainly true that non-participatory textualization is alienation – "not us" – and there is no therapy in alienation.

(Tyler, 1986: 128 my emphasis)

Tyler here is referring to the way that post-modernist approaches to anthropology, themselves paradoxical, offer a double paradox: by affecting to employ various textual and literary techniques in writing texts – including a self-awareness (reflexivity) of their essential nature as "poetics and politics" – they are merely reasserting the search for the holy grail of disclosure. As an alternative to "representation", Tyler proposes "evocation":

The whole point of "evoking" rather than "representing" is that it frees ethnography from *mimesis* and the inappropriate mode of scientific rhetoric that entails "objects", "facts", "descriptions", "inductions", "generalisations", "verification", "experiment", "truth", and like concepts that, except as empty evocations, have no parallels either in experiences of ethnographic fieldwork or in writing ethnographies.

(ibid.: 130)

Such an argument returns us to the tension between subject and object, the core of meaning and understanding, and how to express "findings" as such. Post-modernism, of course, impacted across the fields of human knowledge and one response was to turn its attack as a means of defence. So, if post-modernist "texts" were characterised by their hybrid, paradoxical, a-temporal nature, then we should adopt similar attitudes (implying relationships) to those texts themselves. Rather than define meaning, such "de-centred" it as a means of holding tensions, not denying ambiguity, and thus, somehow, neither subjugating subjectivity nor denying objectivity. If this seems a very unstable, uncertain position to occupy, let alone articulate it, then that is because it is. A sort of refusal of fact all too easily leads to an auto-fascination with the individual, where the researcher becomes more important that the research, and the former is caught within a spiral dive into a nihilistic black hole of self-referential reflexivity. It is a trap that other writers have struggled to escape.

Reflexivity and Knowledge

By now, it should be clear that reflexivity is a complex phenomenon, both in its definition and application. Yet, knowledge and methodology without some degree of reflexivity are questionable for the authority they assume. At the same time, we have seen that über-reflexivity can itself be disarming in actually dissolving research method and its resultant findings in a pool of relativity. We complete this chapter with some direct comments about reflexivity within the fields of linguistic ethnography, since such forms an associate focus for our concerns with language-based ethnographies as read through a reflexive lens. However, as a prelude, this section sums up various ways in ways reflexivity might be expressed.

In looking at the distinction (or distance) between representation (image) and research object (reality), Woolgar (1988b), for example, refers to Garfinkel's foundational ethnomethodological approach to *constitutive reflexivity*; there is an *intimate* inter-relationship between the surface appearance (document) developed to express underlying reality, so that the latter is elaborated by drawing on the former, and the former is elaborated by what is known about the latter. In other words, the two are co-terminus as part of an iterative process. Such, of course would be anathema to the "natural sciences", which affirms a distinction between representation of the studied object of research and the object itself. In so much as they share similarity of knowledge base, it is all to the good since it affirms the objective knowledge of science. What reflexivity might be present is here simply a kind of *benign introspection*, or awareness of doing what one is doing whilst one is doing it, and *retrospection* in the form of *post-hoc* "confessions" from the workbook diaries of the researchers involved. The former represents an undefined general self-awareness on the part of the researcher, whilst the latter is a sort of bolt-on, after the event form of reflexivity that accompanies research accounts. Both have little truck with the constructivist attitudes attributed above to such writers as Marcus and Clifford.

Latour (1986) makes another distinction between *meta-reflexivity* and *infra-reflexivity*. Behind both lies a deep suspicion on the legitimacy of the researcher in action, what justification they call on to do what they do, and the resultant text presenting the outcomes of their activities. They both also raise an issue that we have hardly touched on yet, which is the way that reflexivity needs to be seen not only as the responsibility of the researcher/writer, but also the reader of any text. In other words, research texts assume a reader, indeed, sets up a relationship between author and reader. As such, both individually and together imply an invitation to constitute a reflexive relationship between the two rather than an oppositional or hierarchical one. For Latour, meta-reflexivity operates when the writer discloses the means of their methods, not simply in terms of the conduct of research but in the construction of texts emerging from it. This "calling attention to" the – possibly even deleterious – effect of text inflates method to a level of acute self-awareness. Indeed, it is never ending, since even the attempt to do this can be similarly made explicit, and that attempt in its turn. As can be seen, such quickly leads to a kind of feedback reflexivity where the action of reflexivity is instantly reflected upon, and indeed that action in turn. Such an approach, one often adopted by ethnomethodologists and postmodernist deconstructionists, seems to act on the principle that one can almost transcend thought by the power of thought itself and, by implication, that there is some final resting place when "truth will out". Clearly, both are questionable. *Infra-reflexivity*, on the other hand, takes a somewhat opposite approach, one that might be considered methodologically deflationary. Here, the focus is on replacing method with style and avoiding orthodox forms of scientific narrative. As such, disciplinary meta-language is eschewed in favour of blurred scholarly boundaries and associate hybridised cross-over terms.

Such issues raise questions about a range of topics already raised and researchers struggle somewhat to come up with a satisfactory response to them. We have seen that at base is this issue of the relationship between subject and object, a phenomenon and its representation. This might even seem a naïve question, but we have seen that it has implications also for the relationship between theory and practice, and what we take to be true and dependable. Therefore, not a simple question at all. In attempting to represent their respective disciplinary worlds, social and natural scientists have developed methods that put such issues in sharp relief, and almost demand questions with respect to confidence in their knowledge claims, if only to know the limits and extent what we can be sure of. Reflexivity must be part of such a process, even in its absence. We have looked at the ways that reflexivity might be understood, and how various ones – ethnographers, etc. – have attempted to operationalise it. Finally, and perhaps most importantly in the present context, is a range of issues concerning language: the language used in representation; the relationship between language and thinking; and the way in which language features as part of reflection and reflexivity. All of which pertains to further questions about how one *does* reflexivity – if "does" is the apposite word. These issues and questions really form the core of the rest of the book. Lastly, in this chapter, I turn my attention back to the science of language – linguistics – and consider to what extent reflexivity might feature in its past research endeavours.

Linguistics, Ethnography and Reflexivity

By now, it should be fairly clear that reflexivity is multidimensional and, indeed, it might be best to understand it both as having "hard" and "soft" forms; more-over, that these forms themselves are best seen as a continuum. On the one hand, we can hardly walk one step down the road without a degree of reflexivity entering in. On the other hand, however, there are extreme and rather obtuse forms of reflexivity that pertain to the nature of knowledge itself, and can involve sophisticated forms of philosophy to operationalise.

As noted above, linguistics constituted itself as a "hard" science in its very foundation, and both its structural and Chomskyan forms are predicted on falsifiable theories as robust as any natural science. Which is not to say that more socially sensitive variants have not also emerged; for example, sociolinguistics and social psycholinguistics. Clearly, it is beyond the remit of this book to examine in detail the extent to which reflexivity has featured in such disciplines but, on the whole, it does tend to be implied to a large extent. Even in a book addressing "the social turn in second language acquisition" (Block, 2003), there is no mention of reflection or reflexivity in it.

Linguistic Ethnography

It is worth looking at an academic area in which we might expect a degree of reflexivity with respect to language and ethnography: *Linguistic Ethnography* (LE). First, we might say that LE is not language-based ethnography, which could seem odd as it would appear to share its main focuses. As we have seen earlier in this chapter, various approaches to language study have been taken, and indeed naturalistic ethnographic methods. LE is a relatively recent development in this research tradition. In a seminal article, Rampton (2007b) sets out what we are to understand by this "new" academic field of "linguistic ethnography". He refers to it as "the development of an arena for the analysis of language in society" (p. 1). It is not, he argues, a "school" or a "definitive synthesis" but "a site of encounter" where existing lines of research "interact", "pushed" together as they are by circumstance. Linguistic Ethnography can then be understood as a "hybrid" of ethnography, as a form of anthropological study and linguistics, the technical study of language. The article refers to some of the other qualitative shifts that have taken place in linguistics; including Conversation Analysis, New Literacy Studies and Critical Discourse Analysis. The main virtue of Linguistic Ethnography, Rampton argues, is that "ethnography opens linguistics up" and "linguistics ties ethnography down" (p. 8). By "opening up", they clearly mean developing cultural sensitivity, reflexivity and contextual understanding; by "tying down", they intend technical descriptions, systematic analysis and delimitable processes. What does this look like in practice?

If we take an exemplar of work from exponents of LE, we see the efforts they make to develop a reflexive account of their activities. In *Reflexivity, Voice and Representation in Linguistic Ethnography*, Creese (2015) recounts a project concerning community-run complementary schools in Birmingham. Essentially, this project, the teaching of Punjabi, and the research sets out to explore the literary practices amongst the staff and students involved in such teaching and learning. A primary intent was to move away from a straight linguistic analysis since an assumption that answers lie in the language itself is eschewed by the project team, who are made up of a number of contract researchers (in fact the project extended to various European countries) as well as Creese and other Birmingham-based academics; for example, Adrian Blackledge. Within its opening sentences, the author makes it clear that "investigating the investigation" is central to her concerns and that a range of "practices and routines" were "established for making reflexivity a regular point of consideration" in the ethnography (p. 61). What are these? There is certainly an account of the research process, its questions and conduct. Teams are employed, so that no one view skews data collection and analyses and there is a commitment to *participant observation* (p. 67). So far, so ethnographic.

Data included a range of language recordings, interviews, but these were complemented by field notes and team discussion transcripts, which supported both analyses and disclosure of the processes involved in developing findings and formulating conclusions: "This means that data in our project include not only evidence about our research participants but also evidence about the construction of multilingualism and monolingualism in the research team" (p. 69). Team negotiations then ensued in which "fiercely held beliefs" presented themselves. This approach, where the researcher almost becomes the research, is extended to examples of biographical provenance. The researchers talked a lot about "their own educational background, social class and attainment" (p. 84). One researcher discloses his own history in Birmingham, the school he attended, children. In other words, his "researcher identity" is not discarded and, on occasion, his interpretations are connected directly to features of his socio-cultural provenance (p. 85). It is also made clear how sensitive the researchers were about their presence "in the field" and how this is reflected in the data. The author is sensitive to the possible disruptive effect that her presence might have on a mock examination, and also points out that this is reflected inconsistently is various drafts of field notes. Moreover, she observes how *en passant*, almost "lighthearted" points noted come to have a larger significance once specific themes are developed, which by definition give rise to greater attention being given to them; in other words, the researchers' "stance" towards the notes changes, implying the whole nature of the relationship between researcher and research. At base, however, there is still the "grounded theory" approach of "bottom up" formulations of categories and themes "generated" from the data: "institutional voice", "researcher positionality", "classroom practices" and "social practices". Out of these "emerged patterns" in the "reproduction of distinction about schooling and workplace success" (p. 76), including temporal and spatial dimensions.

Clearly, the researchers in this project have taken issues of reflexivity extremely seriously and have adopted many of the sort of angles and dimensions of reflection and reflexivity highlighted in earlier parts of this chapter. There is certainly intentionality to "objectify" the process of research method, including data collection and analysis, Moreover, there is full recognition of the influence of the researcher and how this can be included as part of the analysis. Clearly, there are tensions, of personal perspective and familiarity, which risk forming a kind of subjective bias. However, the fact that this all takes place within a team allows for a degree of critical scrutiny and verification. That being said, there is more we might ask for. For example, greater systematicity with respect to the disclosure made in terms of the research team personnel; what they shared and what divided them and the symbolic value of each. Also, what was not disclosed: for example, the relationships between researchers and their relative power positions within both the project and the research field they represent. Such extends to the actual relationship between the researchers and the researched. Again, power relations are implied and one wonders to what extent interviewers and interviewees were matched systematically. Finally, although the author makes considerable efforts to define their particular approach to research, there are questions both of how it fits within the academic space of scholarship overall – its epistemological stances – and its position within the larger social sphere. For example, the research was presumably sponsored by someone, a fact which could have constituent influence on its outcomes. These are points, which we intend to take up and further elucidate upon in future chapters, and both from a theoretical and practical point of view. This will be done in the course of our coverage of Bourdieu and reflexivity and the practical case studies, which further highlight aspects of these.

In Summary

This chapter began with considering a common sense approach to reflexivity. We have seen how it has evolved as a concept; from once being a kind of afterthought, or biological nicety, to occupying a central concern for researchers both in the natural and human sciences. We have seen that reflexivity also implies the relationship between theory and practice, and subjectivity and objectivity – briefly, knowledge and knowing. We also discussed the way language is implicated in these sorts of relationships, and the consequences it has once one begins to doubt its foundational nature. Pragmatic, utilitarian deployment of such terms of the "reflective practitioner" are all very well up to a point, but reflexivity is something other. What is it and how do we do it? We have set the discussion within a historical perspective that leads to the dangers of hyper-reflexivity of postmodernism and the problems that result when the researchers become more important than the research. Finally, we have considered Linguistic Ethnography and ways in which reflexivity has been attempted. The whole forms a basis for a subsequent discussion, which develops both a Bourdieusian approach to reflexivity and exemplifies it within a series of practice case exemplars. Such will then allow us to take forward what has been achieved and what more there is to do in order to develop a greater intentional, level approach to reflexivity at all stages of the research process. The next chapter takes us towards this goal by presenting Bourdieu and showing how his methods and approaches developed as a reflexive enterprise, as well as seeing the consequences and challenges such entails.

3

BOURDIEU, ETHNOGRAPHY AND REFLEXIVITY

Michael Grenfell

Introduction

We have seen from the previous two chapters just the wealth and diversity of research scholarship there is within our salient areas of work: language, ethnography and reflexivity. The chapters have thrown issues up in the air from a wide range of perspectives, problems and responses to them. We now want to move increasingly to focus on the core of our concerns in this book, namely, language ethnographies which have been undertaken by our co-contributors taking inspiration from the work of the French social theorist, Pierre Bourdieu. We will, in Part III, then consider the implications of them adopting his ideas in their own empirical language ethnographic investigations, with especial reference to the centrality of reflexivity in this undertaking. Discussions therein will allow us to both assess and extend the potential of Bourdieu's "reflexive method" in language-based ethnographies, in particular, and social science research more generally. This present chapter then moves us in such a direction by presenting Bourdieu, his own ethnographic work, the theory of practice that underpinned it and the extent to which reflexivity is a feature of it. What we offer in terms of reflexivity in this chapter will provide a springboard for further extensions in the final parts of this book.

This chapter offers something by way of introducing Bourdieu in terms of who he was and what he accomplished. Such biographical detail is essential in understanding the nature of his theory and method, and provides some of the grounding themes with respect to reflexivity in developing both. His own formative scholarly disciplines will be presented along with the empirical ethnographies he undertook – and, perhaps more importantly, why. These empirical details will be the basis of an account of his salient key concepts, which he used throughout his research and became focused tools of analysis for him. The chapter will show, given what these were, on what they were based, and how employed, and the way that reflexivity was and is always implicated in the approach. In particular, we shall undertake an initial discussion of the place and role of language within reflexivity, as Bourdieu understood it as an active ingredient of his conducting research. All this clearly is pertinent to other forms of ethnographies besides language-based ones, so we shall make passing reference to these areas whilst also focusing on language-specific issues in ethnographic work. Finally, we shall make a preliminary formulation of *participant objectivation*, a term which most succinctly encapsulates his reflexive stance within ethnographic studies.

Bourdieu – Biography

As we stated earlier, the need for reflexivity in scientific research is predicated on the appreciation that personal bias can enter into the process, which skews the results. Of course, this does raise further questions about to what extent it is possible to escape such bias – and it may indeed "to an extent" – and, if so, how. One obvious bias is the biography of the researcher, as it is pretty evident that a particular socio-cultural and professional trajectory instills a certain way of seeing the world that sets limits on what is and is not perceived. A lot of the rest of the book is about unpacking these statements. In this section, I launch the discussion by considering the biography of Pierre Bourdieu – not simply out of fascination with personal histories but as a prelude to establishing what he did, why, and the way that reflexivity featured in it.

Pierre Bourdieu was born in 1930 in Denguin, a small village in the French Hautes Pyrénées region of south-west France. His family background was quite humble and consisted of little more than traditional peasant life: in fact, his father was an itinerant crop sharer cum post-office worker, and he spoke Gascon rather than French for the first years of his life before going to boarding school in the local town of Pau. Why this is significant is because already life experience set up a series of dispositional structures, which were to shape the rest of his life. Bourdieu talks about the way local town pupils made fun of his rural accent and the way he dressed – the offspring of town-based families came to school each day but spent the rest of the time at home, they wore their own clothes and possessed the trappings of city life, whereas Bourdieu wore a smock and had to "live-in" the school for most of the week, including weekends. There is no judgement here to be made on what is right or wrong; rather, the point is that the experience opened up for Bourdieu a personal *clivage* in terms of socio-cultural positioning, what he later referred to as a *cleft habitus*. Such would clearly be felt at a deeply emotional and psychological level; a social suffering which was later to become central to his professional concerns. Before we tease out the relative constituents of the psychological, sociological and philosophical, it is probably important to ask whether or not this earlier dispositional division opened up further in his educational life – and the answer would be, "yes!"

After further studies in Pau, Bourdieu went on to the *lycée Louis le Grand* in Paris. Again, it is crucial to draw attention to what this would have represented for a young Bourdieu, in that this *lycée* represented "the" training school for one of the most celebrated French *Grandes Écoles* – the equivalent to the English Oxford and Cambridge universities. So, he subsequently passed the entrance *concours* for the *École Normale Supérieure* (ENS), the most prestigious university institution based in Paris, to which most modern and contemporary intellectuals would have gone. Even with this statement, it is necessary to point out that the French intellectual tradition is unique and has given the world many of its most influential thinkers. Dating back to the eighteenth-century *Enlightenment*, intellectualism in France therefore has a more celebrated and secure history, in a way that probably does not exist in an Anglo-Saxon world. It is not a pejorative term to refer to someone as "an intellectual" but more common-place and seen as a way to honour French republican culture. What would have this meant to Bourdieu? The simple answer is "a lot", as he would now have been on the "royal road" to entering intellectual elite of the country, which he did, subsequently being coronated (sic) the leading exponent in his field when in 1981 he was inaugurated as Chair of Sociology in the *Collège de France* – that most august of sixteenth-century French institutions being made up of just 52 professors dedicated not just to "truth" but "free research" in pursuit of it.

Bourdieu graduated from the ENS with a degree in Philosophy – a must for a young Intellectual – in 1955, but the experience was once again multifaceted. On the one hand, the academic route he had taken assured him a secure, if not brilliant, future within the French intellectual field. Yet, on the other hand, in later life, he commented again of feeling out of place, and not just socially but intellectually as well; although, of course, as noted before, the two should never be seen as somehow separate.

Later, we shall need to look into the sort of intellectual ideas Bourdieu was exploring in his formative years as a way to provide a grounding to the way his thinking developed. For the moment, we note that the sort of intellectual climate that Bourdieu was imbibing itself can be characterised by certain traditions. As noted, contemporary view of modern man and rational thinking can be traced back to the *Enlightenment* and beyond. The great French Revolution of 1789 had brought matters to a head – or seemingly – when the Church and Monarchy were rejected in favour of secularity and Republican principles. But, the old authorities were reluctant to lie down and stay dead and, as well as continuing fierce resistance to the modern French state, the experiences of the socio-economic crises in the 1930s, together with the traumas of war and collaboration in the 1940s, meant that reactionary thinking was still alive, well and kicking. Bourdieu would have needed to find a laic route through French philosophy, augmented with his reading of continental metaphysical philosophy.

The philosopher, author and playwright Jean-Paul Sartre – also an ex-pupil of the ENS – was the intellectual star of the day with his brand of French Existentialism, which insisted on individual freedom as a basis of humanism. The other great intellectual of the 1950s was Claude Lévi-Strauss who also had studied Philosophy at University in Paris and was nominated to the *Collège de France* in 1959. However, Lévi-Strauss undertook fieldwork studies of traditional cultures, developing a contemporary brand of structural anthropology which emphasised the underlying "rules" of socio-cultural behaviour. Such figures in the intellectual field would have been significant for Bourdieu when he went to Algeria on military service in 1955. The effects of experiencing a full-blown colonial war at first-hand was to have an epiphanic impact on Bourdieu as he struggled to make sense of what was going on around him. Besides, daily acts of terror, Bourdieu saw the destruction of traditional Algerian rural culture as Berbers were moved off their land to *groupement* encampments. Religions were opposed, as were local customs and modern attitudes. A keen photographer, Bourdieu took literally thousands of photographs, made field notes and drew sketches in order to record what he saw on the ground. It is this, more than anything else, which moved Bourdieu away from pure philosophy to a more applied version of it – in particular, at least at first – in anthropology. This gave rise to an ethnographic regard that stayed with Bourdieu for the rest of his life. The next section goes into more detail on its results.

Bourdieu's Ethnographies

In the last section, we saw something of Bourdieu's empirical biography as he progressed from the son of a French rural worker to become one of the leading thinkers amongst the Parisian intelligentsia. We make these points not out of some kind of *en passant* interest in who he was, but as features which are central to the sort of issues we will be highlighting later on in the book. We noted that Bourdieu trained as a philosopher and only embraced anthropology of the day out of some sort of practical necessity to explore and understand the surroundings into which he was thrust; and, then, a certain sort of anthropology, commanding a particular place within the French academic tradition of the 1950s.

Anthropology more generally can be defined as the study of human societies, in particular with respect to indigenous cultural practices: it is a kind of human sociology, and its roots go back to the seventeenth century and beyond where "man" became an object of study. Later nineteenth-century versions took in Darwinian evolutionism as traditional cultures and non-Western societies became the focus of explorers and anthropologists such as Richard Burton, Edward Burnett Tylor, Franz Boaz, Margaret Mead and Bronislaw Malinowski. Before we look at Bourdieu's "anthropology", it is worth noting, and despite the influence it had on him, that he rarely used the word; and the term "ethnology" is more frequently employed in his work. Ethnology is a branch of anthropology that compares and analyses the characteristics of different people and the relationships between them. In theory at least, it is distinct from ethnography *per se*, which is more concerned with the direct study of single groups in contact with cultures. In practice, of course, it would not be unusual for researchers to be undertaking both ethnography *and* ethnology within a broader anthropological umbrella; and each of these terms have various delineations between its active members. And, then there is sociology.

Once again, sociology is a term used for an activity that goes well back into the annals of history: and its antecedents can be found in Greek philosophy, Confucianism and medieval Arab writings. In modern times, it seems to have been used first by the French essayist Emmanuel Joseph Sieyès in 1760, although is was another Frenchman, Auguste Comte (1798–1857), who is attributed with being the "founding father" of sociology per se when he adopted the term in place of "social physics" to describe the study of society. It is not a coincidence that Comte very much grew out of both the Enlightenment and revolutionary periods, and sociology was first seen as rationalist integration of history, psychology and economics. Most significantly, it presented itself as a "science" with the ambition to formulate rules about society in the same way as one might in the natural sciences. Other founding fathers of sociology would be the Germans Karl Marx (1818–1883) and Max Weber (1864–1920). Bourdieu drew on these writers in his own sociological explorations, as well as another Frenchman Emile Durkheim (1858–1917). It is important to note that when Bourdieu was embracing sociology in the 1950s, it was not the popular discipline it became in the 1960s and beyond. In fact, it was not even taught that much at university and was mostly preoccupied with the social statistics of trends produced by INSEE. This gave Bourdieu space to fashion his own brand of sociology – *La sociologie* – which is best understood as being very distinct from its Anglo-Saxon counter-part, despite sharing many of the same concerns and indeed thematic language. As we have noted, Bourdieu's sociology need to be seen as a hybrid of anthro-pology and philosophy before anything, and linked to an Enlightenment project that forms a core to the modern French intellectual tradition. In approaching "Bourdieu ethnographies", we can therefore expect a high degree of philosophical insight in how they are interpreted, as well as extensive anthropological exemplification drawn from empirical data. That is exactly what we find.

Above, we noted how Bourdieu was a keen photographer, and it is worth keeping this fact in mind when approaching his ethnographic studies; in that, with somewhat of an anthropological eye, his research projects often seem to arise from a single observation. With Algeria, it was his noticing that despite the country commanding so much of the attention of French society and politi-cians, few seem to know or understand exactly what it was. In education, it was his view that again despite considerable discussion about education in post-war France, no-one seemed to know much about the constitutional make-up of students of the day (see Grenfell, 2007). But, it is perhaps in the Béarn that his photographer's eye is most apparent. It is a Christmas dance near to his home village in the Pyrénées. Everyone is celebrating and enjoying themselves centered around music and the dance floor. Children are laughing and running around. But, then Bourdieu notices a group of men gathered together in a place set back from the others. Although they watch, they do not dance. They all seem about the same age, of the same awkward mine and are caught standing as if outside the festivities. After what seems a respectable amount of time, they make their excuses and go off to drink and play dominoes in a nearby café. One can almost imagine Bourdieu asking: Who are these men? Why do they not join in? What are they experiencing? These seem to be almost naïve questions. However, to answer them, Bourdieu involves the most sophisticated methods he can in order to get to the heart of their evident "social suffering". The results of his analyses appeared in 1962 in a journal entitled *Études Rurales* (1962b) under the article title "Bachelorhood and the Peasant Condition". Indeed, it is a long article – one that took up half of the available space of the journal; something that would be unheard of these days. But, then Bourdieu returns to this study ten years later and reworks the analyses in the light of further reflections and work elsewhere (1972) for an article entitled "Matrimonial Strategies in the System of Reproduction Strategies". And, then, once again in 1989 for a further article, "Reproduction Forbidden: The Symbolic Dimension of Economic Domination" (1989a). In these articles, we see Bourdieu employing every methodological technique available to him, including interviews, statistical analyses, photos, maps and ethnographical narrative. We also see the empirical work necessarily prerequisite to his methodological formulations. The study is multifaceted. In terms of language, he notes how domination – by the outside elite of the peasant life style – is affected in the very language with which the peasant speaks of himself with its associations of clumsiness, heaviness and ignorance of the urban world (see Grenfell, 2011). There is also a mixture of French and the local Béarnais dialect, which plays itself out in actual speech and accent depending on geographical locale – the *Village, Commune, Bourg* and *Hammeau*. Bourdieu is therefore able to show linguistic differentiation between standard and local varieties of speech in terms of social positioning. He also shows how women tend to be more linguistically sensitive – and therefore "correct" – than men. But, what of the men he observed at the dance? It turns out they are all bachelors, rendered "unmarriable" by dent of their position of succession within the family vis-à-vis siblings. Before 1914, marriages were in effect governed by strict formal rules. Faced with the changing world, however, such regulation decreased. A wider range of strategies were therefore needed in order to assure successful marriage and inheritance. Two principles operated: first, one which prioritised the rights of elder children so that the inheritance would not be split; second, the distinction between socially ascending and descending marriages. The classic "bachelor" of the dance floor was consequently the younger child of both large and poor families, but for different reasons. In one case, marriage would entail undesirable dowry payments; in the other, fragmentation of inheritance. The conclusion being that marriage and celibacy was not simply an individual but a collective decision; one which was socially prescribed and managed, in this case normally by the grandmother.

Even with this early study, there are various features, which are key to understanding Bourdieu's ethnography. First, is simply the motive for undertaking an ethnographic study in the first – what observation leads one to this kind of "intervention"? Second, is the range and integration of techniques employed. Third, is the way explanation and consequent theory emerge and are logically necessitated by the data. Related to this point, fourth, is a significant distinction between "rule" and "strategy": Bourdieu showed that consciously recognised rules were not enough, a strategic orientation was also necessary in playing for advantage in the social space. (This point represents a significant departure from the line taken by the anthropology of Lévi-Strauss which, as we have noted, was so popular at the time, since for the latter, "objective rules" were the basis of socio-cultural knowledge systems.) Fifth, is the development of a new way of looking at the world – what Bourdieu would later call a "new gaze" or *metanoia*. In other words, his method was able to show up the misrecognised principles of action under-lying the apparent surface actions and behaviours of those involved. Sixth, finally, and perhaps particularly important in our present context, is just what this new gaze meant and in fact did to the one making it. In a later volume col-lecting together the various articles on *the bachelors' ball* (2008a), Bourdieu writes of the "emotional" and "intellectual transformation" – even "conversion" – that was necessary on his part in breaking with his own native "empirical" view; creating, as a result, a world that, although more *realistic*, was more *distant* and therefore *less comfortable*. Moreover, such a move impacted not only at a personal, emotional level, but entailed a discipline shift – from philosophy to ethnology, from ethnology to sociology, which itself had implications for his standing socially (p. 2).

A similar pattern of approach can be observed in his work on Algeria. There is the same recourse to a range of techniques and methods in constructing his ethnographic studies (1963, 1964a); the same imperative to rework the analyses at periodic intervals after their initial publication (1977b, 1990c). Mostly, perhaps, is the need not to take Algeria as a pre-given. In fact, the first line of the first page of his first publication on Algeria (1958) states that "it does not exist", of course, as a single "cultural unity" (p. 5). Rather, it is a social construct created for the benefit of those who had colonised the country. What he offers instead is a kind of socio-cultural topography of the terrain delineated by the borders known as Algeria. This includes its four principal peoples – the Kabyles, the Shawia, the Mozabites and the Arab-speaking people. What he finds on the ground, of course, is that each of these have their own languages, cultures and, with them, ways of seeing the world. This involves religions and traditional beliefs, which affect the way they orientate themselves in economic exchanges. He shows how economic exchanges are *symbolic* and based on honour that prefigures an entirely different orientation to the future when compared to capitalistic systems. There are not social classes as we know them, therefore, but traditional clans and castes make up the Algerian socio-economic infrastructure. At his most Lévi-Straussian, he also sketches out the plan of the Kabyle house, arguing that in its very design that their relationship to the world and universe is reproduced (1979a: 140–141) according to homologous oppositions of fire/water, cooked/raw, high/low, light/dark, animal/human, night/day, male/female, etc.

Language again features, and Bourdieu notes the way that French and Arab languages are used for "different worlds": when Arab is used there is within it an entire "vision" of the world, including God and destiny; whilst French is the language of protest and counter claim (1977c: 94–95). He also notes the widespread "destructuration" that the French operated there, which resulted in inhabitants being moved off of their land and, with it, away from their traditional farming economies, to live in encampment collectivities (2012: 105). Photos taken by Bourdieu show the juxtaposition of "old" and "new" Algerians: traditionally garbed inhabitants riding modern motorcycles (2012: 31) and "modern men" selling their good from mobile shops (2012: 160). Needless to say, such changes had profound socio-political repercussions, with some groups ready to embrace the modern capitalist world, and others wishing to continue with past beliefs. Attitudes to revolution, independence and a new Algeria could all be identified with particular social strata, which only showed up fundamental differences in aspiration and rationale; all of which augured badly for a future peaceful country – as was shown to be true. Colonialism, it seemed, came at a huge cost, the removal of the colonial leaders of which did not resolve consequent problems. Bourdieu writes on the "domination effect", that even when ruling cultures withdraw, their pernicious effects remain. These were formative ethnographies for Bourdieu – rich, dense and tightly argued. Once again, however, the biggest insights seemed to be personal and methodological. As noted before, he later remarked that it took him ten years – at least! – to be able to see the world through the eyes of an Algerian peasant (2000a). This is a salutary statement and again raises questions of reflexivity and method when we come to look at the world through an ethnographic eye.

It is worth pausing at this point to note that these studies in the Béarn and Algeria represent Bourdieu at his most ethnographic: this is Bourdieu "in the field", surrounded by the intensity of first-hand empirical experience; this is where his philosophical eye met real world events and the need to make sense of them; this is where his own background and biography was brought to play as part of his scholastic endeavours. Such implicate issues of theory and practice, the world and the individual, and consequently the limits of scientific knowledge. It also very much puts a focus on the individual and their own relations to the objects of study. These issues will be explored further below. For the moment, it is important to appreciate the way Bourdieu's "ethnographic" understanding and approach were subsequently taken forward into further "field works". In 1964, he took over the directorship of the *Centre de Sociologie Européenne* from Raymond Aron, which legitimated a full-blown embracing of sociology, or at least his version of it. Of course, the epistemological "conversion" had already taken place; all that was now needed was the time and resources to take it forward. Two areas were of immediate attention – education and culture – which in many ways can be regarded as aspects of the same thing.

Bourdieu's early work on education offers a kind of social topography of the student population, in a similar way as he had with Algeria, again with a commitment to find out just who they were (1979b/1964; 1964b). These studies were largely based on ethnographic interviews and questionnaires, and provide a scope of the provenance and cultural practice of French students. It is important to place such work in the context of post-War France, where education was seen as central to the building of the modern Nation state. Education was also considered a critical aspect of defending and implementing French Republican values of Equality, Liberty and Fraternity. It was therefore a scathing attack on such presumptions when Bourdieu's subsequent analyses argued that it was education which acted most centrally in the preservation, through reproduction, of the French social elite (1977a); in other words, the Jacobin ambition of the "democratic school" was an illusion (1966). Subsequent major studies on Education targeted the field of Higher Education institutions (1988/1984) and the role of the *Grandes Écoles* (1996a/1989) within it. The latter, in particular, entitled "the State Nobility" seemed to suggest that nothing had changed from pre-revolutionary times in terms of the preservation of social dominance, and the so-called meritocratic education system was deeply implicated in ensuring it should remain so.

If education in France was one of the pillars in the founding of the modern French state, culture was the other. Culture of course is central to education as well, and often carried in language – literature, theatre, poetry and, indeed, learning per se. In fact, Bourdieu developed the concept of *cultural capital* in schooling to explain why it was that pupils differentiated themselves in the process of schooling; the answer being that some entered education already steeped in the prerequisite "culture of learning", which gave them a substantial advantage. But, culture was more than a backdrop to the French state, and the Republic – and indeed Empire – had always glorified French culture. Catholic intellectuals in the 1930s saw culture as the mean for the "personality to blossom", a sentiment taken on board in the 1950s and 60s when successive governments implemented policies aimed at raising the cultural awareness of its citizens; for example, André Malraux's *Maisons de la Culture*. Bourdieu's early work on culture followed similar paths to that on Algeria and Education, with a major study of museum attendance (1990b/1966). He also focused on photography as a "middle brow art" (1990a/1965). This work grew in various directions eventually culminating with the publication of his magnum opus – *La distinction* – in 1979, which offers a voluminous account of French cultured taste.

It is important to see these studies as a two-way evolution: first, in the scope of Bourdieu work; and second, in methodology. Along with these major works, the publication of *Questions de Sociologie* in 1980 (1993), and various other papers, demonstrate the range of topics Bourdieu's eye was including: Art, Literature, Fashion, Linguistics, Sport, Religion, Law, Television and the Media, Economics, Politics, Music. Many of these can be read as blueprints for larger studies, only some of which were ever completed; for example, later extensive treatments of Manet (2013) and Flaubert (1996b). And, all the time, methodology – *The Craft of Sociology* (1991b/1968), *The Outline of a Theory of Practice* (1977b/1972) – the latter of which included further re-workings from his Algeria analyses, and again in *The Logic of Practice* (1990c/1980). His last major ethnographic study, however, appeared in 1993 with the publication of *The Weight of the World* (1999) which is made up of several first-hand accounts – gathered in interview – of various French men and women with a focus on their quality of life. What emerges is a picture of social suffering, largely as a result of neoliberal economic policy, amongst large sections of the French populations.

By now it is possible to regard Bourdieu's work not in terms of sociological texts per se but, rather, as ethnographies of France in the latter part of the twentieth century. Each of the areas covered of course repay detailed investigation. However, in the context of this chapter, we are heading to a preliminary discussion of Bourdieu's reflexivity, and for that we need to know more about his theory and method.

Theory, Practice and Methodology

Clearly, a fully comprehensive account of the range of philosophical and sociological sources, which Bourdieu drew upon is beyond the scope of this book. That being stated, in this section I want to show something of the theoretical perspectives developed by Bourdieu in the course of his empirical, ethnographic studies.

Of course, sociology was a development of philosophy, and thus an "applied philosophy" of sorts. By the time that Bourdieu was engaging with it, and, as noted, as well as those previously mentioned, three so-called "founding fathers" can be identified: Marx (1818–1881), Weber (1864–1920) and Durkheim (1858–1917). Each of these, of course, came from very different traditions and backgrounds, each maintained very different preoccupations. Yet, they all shared a concern to explain the relationship between the human individual and the social collectivity. For Marx, it was all about the economic "infrastructure" shaping individual agent's thoughts and actions. For Weber, ideas themselves could have a constituting effect on such an infrastructure: the protestant work ethic on the development of capitalism, for example. Whereas Durkheim too was concerned with the way various social structures could display different forms of social cohesions – mechanical and organic solidarity, for example – and could even effect such social phenomena as suicide rates.

Bourdieu was not that impressed with sociology at the outset and even declared himself horrified at having been asked as assistant to Raymond Aron to teach it on his return from Algeria. He would also have been knowledgeable of French philosophy such as the existentialism of Jean-Paul Sartre, although he describes it as a "weak form of humanism", as well as the philosophers of the history of science – Bachelard, Canguilhem and Koyré; in addition to the anthropology of Marcel Mauss, Lévi-Strauss and others. And, all this would have been set against a background of continental philosophy: Kant, Heidegger, Husserl, Nietzsche, etc. If Bourdieu underwent a kind of empirical epiphany in Algeria, he experienced a similar theoretical one when he returned to Paris to teach:

> I had read Durkheim as a student – *The Rules of Method*. Then, I had to read it again to teach it and it began to interest me because it could help me with my empirical work on Algeria. Mauss even more. Then, I went on to Weber. I taught Weber and I found the notion of field which I had confusingly in my mind while teaching it . . . It irritated me a lot and I could not see the logic. And, then, one day, I started to make a scheme on the blackboard and I said to myself, "Well, it's obvious, it is necessary to study people 'in relations'" . . . I was doing structuralist studies of parenthood, the Kabyle house. So, I was reading a pre-structuralist text with a structuralist way of thinking.
>
> (1995: 4–5)

What did this amount to?

Bourdieu came to see the studies of cultures as being made up of two principal traditions: the structuralist one, which sees it as an instrument of communication and knowledge – a *structured structure* (consensual signs, etc.); and the functionalist one, which sees it as an ideological force – *structuring structure* (political power, social order). The anthropology of Lévi-Strauss, with his focus on totems, myths, etc., would be an exemplar of the first; whilst the concern with collective systems that we find in both Marx and Durkheim would be examples of the second. To view cultures in this way – structurally – is useful for Bourdieu since in structure we find the essence of relations and relationships – to the world, things, thoughts and each other:

- That the primary cognitive act (i.e. that of a newborn child) takes place in a social environment and is essentially structural as it sets up intentional (what phenomenologists refer to as "intensional") relations between the social agent and the environment;
- That environment includes both material and ideational structures;

- That the primary cognitive act therefore needs to be understood in terms of a search for social-psychic equilibrium, or control, over Self, Objects and Others;
- That such an act – and subsequent acts – do not establish themselves in a value neutral vacuum, but in an environment saturated with values and ways of seeing the world;
- That such values and such ways constitute a pre-set orthodoxy into which agents are inducted;
- That such values and orthodoxies are dynamic and constantly evolving. However, their underlying logic of practice remains the same: they represent a certain way of seeing the world on the part of particular social factions of society;
- That such a way of seeing the world conditions and shapes the primary cognitive act in a dynamic relationship with individuals involved. In this sense, individuals can be particular all whilst sharing commonalities with those immediately in their social environment.

Structural relationships are therefore actualised within both the individual and the collectivity, and dialectically between both. Ethnographical research then becomes not simply the account of cultures but, "the science of dialectical relations between objective structures . . . and the subjective dispositions within which these structures are actualised and which tend to reproduce them" (1977a: 3). The goal of this undertaking is therefore to recover the principles through which such structures are generated; in other words, the "logic of practice" of particular cultural behaviours. In the above quote, Bourdieu employs the term "subjective and objective", the dichotomy of which he describes as "most fundamental and ruinous in the social science" (1990c/1980: 25); and thus the need to see both in practice as co-terminous, mutually constituting and dialectical. If the "objective" so far has been referred to as series of salient cultural trends in his ethnographic studies, it is equally necessary to see these as made up of individual subjectivities. In this, another of Bourdieu's influences – namely, the phenomenology of Husserl and Merleau-Ponty – become evident with its focus on the distinction between everything we know of the world (*noema*) and individual instantiations of aspects of it at any one time and place (*noesis*).

If all this represents a revolutionary epistemology, it is little wonder that Bourdieu presents the account of his "theory of practice" in terms of a series of "breaks" or "ruptures" with established ways of knowing and doing: the empirical, the objective, the hermeneutic (1977b/1972). Even so, Bourdieu still required a series of conceptual tools in order to represent these levels of human exegesis. The two most basic are *habitus* and *field*. If *habitus* is concerned with the subjective, *field* can be seen as the site of objectivity:

Habitus is defined as:

> Systems of durable, transposable dispositions, structured structures predisposed to function as structuring structures, that is, as principles which generate and organize practices and representations that can only be objectively adapted to their outcomes without presupposing a conscious aiming at ends or an express mastery of the operations necessary in order to attain them. Objectively "regulated" and "regular" without being in any way the product of obedience to rules, they can be collectively orchestrated without being the product of the organizing action of a conductor.
>
> (Bourdieu 1990c/1980: 53)

Whereas *Field* is defined as:

> . . . as a network, or a configuration, of objective relations between positions. These positions are objectively defined, in their existence and in the determinations they impose upon their occupants, agents or institutions, by their present and potential situation (situs) in the structure of the distribution of species of power (or capital) whose possession commands access to the specific profits that are at stake in the field, as well as by their objective relation to other positions (domination, subordination, homology, etc.).
>
> (Bourdieu and Wacquant, 1992: 97)

There are several points to be made with respect the integrity and use of such concepts.

First, although, they emerge from the same epistemological needs and vision, they are developmental. For example, although the concept of *habitus* was already employed in the Béarn, *field* was not explicitly used until into 1966 when Bourdieu saw the way that ideas and actions could be shaped by a certain way of think within a specific socially bounded space. In this original case, it was the way Gothic architecture was fashioned by a scholastic training, but the concept of *field* was immediately brought to bear on such social locales as education, culture and media, etc. Not everything within *social space* is a *field*, but many are, especially in terms of socially sanctioned forms of life.

Second, such concepts are consistent with each other and according to their range of applications; indeed, one of Bourdieu's major research questions would be the extent to which all *fields* behave constitutionally the same.

Third, they do need to be treated as co-implicated: we cannot think about *habitus* without thinking about *field* and vice versa. This itself requires inclusion of both within any research topic and dialectical thinking.

Fourth, such concepts are not simply heuristic devices or metaphors, and it is so easy to equate *habitus* with agency and *field* with context. We hope, on the basis of the above, that it is clear that they are each and together highly charged epistemological matrices: with all that they imply in terms of breaks and ruptures with conventional ways of thinking and doing things. Moreover, they arise in from saturation with empirical data; they are then logically necessitated by what goes on within them.

Fifth, *habitus* and *field* are not the only key concepts that Bourdieu uses; there are many others: *hexis, interest, capital, hysteresis* (see Grenfell, 2012a). Again, it is important to note that each of these concepts arose as necessitated by the data. For example, *capital*, as a sort of *field* currency, emerged as part of Bourdieu's account of what was valued in education and how some pupils arrived with obvious cultural advantages (*cultural capital*) in terms of what is symbolically significant (*symbolic capital*) within the *field*. These forms of *capital* were distinct from straight money wealth (*economic capital*), but still acted as a way of "buying" position (prestige) within the *field*. Next, Bourdieu saw that it was not just *what* anyone knew but *who* they knew, which was significant in social trajectories (*social capital*). Language also acted as *linguistic capital* and was valued as such within the various *fields* – more of less depending on their complexion – as a definition of individual worth.

A lot of Bourdieu's later ethnographies can be understood as "further explorations in field theory", which inevitably entailed the quantities and forms of *capital* held by individuals and groups and how these were expressed and used within *field* manoeuvres. But, finally, what of reflexivity as part of such endeavours?

Bourdieu and Reflexivity

Clearly, reflexivity is a major focus for this book, and there is a lot to write about it. Besides the chapter here in this Part I, the whole of Part III is based around a reflexive consideration of reflexivity in the light of the empirical case examples we give in Part II. In these parts, we wish to apply, exemplify and extend Bourdieu's reflexivity with respect to language ethnographies. This section, therefore, needs to be read as an introduction to this later, more advanced discussion.

The first point we need to make about Bourdieu's reflexivity is that it is both present and absent in his early works: present in the sense of logically implied by the kind of epistemological vision he was beginning to articulate; and absent to the extent to which it is not referred to in explicit terms. This later case would not be true in work in the 1990s, where issues of reflexivity are given a lead in a range of publications: *An Invitation to Reflexive Sociology* (1992), *Science and Science of Reflexivity* (2004/2001), *Participant Objectivation* (2003), etc. Even the 1968 text *The Craft of Sociology* (1991c/1968) does not seem to make reference to it by name. At the same time, it is clearly implied strongly by what can be found in the text and, at a similar time (1966), there is a filmed dialogue between Bourdieu and one of his key collaborators Jean-Claude Passeron concerning "la vigilance épistémologique". The core of this discussion indeed concerns issues arising from the subject-object dichotomy referred to above. What is implied is the very "construction of the research object" (which is openly discussed in *Craft*) that the researcher forms in the course of undertaking their research.

The degree to which the significance of reflexivity was playing itself out as a strand of Bourdieu's work is noticeable from the way an entire section of the original French version of *The Outline of a Theory of Practice* (1972) is dedicated to "the observer observed" (pp. 225–234). Here, Bourdieu acknowledges that a researcher is already a "dominated" member of the "dominant" since undertaking such work presupposes a certain lack of practical/empirical exigencies with respect to the world. It is both a privileged and intellectualist stance. However, acknowledging such a relationship between the researcher and the research is not simply a methodological nicety, but central to the robustness of the resultant science. In other words, to forget the social conditions of the construction of knowledge is to forget possible social conditions that can be founded in the name of the sort of sociology he is wishing to establish. Briefly, it is a form of *scholastic fallacy*.

Such a reflexive position is perfectly conducive with Bourdieu's entire theory of practice, and the language by which it is expressed is central to it. As discussed in Chapter 2, since Saussure, the distinction between a language sign (word) and what was signified (things) was acknowledged. In other words, a single word could never capture the entire practical use to which it is put. A similar relation exists between theory and practice for Bourdieu. He writes of a sense of "unease" when writing about and describing something he first "mastered" in practice (1977b/ 1972: 223) since it risks, giving a false "understanding" both of the "understanding" which such a concept makes possible, and the practical "understanding" which "does not need concepts". Such is to confuse "the things of logic" with "the logic of things", for Bourdieu, as what is incarnated in a object of research is the relation that the researcher has to it – often derived from an academic *field* discipline – rather than the objective thing itself. To fall for this, especially in a *field* like sociology, which both should and does know better, is a kind of act of ultimate intellectual bad faith. This is why researchers need to be careful of "rules" and "models", which render "static" social process which are by definition "ex-static".

All language and theory are, for Bourdieu, nothing more than the "totality" of actions which they instantiate – all the more reason, therefore, to employ a theory *of* practice which is formed in and for practice rather than a straight formalist theory. The ethnographic aspiration of "participant observation" needs, conse-quently, to be regarded with high suspicion; indeed, these two words are tantamount to being a contradiction in terms. Little wonder, furthermore, that increasingly in Bourdieu's work there is reference to the necessity of a "sociology of sociology" (2016b: 1116) at the risk of moving too easily from a "concept of reality" to the "reality of the concept". The whole point of "field theory" is to avoid such a slippage.

Society, for Bourdieu, of which sociology is a part, contains innumerable "traps"; this slippage being one of the most common in social science research. Reflexivity, as manifested within his "theory of practice", is one way to escape the trap. Bourdieu writes that there are three principal presuppositions, or biases, commonly actualised in such a trap (see Bourdieu, 2000b: 10f). First, is the view taken as a result of a particular position within the social space, including social trajectory, gender and the effects these have of relations to objects. Second, is the orthodoxy of the particular *field* space; for example, most academic disciplines have a normalised way of viewing their subjects and, indeed, sanction what can and cannot be a legitimate topic and form of enquiry. Third, as noted above, is simply a certain "ease", or leisure – *skholè* – implied by being in a position to take a non-imperative relation to this aspect of the world. Real *field* players are too consumed by the game to be able to research it. To practice reflexivity means, for Bourdieu, a way to "break" from these biases in a manner which parallels Bachelard's epistemological "rupture". If the subject is to objectify the social conditions of the production of knowledge, then the only way to do this within Bourdieu's perspective is by researchers "turning the instruments of knowledge that they produce against themselves, and especially against the social universes in which they produce them" (2000c/1997: 118). By doing so, researchers create the possibility of escaping the social and economic determinisms of thought production, as well as historical determinism. Moreover, by doing this, the researcher is not simply acknowledging the limits of knowledge as constructed within the "subject", but establishing the social possibilities of true science by bringing to light the limits of objectification. The aim is to renounce both the absolutionist objectivism and subjective relativism. Indeed, for Bourdieu, "the conditions of possibility of scientific knowledge" and "scientific objectivism" are one and the same thing. The rest of this book, one way or another, deals with how one might do this, what happens as a result, and how we should interpret the outcome in terms of this ambition. We shall later see what all this meant for Bourdieu himself; for example, in the way he worked with theory and practice, and, indeed, how and where he objectified his own academic space and research activity within it. Finally, however, a few further preliminary thoughts on what Bourdieu called "participant objectivation".

Participant Objectivation

Participant *objectivation* is, then, quite distinct from the normalised feature of "participant observation" found as part of the ethnographer's methodological training. What is it and how does anyone do it? Clearly, Bourdieu is wishing to distance himself from the kind of self-observing-self approach that can be found in various research traditions: sometimes phenomenological, sometimes post-modern. For him, this approach is both narcissistic and impossible: the pretence, as noted, of acknowledging bias, of being able to transcend thought by the power of thought itself. At the same time, Bourdieu insists that without reflexivity researchers are always prone to import their own primary – pre-reflexive – selves into the object of research, and then pass the whole thing off as science. Whereas, in effect, it is the product of a particular empirical *habitus* presented in the form of an objectivity rooted in a kind of "academic transcendence" grounded in the post-Kantian metaphysical tradition (see Bourdieu, 2003). For Bourdieu, researchers need to "disarm" themselves of the power, which leads them into this epistemological "fall". We saw above how Bourdieu listed the presuppositions which can so easily slip into a research project – almost like a Trojan Horse: of the researchers' social provenance and trajectory, of the orthodoxies of the academic field, of the distance created by being "out of the game". All these need to be objectified as specific value-laded relations for Bourdieu as part of the "objectivation of the knowing subject". But, this is not simply a process of once-only acknowledgement. Rather, it is a procedure that goes to the heart of the relationship between the researcher and the research, and the way that knowledge and understanding of the subterranean features (generating structures) of data are rendered manifest. As opposed to the notion that a researcher can affect a separate, non-involved relationship to the object of research, one that gives them an "objective eye", Bourdieu wishes to exactly draw on the primary knowledge of the researcher and their previous experience in the research *field*. There is then a three-way partnership: the researcher and their empirical *habitus*; their previous scientific experience; and the current object of investigation. By way of exemplification, Bourdieu discusses the way his insights into the marriage patterns in the Béarn came about as a result of him holding up his primary experience of life in the area next to his investigations in Algeria, clarifications about which then led back into analyses of the Béarnais peasant. By this too-and-fro method precisely the sort of theory of practice is built up which we have elucidated above. The researcher is then intimately involved; indeed, their primary "empirical" *habitus* is slowly dissolved in the formation of a new reflexive "scientific" *habitus*. It is when this occurs, not only at the individual, personal level, but at the *field* level, that there is a genuine paradigmatic shift within the critical community. In other words, this is not just, or not only, a personal foundation but holds the possibility of a collective one as well. In later works, for example the *Sketch for a Self-analysis*, Bourdieu shows how this is brought about and accomplished, and, moreover, what are its consequences.

Conclusion

This chapter has covered a lot of ground. As well as introducing Bourdieu we have explored the context of his early work and how it shaped his later studies.

Issues of theory and practice have been to the fore and, with them, further questions about the relationship between primary data and analysis undertaken by the researcher. We noted the importance of language in elucidating this relationship, and the range of concepts developed by Bourdieu in field-work in the Béarn, Algeria and education. We have drawn attention to the dangers of the academic discourse in skewing interpretation and introduced Bourdieu's take on reflexivity as central to the whole process. Next, Part II will report on actual language-based ethnographies, highlighting the researchers own thoughts and understanding about reflexivity before taking the discussion forward in Part III into more advanced and sophisticated ways of working with it.

PART II
Reflexivity in Practice
Case Examples

Introduction

Part II is where we introduce the living, breathing accounts of language and literacy ethnographies that are threaded through with reflexivity. Our chapters encompass: community literacies; a longitudinal exploration of literacy lives over time, which brings a young woman's biography back to life; an account of the idea of "home" in a study of the literacy lives of American Caribbean youth; and a description with two studies of academic literacies that then become much more complex, as wider world events overtake and shift the "field" of study under consideration.

In each study, Bourdieu's conceptual framework of reflexively informed objectivity helps unpack the ways in which the studies themselves were constructed and understood by the researcher. The authors make sense of this undertaking through examining, often simultaneously, where they are in the field. Under consideration are ways of knowing, the life of a researcher, considerations of power, linguistic identity and ethics. All four researchers are women, which is significant both in signalling the ways in which women navigate the world of academia, and the sorts of bias this may give rise to. One of the scholars, McLean, identifies as American Trinidadian, and one, Seloni, is multilingual and Turkish in origin. These complex identities cross and re-cross the studies as they unfold.

In Chapter 4 (Pahl), reflexivity emerges as a community project. The use of collaborative ethnography means that interpretative insights from participants become research insights, and as participants move into the research space, the research itself is changed. This then changes, in turn, the field of language and literacy research. There are implications for this kind of work for the wider field – whose voices count and why?

Chapter 5 (Compton-Lilly) explores different types of reflexivity over time. The researcher's life story is played out in a relational way, between herself and her research participant, and the chapter explores that coming together of the two narratives. The chapter itself becomes a "trace" of that process. Reflexivity itself emerges in this process of "tracing". Ultimately, this offers a fresh glimpse of how reflexivity can itself become the object of study, over time, and within lives lived in tandem with each other, crossing over at key moments to form the narrative. Within this narrative is also the realisation of the ethics of care of a researcher who herself has a biographical piece that she can give back to a research participant, bringing the process full circle, but in turn raising questions about academic biographies.

Chapter 6 (McLean) asks the reader to consider the way in which a reflexively informed objectivity becomes constructed in the field. Issues of power and identity are key here, as the author reflects on the process of reflection, and asks, whose space are we invited into to reflect? The space of "home" becomes critical for these musings. But where do we feel "at home"? The landscape of research is problematised in this process, and the issue of whose voice counts in the space of research, and who is "at home" here, is elucidated by vignettes from the field of practice. This "coming to know" is both a research journey and a reflexive experience.

Chapter 7 (Seloni) provides an insider and outsider account of a multilingual scholar who is working with academic multilingual literacies in two settings. Her work details the field anew and provides an insight into both her reflexive positions but also those of her participants. Bourdieu's work highlights the way in which practice, as well as the making of theory, can be re-thought in these contexts. Observing oneself becomes part of the research process and deepens an understanding of the research itself.

Reading these chapters, some key issues come into play. Co-production, affect, time, space, power and agency leap into the field of literacy and language ethnographies. We are able to create a space for such studies, longitudinal, situated and rich in data, to yield insights about the role of the researcher in that process. In the chapters, ideas about literacy and language are made and re-made through conversations, ways of knowing, new understandings, failures and turn-arounds. In the final part of the book we shall reflect on these ideas further.

4

RE-THINKING LITERACIES WITH COMMUNITIES

Literacy as a Collaborative Concept

Kate Pahl

Introduction

How can language ethnographies work in a context of collaboration and joint, entwined thinking? Here, I consider how collaborative conceptual understandings of literacy can be built within communities in ways that reflexively consider epistemological difference. This is not so much a "how to" as a reflection, from a Bourdieusian perspective, on what it was to do the projects. I explore what was involved in the process of developing a shared lens with participants. This involved conducting literacy and language research in ways that recognised diversity and difference. I discuss ways in which literacy and language practices in communities could be conceptualised through the process of collaboratively working out what the concept of literacy could be, drawing on situated, every day and community knowledge. This involved identifying cultural patterns and everyday practices in communities, much as Barton and Hamilton were able to do in their study of "Local Literacies" (1998). This chapter moves from a singular stance on literacy to a much more diffuse and distributed understanding, informed by the work of a number of key collaborators who worked with me on the projects.[1]

Much of my ethnographic work has been situated in homes, schools and communities in Rotherham, a post-industrial town, east of Sheffield, in the UK (see Pahl, 2014a).[2] Initially, I was interested in what people did with literacy, but united to that was a focus on the meanings and situated-ness of everyday texts, of their cultural resonances and echoes. I derived much of my thinking from the work of cultural theorists such as Raymond Williams (1958, 1965) and Stuart Hall (2007), who identified the need for a "social hermeneutics" of everyday texts that combined the sociological with the hermeneutic to uncover the meanings within everyday life. My work explored, through close ethnographic study, the way literacies were materialised, shaped and felt within home and community settings (Pahl, 2014a). I considered the ways in which literacies were inscribed within textiles, carried across from home to school on bus journeys, were enacted in playground leaps, and became material and (im)material in relation to online and off-line practices (Pahl, 2012; Burnett et al., 2014).

My understandings changed, however, in relation to the collaborations and conversations that developed as the methodologies became entwined within co-researchers' and community participants' understandings of literacy. I began by conducting a more traditional ethnography that involved field notes, collected texts and ethnographic observations and interviews (Sanjek, 1990; Agar 1996). I then turned to collaborative way of working in which participants became researchers. They devised and conducted projects that then articulated emergent conceptualisations of literacy. I turned from a model where I took data from a field to one where I learned from the field, alongside a team of community researchers. Ingold talks of the move from taking "from" to learning "with" as an argument for a more immersive model of anthropology (2013, 2014) where the researcher is wholly engaged in the experience and I was able to apply this in my work, in that I worked alongside the projects and was myself immersed in the processes I was supposed to be studying. This placed me within the projects, and I learned conceptually as I went along with community partners becoming co-researchers during this time.

I was helped in this endeavour by methodological insights from Lassiter and Campbell and their work on collaborative ethnography (Lassiter, 2005; Campbell and Lassiter, 2010; Campbell and Lassiter, 2015). This shift situated the enquiry within a more reciprocal and distributed model of research in which community researchers developed and framed the studies. The way I saw the world derived from my own experience of it, and my view was inevitably limited. I was concerned about my own unconscious bias within the field. Coming from a white, middle class background, but with experience of community outreach adult literacy work, I was aware of the complex literacies that lay within communities that I needed to learn about. I began to work with a co-constructed lens, that took in a broader view of literacy and incorporated insights from people's lived experience. I worked in particular with Zanib Rasool, who brought her own lens as a Pakistani heritage researcher to the project (Rasool, 2017). Community researchers, such as Rasool, became more active within the projects through conceptualising and framing what they understood to be community knowledge production practices. They were involved in bid writing and running the projects as researchers but also community partners. From this process we co-wrote a book about our research in Rotherham (Campbell, Pahl, Pente and Rasool, 2018).

This way of working surfaced new knowledge production practices that themselves derived from traditions resting within intergenerational patterns of thought and ideas. This contributed to a decolonising lens that became increasingly important to our projects. This lens drew on the work of Tuhiwai Smith (1999) by arguing that Western epistemological structures did not account for many forms of knowledge production that have strong genealogies, including intergenerational and place-based ways of knowing (Mahuika, 2008). Rasool (2017) argued that ways of knowing that are situated, relate to the everyday and draw on tacit and non-linguistic forms of knowledge are distributed beyond university disciplinary structures. While collaborative ethnography provided a pathway for my thinking, I also drew on ways of knowing from artistic modes of knowledge production (Barrett and Bolt, 2007; Coessens, Crispin, and Douglas, 2009).

Arts methodologies have created opportunities for researchers to think differently about knowledge creation practices within communities. For example, experiential knowledge, that sits within the body and within a mode of understanding that might be resting within intuitive and non-linguistic practices, can be surfaced through this process (Ravetz and Ravetz, 2016). As the research developed, I began to think about literacy and language practices differently. Thinking was shared and came from many different places. Within collaborative research, ideas flowed through conversations, collaborations and ways of understanding the world. They often came from meeting in a site, such as a community library, or drinking tea in a home. We found that the contexts for research conversations were important. We also found it important to recognise difference and divergence (Mouffe, 2004). Sometimes we disagreed, and the resulting conversations led to publications that were multi-voiced and complex (Campbell et al., 2018). It is impossible to make these descriptions "objective". Instead, the reflexivity was dispersed across subjectivities, sites and spaces.

This chapter describes the process of untangling a conceptual framing of literacies, as the concept moved from more formalised patterns to threads that could be seen spreading out all over the place and re-forming in new ways. Rather than fixing the nature of literacy within communities, re-thinking literacy ontologies became a focus. This then led to a layered and complex account of reflexivity, as my own situated understandings entwined with those of the participants in my study as well as my research collaborators.

In all of these studies we were investigating key issues around narrative, everyday literacy practices, voice and ways of knowing. Out of these came issues of power and ideological conceptualisations of literacy (Street, 1993). Over the ten years of these projects we became more aware that community ways of knowing about writing and literacy affected how we conceptualised the concept of literacy practices. Our work became steadily more co-produced and informed by a community development approach to co-production that involved doing things with, not on communities. This was embedded in practice, and privileged processes of analysis and discussion around findings, and produced emergent ways of doing things rather than an outcome driven research study. Literacy as a static concept unravelled and untangled, then dissolved into gesture, visuals, language, gesture, script and writing (Finnegan, 2015).

Here, I introduce the themes that continued to pre-occupy me as I conducted the studies. I began with the question, how are literacies conceptualised but also shaped and constructed from stuff within the everyday? I became interested in young people's aesthetic understanding of what literacies were, how they worked, how they travelled and what they did. In these studies, the everyday was the site for literacies that were found, repurposed and developed through artistic methodologies that included re-purposing books, working with artists and developing participatory methodologies with young people including film, photography and art work (Pahl, 2012). Literacy was densely patterned, woven through with stories, seeped in material artifacts and layered through intergenerational conceptual framings. This led to an understanding of literacy that was inscribed into material objects. An "artifactual" literacies approach widened the scope of how literacy was understood by linking literacy to materially situated cultures (Pahl and Rowsell, 2010). Writing was both material and also could be found within material objects. This altered its nature. It could also be spoken, narrated and told and re-told, until the story had a "thing-like" status (Brandt and Clinton, 2002). This developing lens then included a collaborative ethnographic lens so that the stuff was also collectively researched and understood.

Researching Literacy Practices in Homes and Communities

Participatory methodologies alongside an ethnographic perspective develop insights from young people that then unsettle what literacy is and could be. During the research process, we asked young people to make films about what language and literacy meant to them (see Escott and Pahl, 2017). This work included film-making and creative writing in schools and community settings. Language and literacy practices became animated as young people created ensembles of meaning making that were alive with possibility. Objects such as sticks and permits were embedded within the communicative practices that unfolded in the film. In our joint work, Hugh Escott and I wrote about the materialities of these episodes (Pahl and Escott, 2015) and explored the potential of theories from the new materialism to make sense of the de-centred role of literacy and language within the films.

The definitional questions about literacy and language that we were exploring led to a focus on what could be described as the, "prior ontologies" of literacy (Massumi, 2002: 66) in which understandings of literacy and language were "de-centred" by objects, activities and non-human encounters (see Latour, 1987). While these were materially situated, there was a movement into other kinds of understanding – silence, tacit knowledge, visual and gestural models of communication – that opened up a space to situate literacy differently. Our work began to consider whether there were ways of looking at language and literacy differently, through the lens of young people's own understandings of language and literacy in practice (Escott and Pahl, 2017).

TABLE 4.1 Dataset – 10 years of literacy ethnographies

Year	Type of data	Site	Collaborators	Project name and funder	Literacy ontology
2006	Interviews	Aliya's family home	Andrew Pollard, Zahir Rafiq	Artefacts of migration Narratives of Identity (AHRC)	Material literacies
2009	Fieldnotes	Community library	Chloe Allan	Inspire Rotherham (Yorkshire Forward)	Community literacies
2011	Writing by young people plus fieldnotes	Lucy's home	Richard Steadman-Jones	Writing in the Home and in the Street (ARHC)	Aesthetic literacies
2012	Interview plus writing by young people	Aliya's home	Aliya Khan	Revisiting project (SSHRC Canada)	Ineffable literacies
2012	Writing by young people	Youth club, Park	Sam Rae, Steve Pool	Language as Talisman (AHRC)	Intergenerational literacies
2014	Writing by women and fieldnotes	Community library	Zanib Rasool, Shirin Teifouri	Imagine (AHRC)	Collaborative literacies
2016	Young people's poetry	Park, Community centre	Zanib Rasool	Threads of Time (AHRC)	Co-produced literacies

Where I started was with a conceptual framework that included, "writing"; "language" and "culture" as terms that could be identified within the shifting sands of observation. I drew on field notes, written texts by young people, films, artifacts, interviews, discussions, conversations and school projects. Where I finished was in a space where writing singly about these phenomena was less possible, as the ownership of concepts, ideas and research thinking on literacy and language became shared and co-constructed. This happened with the aid of researchers such as Zanib Rasool, whose work on "girls'" and women's writing practices became central to the projects (Rasool, 2017). The way in which literacy and language ethnographies were conceptualised became shared across the domains of the projects, and across the dispersed subjectivities of the research teams (Pahl, 2017). These subjectivities were threaded throughout the projects. Below, I examine, through field notes and writing by young people, the way in which subjectivities can be traced within the projects, with a focus on the themes of this chapter – voice, stories, materialisations, traces and embodied and affective literacies. I conclude by arguing that we need a new mode of understanding of the processes of constructing the field and of making sense together of what things might mean.

Here, I present data, collected over ten years, in order to explore these changing understandings of literacy. Going close to the data brings a different perspective. Taking my cue from Hymes in the "Warm Springs Interlude" (1996), I walk around the experience of being in the field and live the literacies through my personal interaction with the field. I look at written texts and excerpts from interviews, reflections and observations. This data was collected in different ways; some was recorded as interviews, some as field notes, some are pieces of writing that were shared and some are personal recollections. Much of the data was developed in a situated, emergent way, and many of the written texts and artifacts were produced by young people in response to traumatic experiences such as racism. These emergent literacy artefacts changed how I thought. As I lived through the projects, the lenses shifted and developed. Researching literacy and language practices in communities involves an understanding of the sites and contexts of the research as a generative starting point for thinking. In our case, the studies took place in Rotherham, UK.[3]

I anchor my work in the sites and spaces of the research. I focus on sites (a community library, homes) and people (young women, women writers, collaborators and co-researchers) and specifically, on writing and literacy research co-created through and with people in communities. I call this a "living literacies" approach to understanding literacy (Pahl and Rowsell, 2019).

Cultural Literacies and Travelling Stories

When I first worked in Rotherham, while some of the descriptions of the town were depressing (e.g. Charlesworth, 2000), it was also a place of artists and writers and poets. The town centre was inhabited by a small but stable British Pakistani community that was collectively interested in exploring issues of their cultural heritage and identity. I began to conceive of a project that could start to re-situate the cultural experiences of the families in Ferham, Rotherham, in relation to the local museums. This project began the series of studies that became the Rotherham studies, and focused initially on the relationship between stories and objects in the home. This work reflected how family stories were carried across generations, often narrated alongside everyday objects, that were narrativised in homes and created conditions for oral storytelling and multimodal drawings and productions (Pahl, 2002). I began working with a small group of British Asian families, together with an artist and a museum curator to develop a project that listened to the stories of migration together with discussion of special objects of the families. The intention was to develop a local exhibition that would celebrate people's heritage and culture and family values, but also draw commonalities across the experiences of the different communities of Rotherham, to find out what they shared. Our approach was led and co-constructed by the involvement of artist Zahir Rafiq, and through the ideas that emerged through interviews with the families. Together, we identified a small number of families who were willing to share their stories and objects, in order to create an exhibition that would describe the everyday lived experiences of families in central Rotherham. This exhibition was initially called "Ferham Families". A website, "Every Object Tells a Story" (www.everyobjecttellsastory.org) which was curated by Zahir Rafiq, was set up to document family stories and objects. The project team worked to listen to the stories of a core group of families who migrated to the UK from Pakistan in the 1950s. We drew on an ethnographic perspective, taking the time to listen to families but we also began to co-analyse our findings with the families as a way of ascertaining their interpretations and ideas about their stories (see Pahl and Pollard, 2010; Pahl, Pollard and Rafiq, 2009). Our approach was to co-create both the exhibition and to listen to the families so that we could develop a series of themes emerging from the stories. We did this jointly. We discussed the themes with the families and these emerging themes became the display cases that were presented in the exhibition. These themes included: gold, travel, toys, transport and weddings. These themes emerged naturally from the interviews and turned into display cases that themselves were a collection of objects from the families.

Reflecting back on the project, however, it was apparent that some of the initial themes, while still strongly resonant with the families, did not reflect the whole picture. Within our interpretative framework, inevitably, some things were missed. Our focus reflected our starting preoccupation – we conceived of the project as being about the relationship between everyday objects and stories and that is what we heard. What we did not hear so much was the ways in which the participants lived within the stories that they told us and how they perceived the nature of those stories within their everyday lives. In this case, understandings of literacy were refracted through experiences and feelings.

Home Literacies: "A Candle for My Thoughts"

In 2012, I was invited to revisit this project, as part of a Social Science and Humanities Research Council in Canada funded project that encourages researchers to revisit original studies. I went back to the family members and asked if they would like to revisit the original study (Sefton-Green and Rowsell, 2015). I interviewed Aliya, aged 17, who was 10 during the original study, about her memories of the study as well as about her stories. She decided to interview her aunt, who had been in the earlier study. In this interview, and in my conversations with Aliya, new themes emerged. Crucially, the importance of literacy, for women and across the generations, became clear (Pahl and Khan, 2015). In this later project, my conceptualisation of literacy rested much more on a co-produced model of literacy, now understood through the eyes of the participants, not through my own perceptual framework. Literacy, as Aliya Khan described it, was an investment, a means to a better life, but also a thread that created opportunities for poetry, enabled feelings to emerge and provided an articulated identity, expressed through the reading of written texts, such as Harry Potter, that could be carried through adolescence and beyond.

Aliya once more returned to this experience of stories and reading when she was talking to me about her grandmother:

> I used to share a room with my grandmother before I moved here, and we used to bicker so she used to tell me stories to mellow me down a bit, she used to tell all sorts of stories, religious stories about my grandfather about relatives, and it would be like bedtime stories to get me asleep and she taught me a special prayer which I still read to this day three times so it protects the household, from any spirits or any things happening while we are sleeping, sleep peaceful, I was four years when I learned that, yeah so for the past thirteen years I have been reading that (laughs).
>
> (Aliya, interview 17th July, 2012)

Literacy here was embedded in a bedtime routine, and in the cycles of the everyday. Stories are about identities and about everyday routines, about love and feeling cherished. Aliya described a special prayer which was part of her everyday experience of creating a safe and protective space. Aliya's literacies were still entwined with identity, and everyday life. Aliya wrote a poem at school, during those years, which described a candle that held her thoughts and family together:

> A candle of my thoughts, how the wax melts, the smell, the feel, everyone, my family around . . .
>
> (Aliya interview 17th July, 2012)

She here articulates how the wax, like the gold in her family, melts, but that intangible melting also signifies the family, the core values that lie beyond the material world. The collaboration with Aliya surfaced a more nuanced and embedded model of literacy that was about ways of knowing and being as much about writing. It was in the material objects, the candle, and in the ephemeral smell of the wax candle. Here, material objects offered a space for literacies to be subsumed in something wider, akin to feeling, smell and affect.

Literacies in a Library: "I Don't Know what Literacy Is"

I now move onto describing a project in a community library in Rotherham. Inspired by the studies of Neuman and Celano (2001; 2006; 2012) that investigated the effect on children's literacy of public libraries in low income areas in Philadelphia, I was interested in how literacies were understood and used within a community library and the ways in which they were mediated and conceptualised. I first conducted a study in which we investigated everyday literacies in the library with a fieldworker, Chloe Allan, in 2009. The library (situated in Rotherham) was a space where parents and children formed groups, to meet and to drink hot chocolate and keep warm. In our joint article (Pahl and Allan, 2011) we described the library as a place of refuge and somewhere that children could escape to, a kind of "treasure island". When we started doing the fieldwork, we spent time in parents' groups and watching craft groups. One observation we had from the data was the way in which literacy was both invisible and also sometimes not recognised by the people who came to these groups. From our field notes we observed this:

One woman said she had done a literacy course in her child's school, or at least she thought it was literacy – "I don't really know what literacy means", (field notes, Chloe Allan, 19th November, 2009)

We also noticed that there were many literacy activities, for example, reading labels, using the computer, looking at some products, which were not recognised as literacy. From her field notes, when Kate was sitting with a group of parents, she noted:

> The parents were sharing Body Shop products. We all sat on a table and sniffed them. One smelt of cranberries. One of the women holds parties and sells them. It was a sensory experience, sniffing the products and feeling them.
>
> (field notes, Kate Pahl, 19th November, 2009)

Through conversations with different community members and library users, including parents and children, it became apparent that the library was a central hub. The community used it for various activities, such as parent and toddler groups, English language classes and after school activities, and as a meeting place for groups such as walking groups. Chloe Allan's field notes, collected while talking to a mother and daughter about previous activities at the library, noted,

A few children arrived for the crafts. The lady with three young children ("don't understand literacy" woman) was here again, along with a young woman with her daughter and the 3 children with the crafts woman. Another little girl came over a few minutes later with her mum. They all sat around the tables and started colouring their pictures, sticking them onto their cards and stamping "merry xmas" stamps onto them. Some of them also wrote stuff inside for who they were making them for. There was not much direction from the crafts woman – it was a bit of a free for all.

(Field notes Chloe Allan 10th October, 2009)

Literacy, like water, flows through this episode, it is inscribed in the sites and spaces where the activities such as the craft activities described above, took place. Our understandings similarly grew in response to the ways in which people "did" literacy in community settings.

"Listening Voices: Telling Stories" Women's Voices in a Library

In 2014, we started another project with the support of the library. "Listening Voices, Telling Stories" was jointly constructed and developed by Zanib Rasool, Shirin Teifouri and a community volunteer. The project involved women reading poems and writing their own poetry. Through this experience, I learned to understand literacy differently. Echoing the previous understandings of literacy as embodied, and flowing through gesture, and story, I began to conceive a much wider conceptualisation of language than simply written or narrated texts. Ruth Finnegan articulates this perfectly:

> I too was once confident of what "language" was, where its boundaries lay and hence what might count as data for documenting it. But I am no longer sure. Nor am I clear where information about a given language should be found, or how, by, and for whom a language should be documented.
>
> (2015: 1)

Finnegan argued that the performed stories she transcribed lost so much in translation that they were almost useless without the experience of hearing the performance:

> The reality lay in the performance. It was this that the written texts had failed to capture. They missed the subtle characterisations, the drama, the way the tellers used volume, pitch, tempo, repetition, emphasis, dynamics, silence, timbre, onomatopoeia, and a whole plethora of non-verbal indications to convey humour, pathos, irony, atmosphere . . .
>
> (p. 3)

Sitting with a group of women, telling stories, reciting poetry, one of the women, with fleeting hand movements, spoke and outlined the jumping of a fish through a river:

> Saima [pseudonym, a British Asian woman] immediately took out a piece of paper on which she had written, in Urdu, phonetically and in the Urdu script, the poem she had told me a few weeks before. The poem, roughly, translated, was about the eggs that spawned the fish, and then the fish swam down river (at that point she made a nice wavy motion with her hands) and then the fish was caught by the son, who took it home and the mother cooked it and the family was happy. This seemed to be about completion and the experience of completion through the fish, river, son, mother, eating, happiness.
> (field notes Kate Pahl 30th January, 2014)

My understanding of this text was as enacted in the performance, in the act of waving the hands, enacting the downward spiral of the fish and the articulation of happiness and completion of the act of swimming, catching, eating and being together. The "compressing" of this experience into one dimension, literacy, was not adequate to account for it as a text. Understandings of literacy and language were spread and diffused across the projects in this way. Rather than being located within a person, or a set of texts, or within the lens of one particular researcher, the lens was dependent on who was looking at what and why. Saima's literacy was as much in the wavy motion of her hands as in the poem and in her own relationship to family, which was very strong.

"How to Drown a Blondie": Writing in a Home

Lucy was a British Asian girl who was eleven when I began to work with her and visit her home. Lucy produced stories that were vivid, expressive and powerful, in the context of a climate of racism within her school. One of her stories, "How to Drown a Blondie" expressed a powerful metaphorical and embodied rage against "Lauren", a blond girl who came to a bad end. As in Toni Morrison's "The Bluest Eye" (1970) the story of the Blond girl (the "Blondie") was an enactment of rage, against racism but also a graphic and powerful account of a young person's perceptual framework of the world:

> Right let's get this straight. I am writing a story about a selfish, evil, cold-hearted girl whose life I took away. Everything in this story is the truth. 100% I guarantee you.
> The girl's name was Lauren. She had beautiful hair. It was blond and shoulder length with beautiful eyes which were Indigo-blue. But if you looked closer you could see her eyes were raging with fire and jealousy if she met someone more beautiful than her. Her dad was a very rich man,

a billionaire who not only loved his daughter but was scared of her as well. As she was demanding and can turn anyone around her little finger with a click (but not me) as you couldn't be sure of what she was capable of doing. I'm not even going to tell you what she did. Because it is too evil.

(from "How to Drown a Blondie" by Lucy, 2011)

I wrote about this as an example of an aesthetic consciousness that was imbued with a post-colonial and anti-racist sensibility (Pahl, 2014b). Lucy drew on aesthetic categories to create the effects she sought; for example, she used colour and vivid language to make her point. These aesthetic categories created the effects she wanted. They shaped my understanding and reception of her work. Alongside, "How to Drown A Blondie" Lucy also wrote a series of stories, including one, "Bloody Boots" that begins like this:

I am going to tell you a story that you may not think is true. But I wouldn't want to waste your time writing a load of garbage, and I am warning you now if you get nightmares if someone tells you a ghost story; immediately put this story down before it is too late for you and you may regret it for the rest of your life! Right now that I've got that over with. Let's begin . . .

(from "Bloody Boots" by Lucy, 2011)

The rhetoric is declamatory, addressed to the reader, and opening up a conversation that is designed to shock and scare the reader into submission. This discourse constructs an oppositional space that dares the reader to take part. Inviting rebuffs, it seduces the reader. Lucy's stories were set within her own experience of marginalisation and her experience of racism at her local school. Over time, Lucy shared these experiences with me and I came to realise these were a key backdrop to her story writing.

"Language as Talisman": Oral Stories in a Park

Stories resonate across sites and spaces, united by a common "structure of feeling" and social haunting (Bright, 2012). These stories linked to another story, told by a group of girls in Rawmarsh, once a village now subsumed by the borough of Rotherham. These resonances and echoes were interesting in that they captured the ways in which stories were generated by sites and by themes. In both cases, ghosts and girls' experiences were key to the telling of the story. The tellers of this story, "Reunion", were three working-class 13-year-old girls who attended a youth club in a park. As part of a project called "Language as Talisman" we undertook collaborative storytelling sessions in the park. From a joint storytelling session emerged the story of two girls who died in the second world war bombs (see Pahl, 2014a). This story was narrated by Chloe, Ella and Georgia, in a round circle, together with Sam Rae and Steve Pool as inscribers and recorders of the story. This excerpt from the story was narrated by Chloe, and describes an incident in the story when the main character, Maria, wandered into an abandoned warehouse and heard two little ghosts:

> Little girls' laughter. She opened up a box lid; the kind that open in two ways and make a bang. She'd seen people that nobody else had seen before, because those people were ghosts. She never told anybody this because she didn't want people to think she was weird and everything, or not believe her. But looking in the boxes, she thought she might maybe see some more ghosts – if she carried on looking. Then she'd have proof and people would have to believe her.

> (2012)

Like Lucy's story, there is something about the invisible becoming invisible, the ghost but also the issue of being believed. This story, again, is about being believed, being heard and being recognised. It is also an extraordinary act of description of a box ("that open in two ways and make a bang") resting on observational drawing, that is, drawing based on direct experience of an object. Chloe also drew the box. At that time, Rotherham became haunted by a set of incidents in which girls were successively not believed over a long period of time. This experience led to a report that argued strongly for the need to believe and trust the testimonies of young girls in Rotherham (Jay, 2014).

"Threads of Time": Poetry with a Group of Girls

The projects gradually became more collaborative. My final example is from a joint project, one directed by researcher Zanib Rasool. Collaboratively developed with poet Helen Mort, "Threads of Time" sought to work with young women to explore their identities. As Rasool (2017) writes,

> The Threads of Time project explored minority ethnic girls' identity and their understanding of citizenship linked to place, culture, faith, history and tradition, and examined what it means to be British. This type of research increases our understanding of how minority ethnic girls see themselves, and has been an under-researched area. The research questions were formed around British identity and the national narrative, exploring cultural heritage and how young people identify themselves, links to the past and visualizing a better future. Participants repositioned themselves using their personal lenses, thus defining their own citizenship captured through methods of creative writing and visual arts.

> (Rasool 2017: 315)

Lucy, whose writing I described above, was one of the participants in this project. As described above, she attended a poetry writing session with poet Helen Mort that took place in a park called "Clifton Park". In a poem written as part of the project, she wrote about a historical person – Lady Walker, who lived in the "big house" in Rotherham, known as Clifton Park. Here is her poem:

I am Lady Walker

More than a maid but less than an equal to my superior
More than a simple peasant but less than Royal blood
Thy sings and doesn't bathe in mud
Thy is purer than white
Fresh as snow
My purpose is to be pretty
Certainly not witty
I don't speak my mind
Because I'm supposed to be kind
I am oppressed because of my femininity
Oh I so wish I had more masculinity
They give me flowers
My husband powers
They don't acknowledge me
They only look at me.

Here, the themes expressed in "How to Drown a Blondie" and "Bloody Boots" – revenge, powerlessness, voice and identity – echo across the years between 2011 and 2016. Lucy's writing had matured but her determination to be heard continues. Her work, ably described by Rasool (2017) describes the "structures of feeling . . . the deep community that makes the communication possible" (Williams, 1965: 64–65) that is emergent, and led by issues of voice and identity. Learning from the work of these girls is something that requires an attention to the ways of knowing and the issues within the context of Rotherham. The need to believe and trust what the girls said, and to recognise their voices, became stronger as the projects continued. Capturing those voices through collaborative work and listening to the voices of the young people was an important part of this process.

In Summary

What does this mean for language and literacy ethnographies? These layered understandings of literacy are presented as different research projects, but form a single journey for me. They start with the initial accounts of literacy in objects and develop into accounts of literacy within intangible, affective gesture and feelings, in the library. This then produces an account of literacy that is about the verve, voice and power of written texts. Literacy looks different wherever you look in the data. These competing analyses were also collaboratively constructed and reflexively analysed. The literacies were lived and experienced with people, and the construction of the data was produced in experience and within sites and spaces. This was not a model of research that took data "from" a site but instead, produced it within a site, as a co-production. The co-production process included co-analysis, and co-inquiry as projects were developed in collaboration with community researchers such as Zanib Rasool (Rasool, 2017; Campbell et al., 2018). As a result, the research direction changed and shifted.

This shift in perspective is significant as it decisively changes the way the layers are reflexively experienced. The process was not neat and tidy but was emotionally laden, with some tensions and difficulties. While these stories resonate with the lived experience of the people described within them, I navigated the experience of recording these stories in many different ways. In some projects our field notes were settled and agreed; in other projects, they did not agree (Pahl, 2017). Here, I recognise the living of those lives and this chapter, also, is a trace of the literacies of those relational projects. Returning to the Boudieusian project in this book, I now consider the layers of reflexivity within these studies and the epistemologies that lie behind them. Taking apart these layers and identifying them with traditions, I can see within these studies some key strands:

- *Ethnography, Linguistics Narrative Inequality.* Del Hymes' focus on voice, power and the narrative pull within the everyday (1996) informed the work in the library and within the community settings. In the telling of the ghost stories and the articulation of the "Bloody Boots" and "How to Drown a Blondie" new articulations of identity and voice surfaced.
- *Local Literacies.* In an understanding of the sites and space of literacy, I could see how the community library produced literacies that were collaborative, invisible and nurturing, imbued with the literacies of place and space (Barton and Hamilton, 1998).
- *Artifactual literacies.* In my work with Jennifer Rowsell (2010), we explored the ways in which material objects interacted with literacy practices but also how literacies themselves were materially situated.
- *Ideological literacies.* Echoing the work of Brian Street's (1993) account of literacies as always ideological, these studies are themselves imbued with the meanings that surround them. In that, literacy is always seen as ideologically situated.
- *Living literacies.* This is a conceptual framework for literacy which understands literacies as lived through the optics of Seeing, Knowing, Disrupting, Creating and Making. This then situates literacy within lenses that acknowledge its diverse relationship to lived experience (Pahl and Rowsell, 2019).

By seeing these theoretical traditions and methodologies as layered, a more process-driven and emergent conceptual framework for research can be traced that recognises the "prior ontologies" of literacy that are being constructed in the field (Massumi, 2002: 66). I recognise that these ontologies are constructed, relational and site specific. By taking a layered approach to reflexivity and separating out the strands of thinking within the projects, I explored the ways in which literacy ontologies emerge from sites, space and people. They were not "found" independently by an independent researcher. They were entwined within lives. This relational understanding of literacy was ideologically situated. This entails seeing literacy differently as an engaged, sometimes invisible articulation of feeling within a social structure that requires articulation to make sense. Part of those articulations lies the researcher, living life within the fieldwork. This book surfaces this knowledge and experience, and explores how reflexivity constructs the field anew, and is in process within this, these studies sit as a trace of that process.

NOTES

1 I would like to acknowledge the work of the following people who worked with me on the projects described in this article: *Artefacts of Identity and Narratives of Migration*: Andrew Pollard, Zahir Rafiq, Aliya Khan; *Inspire Rotherham*: Deborah Bullivant, Chloe Allan; *Writing in the Home and in the Street*: Richard Steadman-Jones, Zanib Rasool; *Language as Talisman*: Hugh Escott, Steve Pool, Sam Rae, Marcus Hurcombe *Imagine*: Zanib Rasool, Steve Pool, Sarah Banks, Angie Hart, Paul Ward.

2 Rotherham, is a post-industrial town in the UK, with a history of mining and steel works. This research was funded in part by the AHRC Connected Communities programme and also by the ESRC *Imagine* project (grant number ESK/002686–2) as well as by *Inspire Rotherham*.

3 Rotherham had experienced some hardship following the closure of the mines in the mid-1980s and the steel industry in the decade previous to that. This meant that many of the secure jobs were gone. Rotherham grew rapidly following the industrial revolution, experienced deep and profound changes which created an industrial community, which then had to adapt to changes brought about by outside forces. De-industrialisation led to high levels of unemployment and poverty in the 1980s, some of which has proved difficult to shift over the last thirty years.

5

REFLEXIVE LAYERS AND LONGITUDINAL RESEARCH

What we Might Know Across Time

Catherine Compton-Lilly

As Grenfell argues in this book, the crux of what Bourdieu asks of scholars is not how to *do* research, but "how *to be* it". Gaze is personal, embodied and enacted. With this in mind, I explore my own gaze through three different positionalities – as a teacher, researcher and scholar, and archivist and ally. Specifically, I focus on Christy a former student whom I followed for a decade (Compton-Lilly, 2003; 2007; 2012; 2016) to explore layers of reflexive attention that Bourdieu described as essential (Bourdieu, 1993a, 2003). Arguing that the researcher's goal is to reveal the strategies and the habitus of the field in which participants operate, Bourdieu (2003) maintained that understanding systems and making sense of people's experiences always involves the researcher. As Deer (2008) explained, Bourdieu lamented the "unconscious failure by most [researchers] to recognise and control the effects and influences of their own relation to the object of the research" (p. 201).

In short, our understandings of the world are not separate from the language we use, the communities we participate in, and the histories within which we reside. In particular, Bourdieu focused on how researchers must move beyond the common sense of the researcher, the participants, the community and the particular academic field that claims the researcher.

First, I briefly describe the methodology for this longitudinal study. Then, I turn Bourdieu's methodological gaze on myself as I consider three reflective stances that I brought to a longitudinal research project. These stances highlight the ontological – my being and becoming in the field (Parkin, 2016). I end by considering how engaging in reflexive analysis of self contributes to what we can learn relative to the questions we ask. Along the way, I explore previously unrecognised and unspoken dimensions of the longitudinal research process as I reflect on the role I played in Christy's life. I work to explore my own position as a researcher within schools and the academy alongside the intellectual biases and presuppositions that limit and direct ways of thinking about Christy, her literacy learning, her family and my relationship with her over time.

The Longitudinal Process

I met Christy and her mother, Ms. Green, when I taught at Rosa Parks Elementary School – a large urban school where 97% of the students qualified for free or reduced-price lunch. Most of the children walked to school from the housing projects and apartments that surrounded our school. While the neighbourhood was often described as violent and drug-ridden by the local media, the dedicated parents who sent their children to Rosa Parks Elementary School continuously impressed me. At the time of my research, our school had been placed on our State's list of failing schools. If reading and math test scores at our school did not improve, our school faced closure.

It was in this context that I began my doctoral dissertation. My goal was to document the literacy practices of my students and their families. Ten families participated in what I thought would be a one-year study. Eventually, I was able to revisit eight of the families when my former students were in grades five, eight, and eleven. During grade one, I collected multiple classroom observations and student work samples. During each phase of the project, I interviewed children and parents. I also collected reading assessments and writing samples.

I was deeply inspired by the work of critical ethnographers (i.e., Barton and Hamilton, 1998; Heath, 1983; Street, 1995) who documented literacy and language practices in thoughtful and respectful ways honouring the ways people learned and used literacy in their daily lives. I adopted their methods as I observed, listened and documented children's reading and writing over time. Throughout the study, I kept field notes that are central to the analyses presented in this chapter. Across the study, children and parents were asked to talk about their reading practices, their use of technology and their satisfaction with school. Parents and children described their favourite books and spoke of their plans for the future. Over time, children and families increasingly commented on school expectations and the challenges they faced at school. In addition, the focus of the study expanded beyond literacy as identity negotiations and peer relationships became increasingly salient. A small grant from the Spencer Foundation allowed me to observe the children in high school and interview their teachers.

Across the study, data analysis involved transcription and grounded coding of interviews and field notes (Strauss and Corbin, 1990). Over time, it became apparent that content coding was insufficient. Specifically, I realised that data collected during early phases of the project gained significance when viewed in relation to data collected years later. Thus, the longitudinal patterns that eventually became apparent had been obfuscated by my sequential grounded coding of data from each phase of the project. Longitudinal analysis required reading and rereading stacks of data and using the search function on my word processor to locate words and ideas that recurred across the data set. Eventually, I began to conceptualise what I describe as *temporal discourse analysis* to track discourses and stories over time (Compton-Lilly, 2014b; 2015). While my teacher research perspective and my field notes were informed by my proximity to the children and our shared experiences in the classroom, my researcher perspective benefited from the luxury of contemplating the data across a decade. The case presented in this chapter is drawn from a collective case study; that study involved "periodic restudy" (Saldaña, 2003) – every three to four years – across a decade. While the full study entailed eight students over a ten-year period, this chapter focuses only on Christy. While I offer this account of my procedures, methods, and analytics – how I did my research – to fulfill the norms of the field, in this chapter, I reflect on my own role in the project. I explore what I wrote and how I wrote about Christy with an emerging awareness of the intersectional relationship between the language and textual structures that define academic writing and being an academic.

I argue that longitudinal qualitative research provides an important space for the investigation of reflexivity. As Grenfell argues, research must be "interactive and cyclic, so that outcomes remain open to revision in the light of further investigations" (Grenfell, 2012a: 195). Revisiting findings, reworking claims, and complicating conclusions has been inherent in the longitudinal research process as findings presented in early books and papers are revisited and data collected in later phases begs the re-analysis of data collected during earlier phases (Compton-Lilly, 2003; 2007; 2012; 2016). In short, longitudinal research provides opportunities to revisit what we think we understand over time as children's lives emerge and shift. My own gaze is revealed as constituting what I believe when what I think I understood is complicated and challenged, revealing the emergent and situated nature of my own knowing. Thus, I was left to grapple with layers of reflexivity that created an eternally tentative and emergent stance that continually troubled my research.

My current focus on reflexivity was prompted by an ongoing attempt to create a fictionalised account to capture Christy's experiences outside of the expectations and constraints imposed on academic research. In short, I wanted to tell Christy's story in a way that allowed me to make inferences and add details that could not be fully supported by the data and thus present a fictionalised story that might interest and inform a larger audience. To do this, I again reread Christy's entire data set. This process not only invited reflection on Christy and her trajectory but also on my own trajectory and my changing positionality as I moved from being a classroom teacher to being a university researcher. In writing this chapter, I suspect that the passing of time has made reflexivity easier. For example, it is much less threatening to write about my positionality as a teacher 15 years ago than it would have been to write about that same positionality as it was being lived. My shifting relationship with Christy and my current role in the field created spaces for reflection unavailable to me as a classroom teacher. For example, as a university researcher, I regularly spend entire mornings writing; this never happened as part of my employment as a classroom teacher.

A Traditional Statement of Reflexivity

In this brief section, I offer a traditional and decidedly incomplete statement of my own reflexivity as a researcher. Bourdieu argued that while this layer of reflexivity is essential it is not enough. Most of my publications include statements that position me as a White, currently middle-class, female, American scholar who grew up at the poverty line. I often highlight my eighteen years of teaching in a high poverty urban community. Sometimes I write about the unique juxtaposition of growing up in a highly academic family and being surround by books from a young age, alongside a lack of economic resources – thus a relatively unusual mix of high academic and cultural capital alongside a lack of economic capital. When relevant, as in Christy's case, I mention the history of debilitating mental health issues in my immediate family.

While I choose to disclose different dimensions of my experiences as I write different papers, these markers of my habitus are relatively stable. As will be evident below, Bourdieu argues that researchers must consider much more. In short, the biographical experiences of the researchers are not enough, researchers must acknowledge and grapple with the field and their struggle for legitimation within that field which involve links between their habitus that resonates, or does not resonate, with academic performance, the capital they have accumulated, and the ways that capital operates within a particular academic field (Grenfell, 2008; 2011).

Three Layers of Reflexivity – Teacher, Researcher and Ally

In this chapter, I draw on data from Christy's longitudinal case to explore three dimensions of my own reflexivity that continue to inform my ongoing analysis of the data. As reported elsewhere in this book, literacy is a hazardous field. It is difficult to define. Literacy means many different things to different people and thus is a contentious space in which to position one's self. No matter what you believe and enact in terms of practices and policies, there will always be a critical mass that views literacy learning differently. For example, what counted as capital in my classroom and school (i.e., high test scores, a quiet classroom) was very different from what mattered at the university (i.e., critically reflective students, progressive educator stances, engaged learners). Thus, what counted as capital shifted as I moved through my school, as I travelled into the community, and as I transitioned to the university. The three layers of reflexivity that I explore in this chapter – as a teacher, researcher and archivist/ally – are not comprehensive, yet they are an attempt to recognise and respond to the complexity of reflexivity. The accounts that follow reflect dialogical relations among me, Christy, the structures that define our experiences and our perceptions and the dispositions we assume. They cannot help but act as embodiments of my thinking as the worlds I occupied and occupy constitute sense that speaks to me of myself as I attempt to tell Christy's story.

Being Christy's Teacher

When I revisit my field notes from when I was Christy's teacher, I note that they are filled with concerns related to school politics and my commitment to being a good teacher. In my mind, this translated into making sure that all my first grade students learned to read; I was not always successful. My primary interests focused on how I was expected or allowed to teach and on how well my students learned based on imposed criteria and assessments.

In October of 1997, I described Christy as the "best reader in the class". Having repeated first grade, Christy was a year older and brought reading skills to the classroom that the other children did not. Christy's Mother was White and her father was Black. She lived with her mother on a street that was associated with drug arrests. While the neighbourhood certainly struggled and I regularly observed drug transactions when I visited Christy's neighbourhood; there were several families raising their children on this street. Media reports about the community focused on drugs arrests and shootings, never reporting on the community's strengths or their lack of resources.

As my account will convey, larger issues related to social justice operated when the house Christy and her mother rented was condemned with over 30 housing code violations that the landlord had managed to evade for several years. At that time, there was no grocery store within ten miles of my school despite it being located in the middle of a city. The local library was in the process of being closed and the children were not allowed to play on the school playground due to disrepair and safety issues.

Our school was one of the first schools in the country to be placed on a state list of schools to be annexed by the State unless our test scores improved. Forefront in my mind was not only our increasingly controlled and surveilled curriculum, but also my concerns about being a good teacher and teaching children to read in a context where standardised testing was gaining ground and expertise in teaching reading was increasingly dismissed. In short, I was constantly reminded that the success of Christy and her classmates was a reflection on me as a teacher. My desire to "help" Christy was complicated by being a White teacher in a predominantly Black and Puerto Rican community in which race was salient.

During September of the first year of the study, the teachers at my school were *inserviced* on the new basal program. My field notes read:

> Today was a very frustrating day. The woman who gave the basal inservice seems to think that her textbooks are a lot smarter than we teachers are. Some

of her comments were really incredible. I wrote the following down in my notes. She said, "at first it is ok to hang on to some of the practices you have used in the past. But soon you will wean yourself from that other stuff." It's like saying everything I do is wrong and the program is right. I doubt it!

My field notes went on to describe my concerns about the new and very detailed forms for weekly lessons plans that had to be completed and handed in each Monday for the coming week, my disdain for policies that mandated that all children be reading grade level texts even if they could not read those texts, and my worries about the numerous and ever-changing assessments that were imposed on the children. However, these concerns were not just my personal reflections on being a teacher. Concerns about teacher autonomy, increasingly scripted curriculum and pre-planned instruction reflected much of what I was reading in my doctoral classes at the university. We were reading work by John Dewey, Paulo Freire and Michael Apple and I aspired to be the "transformative intellectual teacher" described by Henry Giroux (1988). Resistance to the mandates imposed on my school reflected the mantra of progressive educators during the late 1990s as we faced the beginnings of the standards movement, which eventually brought us the Common Core State Standards.

While there are many things I could have written in my field notes, most references to children noted their abilities with reading and sometimes writing. I wrote extensive field notes about Christy's journey to become a capable reader. These accounts are filled with references to the basal reading program, Christy's text reading level, mastery of sight words and decoding strategies revealing my ongoing negotiation of Street's (1995) autonomous and ideological models of literacy.

> **October 1996:** Christy was in first grade last year. She also attended the summer school and is now reading at level 9. Christy uses letters and sounds as well as meaning clues and usually syntax to solve unfamiliar words.
>
> **November 1996:** Christy continues to do well but her accuracy and willingness to reread, closely monitor and self-correct is not strong. [When reading the story "Bet You Can!"] she substituted "but" for "bet" four times with no self-correction. The error was not obviously meaningless but it did not make good sense.
>
> **December 1996:** Christy brings challenging books to read to me and generally does well. Her errors on familiar text generally make sense (i.e., "fun hat" instead of "funny hat").
>
> **January 1997:** Christy chose a tricky book (level 12) – Tiger is a Scaredy Cat. She read well but mixed up "strong" and "scared". Again the meaning is not coming through. She is not thinking that the cat is scared [which is important to the story].

February 1997: Christy read at a level 19 the other day. I was impressed. She is doing more self-correcting though she still reads so fluently that she does not slow down to self-correct especially if meaning is maintained.

March 1997: Christy got all the review [sight] words [right] except she said "went" for "want". On list three, she said "loon" for "long" and then self-corrected when she realised that "loon" did not make sense [to her].

Reflecting on these field notes, my habitus as a teacher and as a particular type of teacher, came through. During the early 1990s I had been deeply involved with the *Whole Language Movement*. My comments about Christy as a reader are peppered with attention to meaning. I write about her using "meaning clues", making "good sense", as well as the meaning being "maintained" or meaning "not coming through". While decoding and accuracy are mentioned, as one would expect from a good whole language educator, phonetic analysis is addressed in the service of meaning construction. Notably, I sought and found models of the reading process and reading instruction that provided me with ways of making sense of reading as a meaning-driven practice. These included attending to the three cuing systems people use when they read (Clay, 2001), the Four Resources Model (Luke and Freebody, 1997) and balanced literacy (Pinnell and Fountas, 1996).

As I read back through my notes and revisit Christy's story, I ruminate on the themes that recurred in my field notes. I wrote extensively about what I viewed as impositions placed on me as a teacher. The prescribed reading program imposed testing and surveillance by school administrators through both observations and the monitoring of lesson plans as recurring motifs. While these rants may have been understandable, they also allowed me to present myself as a thoughtful, progressive educator who was committed to developing expertise as a teacher. I operated within a community that recognised my critiques as I crafted a space for myself within that community. My ways of making sense of literacy instruction were deeply embedded in my professional habitus as a teacher and embodied in my instructional practices, language practices, affiliations and the ways I set up my classroom (Grenfell, 2012a). While at the time I was unaware, the field was directing me to attend to some things and not others, to see things in particular ways and to think what was thinkable for a progressive educator to think.

Bourdieu might argue that making sense of my field notes requires recognising and attending to the field beyond my classroom. *No Child Left Behind* (2001) with its mandate for statewide testing, the *National Reading Panel Report* (2000) and *Reading First* grants (2002) were on the horizon. The vision of reading associated with these assessments and policies featured the five pillars of reading – only one of which referenced meaning construction. These reforms were the antithesis of the views shared by progressive literacy educators and in order to claim a space in the field of progressive education, I needed to join the rally against those foes. This is not to say that I was wrong, or that the commitments that progressive educators make to child-centred and responsive pedagogies were misguided. It is merely to acknowledge the field within which I operated and how I played by their rules to establish myself as a progressive educator. Notably, this brought me particular rewards. While at my own school my views and "expertise" were not always appreciated, I became recognised locally as an accomplished reading teacher and was invited by my district to mentor and coach other teachers. Nationally, I began to present at conferences, published in teacher-oriented journals, signed a book contract and was one of the few teacher/researchers to ever be awarded a National Academy of Education/Spencer Postdoctoral Fellowship. I was gradually inducted as a practitioner scholar into a community that required particular allegiances and alliances. As Bourdieu (1993a) maintained, every field brings its own set of stakes and interests and people, whom in order to operate successfully, must play the game.

Being a Researcher and a Scholar

I am now a researcher who has survived the tenure process, become a full professor at a top-ranked university and later assumed an endowed chair at another prestigious university. Obtaining tenure involved a complicated dance – establishing a presence in the field, publishing in the right journals, adhering to established formats for writing and citing the right scholars. What I study and how I write are influenced by current conversations in the field, the IRB (Institutional review board) process, my relationships with senior scholars and the politics of professional organisations.

Along with my position at the university, I have assumed the positionality of a scholar who has *retired* from the social world (AKA public school teaching) (Swartz, 1997). This allows me the privilege of sitting in a sunny coffee shop and thinking and writing about eight students whom I taught over ten years ago. As Bourdieu maintained, leisure time to write and reflect and a "pure gaze" uninhibited by the need for ongoing decision-making and action are luxuries unavailable to practitioners who are "immersed in the flow of everyday life" (Grenfell, 2008).

Time has also passed for the children and families who participated in my study. When we started, I was in my late 30s; most of the children's parents were approximately my age. Since then, most of us have become grandparents and some of the children have had children of their own. Some parents have retired and more than one parent has passed away. As I write about my former students and their families, I think a lot about time. Perhaps it is entering my mid-50s, watching my daughter graduate from college and losing both my parents that has personally affected my thinking.

Time also haunts me professionally. I think about the trajectories that awaited my former students and the apparently severe consequences of attending underfunded schools in a high poverty community. I think about the six-year-olds that I taught and their potential. I consider their parents and the hopes they had for their children. I also think about the opportunities they did not find in school, the stifling instruction that they described and the markers of failure that they encountered in the forms of failed tests, low report card grades and stringent behavioural policies. This is not to say that they did not encounter excellent teachers. All of the students described teachers whom they loved and whom inspired them in school.

My professional experiences have also led me to conceptualise time as a constitutive dimension of people's identities and experiences that significantly affects how participants make sense of their worlds. As I consider my role as a researcher, I tracked students from grade one through eleven to explore their experiences and trajectories. As a good scholar should, I have theoretically grounded my work. Most recently, I have moved among various temporal theories. I have used Lemke's (2000, 2005) descriptions of timescales to explore how my students have situated themselves within multiple scales of time (Compton-Lilly, 2011). I have accessed Bakhtin (1981, 1986) to identify chronotopes – the intersections of time and space that contribute to definitions of students as successful (i.e., passing the fourth grade ELA test) or as failures (failing sixth grade) (Compton-Lilly, 2013). I have also accessed Bourdieu (1990c) to examine how various dispositions that contribute to a person's habitus are embodied over time contributing to ways of being, or not being, a student and ways of being or not being a writer (Compton-Lilly, 2014a). Each theory highlights a different yet intersecting dimension of time.

As a good scholar, I have also explored methodological issues that accompany collecting data over a ten-year period. I read books about case study, explored the affordances of data analysis software, revisited my methodological plans and considered my own subjectivity as a researcher. As a study that was not planned to span a decade, the project took unexpected directions. In particular, I have explored what I call *temporal discourse analysis* to attend to how language and stories are situated within time and how language and stories are used and told across time and how they contribute to the ways people make sense of their worlds. While my explicitly temporal way of thinking about discourse may seem new or original, it is essential to recognise that my conceptualisation of temporal discourses analysis is tightly embedded in existing fabrics of thought. I build explicitly on existing conceptualisations of discourse (Bloome and Carter, 2004; Gee, 2014) and operate within the parameters offered by those methodological constellations of meaning. In particular, my focus on temporality aligns nicely with and perhaps extends current conversation that highlight the role of social context.

As I look back on how I wrote about Christy, it becomes clear that while I thought I was trying to convey her experiences, my writing was also in service of my own professional goals. I told parts of her story to make arguments and to support claims that would make sense to other people who shared the academic field in which I operated – other scholars who might recognise my work as worthy, substantive and significant.

When Christy was in fifth grade, I was interested in how the students were situated in relation to the new State tests that were implemented as part of *No Child Left Behind*. I included the following quote alongside similar quotes from David and Javon:

> CL: What happens when they [children in your class] have trouble on tests?
> *Christy*: Like if you doing the test, they have trouble and they [the children] act mean . . . if they don't know the answer, they will try to ask somebody else.
> CL: And then what happens?
> *Christy*: They get in trouble.
> CL: Yeah. What happens if they take the test and they get a really bad grade on it. What will happen to those kids?
> *Christy*: When they go home, their mom or dad will get mad.
>
> (Compton–Lilly, 2007: 40)

I then go on to explain:

> David, Christy and Javon all used the word "mad" to describe the ways children, teachers and parents react to poor performance on tests. They say that kids "act mean", "get in trouble", and "bother other kids." The children's association of anger and aggression with testing challenges official stories about testing that argue for a logical and scientific approach to school improvement.
>
> (Compton–Lilly, 2007: 40)

In my writing, I ventriloquised the voices of progressive educators who were distraught at the increased amount of testing that has accompanied *No Child Left Behind* policies that required States to administer a literacy tests in grade four. Christy and her peers were part of the first cohort of students to take these tests. My account of the distress they associated with these tests is part of a much larger argument about testing policies, the privileging of *best instructional practices* and research that claimed to be scientifically based.

When Christy was in grade 8, I drew on interviews with Christy to make several points about children's reading practices. I identified Christy as one of two children in the sample who mentioned books that had been assigned in school.

Christy identified chapter books, the Arthur series (Brown, 1982–current) and *The Kid in the Red Jacket* (Park, 1988), a book she had been assigned to read in school. In grades four and five, schoolbooks were no longer predominant and only two children mentioned books that were assigned at school.

(Compton-Lilly, 2012: 41)

I noted Christy's clarity about the kinds of books she liked and did not like.

Christy: [I don't like] Mysteries. I don't want to go through all that . . . [And I don't like] this book we read in English . . . *To Kill a Mockingbird* . . . It's boring . . . I ain't getting into it yet.

(Compton-Lilly, 2012: 42)

Later in the interview Christy spoke about the passive pedagogic practice that accompanied the class' reading of *To Kill a Mocking Bird* (Lee, 1960/2002).

[It was boring because] "We read that *To Kill a Mocking Bird* together. The teacher read it to us and we followed along." Listening to the teacher read, involved passivity and reception rather than enactment and investment.

(Compton-Lilly, 2012: 45)

Finally, I identified Christy's reading practices that extended beyond books and magazines.

Christy, whose biological mother was then living in the Southeastern United States, described reading and rereading the greeting cards she has received from her mother and her mother's relatives. She showed me her collection of sixteen cards that she and her sister had received. She read some of the notes in the cards into my tape recorder and explained that she still missed her mother despite having lived in a foster home and later an adoptive home for the past five years.

(Compton-Lilly, 2012: 45)

In short, I drew on interview data from Christy and the other children in the sample to make what I continue believe to be important points. First, I highlight the rich range of reading practices that occurred within this urban community, often outside of school. Next, I espouse the importance of student-centred pedagogies that include book choice and active engagement with texts. These are not new ideas. Instead, I am contributing to a larger discourse that is currently popular among literacy scholars and educators who share the literacy field. Other stories could have been crafted from this same data. It is not a question of whether the story I crafted is right or wrong. What is significant is that the story I crafted fits with existing literacy discourses and my crafting these accounts contributes to the capital I continue to accumulate in that field.

Until now, I have not told Christy's story in any detail and I have often wondered why. Sometimes I suspect that it is because Ms. Green's story can be read as a quintessential example of the single mother in a high poverty community who made a series of questionable decisions. Telling that story could feed into deficit discourses and would expose me to heavy critique by my colleagues. Sometimes, I think it is because the stories move from the familiar spaces of schools and classrooms into contexts that I know little about – foster care and adoption of children who have been removed from their parents' custody. Sometimes, I think it is because I see Christy and her mother as victims within a system that I do not understand. As Christy's first grade teacher, I recognised that if Ms. Green did not get more support that she would not be able to take care of her daughters. She was on the brink of her life falling apart. I knew it. Other people at my school knew it as well. But we all watched as things unravelled and Christy and her sister were removed from their home and permanently separated from their mother.

My researcher stance allows me to selectively reveal my experiences and to decide how to craft the stories I choose to tell. I can decide what is and is not relevant to the research questions I ask. In my early work, I challenged deficit discourses related to parents in the poor urban community where I taught Christy. This work served me well. It reflected ongoing conversations about the prevalence of deficit discourses that are imposed on diverse students and their families. I was making the right argument at the right time and the field found my argument useful. It served the larger purposes of the progressive academic researchers.

Since then, I have transversed similar ground as I have moved through the tenure process. Specifically, I learned to manipulate methodology and theory to serve my purposes and to establish myself as a scholar. Methodologically, I stumbled into longitudinal research. My analysis of longitudinal data led me to a rich theoretical space that offered a compelling lens for exploring the experiences of my former students. Longitudinal research and methodologies that honour temporality (Bloome, Beierle, Grigorenko, and Goldman, 2009; Wortham and Reyes, 2015) allowed me to explore new territory (Compton-Lilly, 2014b, 2015) while also staying within the boundaries of socio-cultural visions of the world. In particular, my work points to temporal dimensions of context that extend existing visions through negotiations involving previously constructed under-standings.

As argued elsewhere in this book, it must be recognised that I am operating within an established field in which it matters that we all read and cite Heath (1983), Street (1995) and Bourdieu (1990c, 2003). We recognise people's literacy practices, we honour cultural and linguistic dimensions of literacy and we challenge institutional mechanisms that privilege some students over others. As I write these words, I am distinctly aware of the academic capital that is associated with my publishing a chapter in a book that highlights Bourdieu's theories and is edited by recognised Bourdieu scholars. Not only is this an intellectually riveting experience, but it is also a good career move. According to Wacquant (1992), Bourdieu strives to break up "small circles of mutual admiration" (p. 57) that tend to characterise academic fields. Swartz (1997) is particularly direct in his interpretation of Bourdieu's concerns with our lack of reflexivity. Specifically, he notes that too many scholars "refuse to recognize their drive to achieve an objective view for what it is, namely accumulating symbolic capital by discrediting others' views" (p. 275). As Swartz notes, "Reflexivity means viewing intellectual practices as being interest-oriented rather than being motivated exclusively by objective ideas or values" (Swartz, 1997: 279).

Being Christy's Archivist and Ally

I am not sure what inspired the analysis below. Unlike the two accounts presented above, this account is not grounded in the institutional spaces of school or university. It does not reflect practices valued within a particular institutional field. However, I suspect that caring about others, considering their situations and wondering how I could be helpful contributes to an abiding set of dispositions that contribute to my habitus as an ally. These issues were critical to Bourdieu who was concerned about the plight of the Algerian people who were the focus of his initial research (see Wacquant, 1992). What is the researcher's role when people's lives are at stake? How can empirical and theoretical work catalyse each other to improve people's lives? This is the dimension of reflexivity that consumes this section of my chapter. In short, this reflexivity is tangential to the fields of school and university and not directly implicated in my success in either field.

Notably, I do not think that the ways of being that are described below are unique to me nor do they make me special. Instead they are common characteristics of people; most people have an immense capacity to care about others whom they have come to know in rich and nuanced ways. While I am not sure I could identify a particular field of practice within which these dispositions act as capital, these dispositions have indirectly served me by contributing to relationships with colleagues both in schools and at the university. However, they are rarely articulated in educational forums and academic publications.

As I write this section, I wonder at the emergence of this account. Was it made possible because I was both Christy's teacher and a researcher documenting her school trajectory? Did it emerge because I followed Christy for a long period of time, which may have revealed insights and raised issues that I might not have considered? Or is this account the result of a conscious effort – grounded in my reading of Bourdieu – to explore the limits of my teacher and researcher eyes?

My analysis may have been affected by my emerging awareness that I was the only person Christy regularly spoke to who knew her when she was six-years-old and who knew and respected her mother. Christy's experiences, as a foster child who was later adopted, have invited me to revisit the difficulties faced by Christy's mother (i.e., mental illness, drugs, AIDS) across time and how these difficulties were contrasted with her adoptive parents who were constructed by teachers and social workers as saintly. In addition, her foster mother and her adopted mother were paid by the state to take care of Christy and her sister; their stipends far surpassed Ms. Green's welfare benefits.

Almost twenty years ago, Nespor (2013) identified a critical mismatch between how parents and teachers make sense of schooling over time. He wrote that "teachers" acquaintance with kids generally begins and ends within a single school year" and the "histories of students in earlier grades are generally hidden from view" (p. 32); meanwhile, parents view schools as "accounts of how kids matured and took their places in society" (pp. 31–32). Parents know children across time and across multiple social spaces. They live beside children. Teachers only know children for short periods of time and often focus on academic skills and abilities. Each year, teachers are faced with new groups of children who consume their attention. These two conceptions of time and children are antithetical to teacher conceptions generally trumping the embodied and lived conceptions of time experienced by parents.

In middle and high school, Christy and her sister still received the occasional letter from their mother. With the exception of one visit when Christy was in middle school, these letters were the only contact Christy had with her mother across the final six years of the study. When I visited Christy, she sometimes read her mother's letters aloud. They were filled with news about getting a new kitten, the weather in New Mexico and her mother's accounts of trying to quit smoking.

Starting in middle school, when Christy had been living in foster homes for over five years, I started to notice Christy's interest in the past and her requests for me to tell her stories about herself. Christy had no photographs of herself as a child. There was no one to tell her what she had been like or what her mother had been like.

This silencing of Christy's past was complicated by her foster care placement and the often-difficult relationship between the foster family and Ms. Green. Before moving to New Mexico, on several occasions, Ms. Green attempted to see or speak with Christy by visiting her school or attending church. While Ms. Green's actions were driven by her intense desire to see her daughters, they were not appreciated by Christy's foster mother or by school professionals. This resulted in Christy often being privy to people criticising Ms. Green and warning Christy to avoid her mother. Meanwhile, Christy was forgetting her childhood and increasingly recruited me to tell her about the past. During multiple interviews at Christy's request, I shared my memories about Christy, her sister and her mother. When children grow up with their parents, childhoods are documented through photographs, repeated stories, comments from relatives and traditions as well as sharing ways of viewing and understanding the world that are conveyed through shared discourses and perspectives. This did not happen for Christy. At Christy's request, I described her as a first grade student who enjoyed reading and read well. She hated maths and behaved well at school. Christy reported that she could not remember her teachers from elementary school and in one interview even asked me my name.

I remember her being interested when I recalled that she had repeated first grade. Christy thought for a moment and then said, "I guess ninth grade is my right grade but I'm in eighth right now". Christy asked about her original first grade teacher and how her mother had felt about her being retained. When Christy spoke about playing the trumpet in the school band, she was surprised when I mentioned that her mother had played the flute. One of the few memories that Christy recalled, and I confirmed, was having a big dog when she was in first grade. At another point in the interviews, Christy turned to me and asked if I could tell her "stories about me when I was little". We spoke about her mother having attended college and her mother's love of reading. Together Christy and I *re-membered* a time when she and her sister had spent a weekend at my house.

As I view the field notes and interview transcripts from my longitudinal study, I am poignantly reminded that they are perhaps the only existing records of Christy's childhood and that I hold something that is not my own. I have been an archivist of Christy's life. I have given Christy copies of books I have written about her and the other children and revealed her and her mother's pseudonyms. Certainly, the Internal Review Board at my university would bristle at the thought of my returning raw data to Christy, but clearly deeper ethical issues are raised. Whose data is it? It is important to recognise that the data I collected during the first year of the study captured a relatively happy time in the family's history. Christy, her sister and her mother were together. While fighting her own demons, Ms. Green was entirely devoted to her children. I can still see Ms. Green walking toward me as she dropped her daughters off at school each morning, one daughter clinging to each hand. Ms. Green told stories about Christy's abilities to negotiate bus schedules, the pile of chapter books that she was saving for Christy when she got older and Christy's favourite books. While the stress of mental illness, poverty and a lack of resources needed to negotiate these challenges eventually took their toll, there had been better times and Ms. Green was a caring and resourceful parent. I have recently encountered a similar dilemma when I learned that Ms. Rodriguez, another mother in the sample, had passed. I thought of the decade of audiotapes in my closet of Ms. Rodriguez talking about her children and again wondered about ethics.

I argue that this analysis is not directly connected to my being a good teacher or a successful researcher. Writing this reflection might highlight me as a caring and thoughtful person. People may like me more and that liking may result in social capital and networking possibilities, but it is unlikely that this account alone will elevate me in the teacherly or scholarly world. However, I would argue that it is just the sort of account that does not get told, except perhaps over a glass of wine with close colleagues. I would also argue that it is a viable account and perhaps an account that points to actions that may actually serve Christy.

In Summary

As Deer (2008) argues, a goal of reflexivity is to privilege the consciousness and the experiences of participants above our own. As I continued my research with Christy and her peers, I thought I was telling their longitudinal stories as they moved through school. In doing so, I was also writing my own career and carving out my place in the academic community. I was beholden to the orthodoxy of the field, my own background and experiences and the relationship I had with Christy. Unbeknownst to me, I was also playing a profoundly personal and powerful role in Christy's life. I told her stories of herself that she could carry forward. Bourdieu believed that "a reflexive practice can help free the researcher from the particular economic, cultural and social interests that distort that singular pursuit of ideal interests of scientific knowledge" (Swartz, 1997: 282). Too often "researchers do not know, and do not want to know, the limits of their thoughts or to acknowledge the social conditions of its construction" (Grenfell, 2011: 215). This was true as I returned to interview Christy. It was not until she asked me about her past, that I began to recognise the limits of my own thinking and practice.

While it is highly questionable whether this exposé of my own reflective failings, written many years after the data was collected and after hundreds of pages of manuscript have been published, alters anything for anyone, it is my hope that it serves as an example and as a reminder to myself of the limits of my own vision and my need to continuously peel back layers of habitus and accumulated capital with an eye to the academic fields in which I operate and the people I encounter. As Jenkins (2002) eloquently noted, "social agents are typically unaware of the supporting, life-affirming water, the match between their habituses and the fields in which they flourish or feel at ease" (p. 59).

In this chapter, I explored my actions as teacher, researcher and ally and activist revealing the dialectic that informed the ways I made sense of Christy's story and the language I used to tell that story. I presented a certain truth in which my own interests populated its expression. Specifically, the worlds of educators, researchers and people are infused with assumptions, forms of knowledge and ways of thinking that are socially constructed and negotiated. Just as Bourdieu revealed the falseness of scholastic vision, we must recognise that schools and research communities create their own realities that are no more real, and sometimes more dangerous than others. As I have returned to work with Christy across the decade there have been changes for me, Ms. Green and for Christy. These changes as well as the assumptions I brought and bring must continuously be reconsidered. The awkward and imperfect ramblings presented above cannot help but be informed by New Literacy Studies and linguistic ethnography – the communities to which I have aligned myself. At the same time, these awkward and imperfect ramblings may be the only way to approach a reflexivity that is itself emergent in its eternal state of *being* and becoming. Research across time, because it involves explicitly changing positions, roles and ethical considerations, brings to the surface issues related to knowing and reflection revealing critical understandings, insights and what I believe present ethical and humbling dilemmas.

6

INSIDER IDENTITIES

Coming to Know the Ethnographic Researcher

Cheryl McLean

Introduction

As a literacy researcher, I view ethnographic research as a process by which I "come to know" (an)Other *person*, *group*, *context* and/or *environment*. However, this process of knowing is not unidirectional or linear, nor does it operate in a vacuum; rather, it is bidirectional and reciprocal, occurring on a continuum that acknowledges the dialogic struggle between participants' and the researcher's identities and voice. It is a process that speaks to the politics and power of being *a part of* yet *apart from* the research. Thus, in order to more deeply understand and account for the role of the researcher, and make explicit some of the tensions of conducting research on language and literacy, I too must *come to know* my Self as researcher.

The process of "coming to know" my researcher-Self, requires reflexivity – a critical and public reflection on the private Self. Researcher reflexivity involves the self-conscious and critical study of the researcher's own standpoints and assumptions (see Preissle and Grant, 2004), and it demands that these social identities be made public (Maton, 2003). The emphasis on reflexivity in the social sciences signals a collective understanding that the qualitative researcher, her subjectivities, identities, ideologies and biases have some influence on how and what data are collected, the nature of actions, interactions and relationships with participants and the interpretations and representations of the research. Indeed, the need for reflexivity as a researcher is even more relevant given the social nature of my ethnographic work that involves sustained periods of fieldwork focused on interacting and building relationships with my adolescent partici-pants in order to study their literacies and identities as learners. Given the social nature of learning (Gee, 1991; Heath, 1983; Street, 1984) within the researcher-participant relationship, there is an intertwining and reciprocal shaping of identities and belief systems that not only needs to be acknowledged, but also explored. What this means for my research is that, through reflexivity, my identities (ascribed and achieved, personal and professional, social and cultural) help me directly shape the research process and the product. I would argue that, for example, my dual insider-outsider perspectives and identities (Caribbean-Black-immigrant and teacher/teacher educator-researcher), directly and indirectly inform my work with adolescent immigrant participants, and the contexts in which I conduct research on adolescent literacy. In fact, I agree with Maton's (2003: 54) view that reflexivity is commonly understood as a way in which "authors explicitly position themselves in relation to their objects of study so that one may assess researchers' knowledge claims in terms of situated aspects of their social selves and reveal their (often hidden) doxic values and assumptions". However, for me to speak only of coming to know my participants, their communities, practices, identities and experiences is not enough; it is also important for me to look objectively at and come to know my own identities, practices and experiences within that research context.

This chapter, therefore, presents my reflexive self-study – a way to come to know my researcher-Self by critically examining how, as researcher, I shaped the research process and product. I explore the researcher's role in the ethnographic research process by asking: *How does my understanding of my ethnographic work on adolescent literacy change using a reflexively informed objectivity?* (Bourdieu, 2000c). To do so, I draw on the idea of reflexively informed objectivity – from Bourdieu (1977) and Grenfell's (this volume) description of "participant objectivation" and "reflexive objectivity" – as a form of objective practice that is reflexive in that it affords the researcher the opportunity to re-view her participation and intersecting positions in the research context. It is in the movement *away from* the immediacy of the fieldwork and write-up, that I find myself better able to move *toward* a deeper understanding of the power of my own subjectivities, identities and ideologies on the research process. The notion of reflexivity becomes a meta-analytical tool to generate differentiated and nuanced points of view of how researcher position-taking is central to the interpretation and analysis of the ethnographic process and product. Reflexivity then becomes a tool for "objectivism" of social, cultural and academic relationships and points of view of the researcher *within* the research by asking the researcher to consider the particularities and commonalities within the research. From this perspective, when re-visiting ethnographic research, the subject-researcher is framed *as object* to be explored. Yet, I do so with the understanding that, as noted by Grenfell (this volume) and Maton (2003), the challenge or conundrum that persists is that while reflexivity should be integral to the theory, and the practice of research, there is little agreement on what comprises reflexivity and *how to do it* (Grenfell, this volume) i.e. how it may be enacted in research practice.

In this chapter, I re-view data across time (years) and space/place (students' homes, schools and communities) as part of a reflexive self-study. I re-visit data from three of my ethnographic case studies involving immigrant youth and adolescents from historically underrepresented groups in communities in two metropolitan cities in the eastern United States. I apply the reflexive-objectivity by re-visiting three 2005–2015 ethnographic case studies of the literacy practices of Caribbean immigrant students. I frame this self-study by first addressing the theoretical underpinnings of how I have traditionally approached reflexivity in my research. Next, I re-view key pieces of data from three case studies using a Bourdieusian approach to reflexivity. I use narrative as a method of inquiry to interrogate the reflexive practices-in-action, the social contexts and the ways in which the researcher's identities can position her as *a part of* and *apart from* the research. I then reflect on the findings in terms of the ways reflexivity features in the study and its implications for ongoing and future research.

Theoretical Framework

I draw on the idea of a reflexively informed objectivity from Bourdieu with which to come to know the ethnographic research process. From this perspective, the subject/researcher is framed *as object* within the research context, and therefore, is viewed as central to the analyses and interpretations. What this view implies is that for there to be reflexivity – i.e. deeply crucial and public self-reflection – there needs to be a repositioning of the researcher: removing the researcher from the traditional "objective" position of supposedly neutral observer and firmly repositioning her as active participant in the social worlds of the research site. This then involves applying this Bourdieusian approach of a reflexively informed objectivity as a lens through which to re-view the role of the researcher.

Coming to Know Reflexive Practice

Some basic ways, in which reflexivity is traditionally enacted, include auto-biographical reflection that makes public private identities, and sociological reflexivity that focuses on one's social position and how it affects the *process* of doing research. However, as a literacy researcher who uses ethnographic research methods to examine my participants' lived experiences, I found myself drawn to a form of reflexivity, from Bourdieu, that places the author as the object central to the research, and thereby situates the researcher within the particular context. As Grenfell (this volume) reminds us, objects of research can never be understood as objects in themselves; instead they are understood *in relation* given that they are situated within their specific socio-historical environment. From this perspective, the researcher must therefore be viewed as *research-participant*, i.e. both subject and object of the research.

However, from a practical standpoint, while reflexivity is encouraged as standard protocol for qualitative researchers in general – and ethnographers, in particular – it is often approached as a way to triangulate or cross-verify two or more sources of data; i.e. a controlled approach that may be likened to trying achieve a form of objectivity secured through consensus in order to ensure consistency across sources and approaches, provide transparency and to keep the researcher ethically "honest" by allowing her to declare her biases up front. In this vein, when a traditional notion of reflexivity is applied to my own status as immigrant to the US, and to my research with my immigrant students, I liken this traditional reflexive process to the customs and border protection checkpoint that asks of the immigrant/visitor who might be alien to or unfamiliar with the norms and practices of this "foreign" site: "*Do you have anything to declare?*". The question demands that she lay bare her accompanying baggage by declaring which of her possessions – values, views, practices and experiences that have been consumed, produced and/or acquired – might benefit and/or harm the host and the site's community. From this perspective, reflexivity is a normative social practice in which the researcher is repeatedly called upon to declare her biases and allegiances (to the USA, academia and research contexts), and to qualify her social, cultural and symbolic capital by conforming to, participating in, and consequently, validating these practices.

When I reflect on the ways in which I have documented and presented my research, I recognise that I have made a conscious effort to publicly declare my identities to my reader and audience. What this means is that there is an implicit expectation that, as a researcher – and as an immigrant to the USA – I must make my *Self* explicit to my readers and audience: my ascribed status (ethnic, racial and gender identity markers); my achieved status (social positions/titles and accomplishments); and my avowed status (affinity group affiliations). In one sense, such declarations acknowledge and honour my identities and that of my research participants. In another sense, by conforming to such specific academic literacy practices, I indirectly declare myself as "insider" to the research community and the academy. Even so, I concede that such a traditional approach to ethnographic fieldwork can sometimes be viewed as a singular act or event – which, once completed, permits the researcher to then seemingly get on with the business of the fieldwork (oftentimes with limited accountability for how the researcher subsequently navigates and leverages the power of such declared – and undeclared – baggage).

Upon review of the three original case studies, I found that I had consistently applied the notion of reflexivity in this traditional vein by considering the questions, *Who am I?* and *What do I bring to this study/the research process?* For each of these three cases, in order to answer these questions, I had typically considered how my background, experiences and identities might influence the process in the field (i.e. data collection and analysis and interactions with participants), as well as the product (interpretation and write-up of findings). Like the "good" and "ethical" ethnographer, I accounted for these factors through checks and balances that were built into the research process, such as: (1) member checking; (2) multiple data sources; and (3) educational research and theories, intended to validate my analyses and interpretations, and thereby minimise subjectivity and bias in my work.

I argue here, that the appearance and claim of "objective" researcher who is participant-observer is exposed as a façade when viewed through a Bourdieusian lens. Objectivism attempts to explain the social world by sidelining or ignoring the social or symbolic reality (i.e. individual's subjective conceptions and representations) and needs, instead, to focus on the material or objective conditions of existence (i.e. social ground that shapes consciousness) (Bourdieu, 1993: 4). Part of the process of applying a reflexively informed "objectivity" involves confronting the issue of how I go about brokering the contested literacy practices that establish specific boundaries for representation and communication. For example, my representation of my research is often defined by the scholarly and social norms of the academy. The forms and ways in which I use language – even as I write this chapter – are shaped by my understanding and knowledge of the literacy practices that are valued in the field.

Contrastingly, the notion of "reflexive objectivity" as outlined by Grenfell (Chapter 9), does not sideline the researcher in the research process. Instead, it places the researcher in a central role – *alongside* and integral part of the participants – thereby acknowledging the shared culture of the research context. In so doing, it signals that interactions, experiences etc. change and are shaped by virtue of the researcher's presence, observation and participation. For example, when I am actively involved in my adolescent-participants' daily activities and lives, these *adolescents*' experiencing of those activities, events etc. are also affected by my very presence and interactions with them and the members of their communities. The relationships, modes of communication and literacies suggest that, in our actions, interactions and evolving relationships, my participants and I adapt to and accommodate each other. On the one hand, one can argue that my role as researcher compromises what may have been the "true" experience had I not been a part of their lives "doing research". On the other hand, my presence and participation in these young persons' lives may enrich *their* experiences by provoking reflection, dialogue, and even action. Consequently, by situating the researcher directly into the research, this notion of reflexivity forces me to confront how I am positioned, and how I position others in the research process.

Coming to Know Cultural Dialogue

Bourdieu's notion of *habitus* offers a way of understanding the relational and dialogic (see also Bakhtin, 1981) nature of the ethnographic research process, which, is itself grounded in the reciprocal and dynamic interplay of social interactions, relationships and contexts. Bourdieu suggests that ways of being in the world are socially constructed and, in turn, reproduced through social interactions i.e. they are a set of "durable, structured and transposable" dispositions evident in a broad range of cultural practices that become "second nature" as a result of a long process of socialisation. Because my research on immigrant youth identities and literacy practices places cultural identities and literacy practices at the centre, then according to Bourdieu, the social practices and events in which my participants and I engage, play a key role in shaping the relationships, views, dispositions and enactment of social norms in the field/research site. It is not only the identities and literacies of the participants that are at play in the field – there are also the researcher's identities and literacy practices as she engages with the participants and their environments. The researcher and participants communicate, interact, form relationships and have shared experiences – all of which are integral to the ethnographic process. The concept of the "relational" acknowledges the shared experiences, identities and literacy practices between my participants and me as immigrants to the US; it makes explicit the overt and covert cultural literacy practices that identify the identity group.

Linked to the idea of the individuals' social worlds are the affordances and constraints of literacy practice – normative and marginalised. Because homogeneity of habitus implies consensus on meaning, with it comes the objective homogenisation of a group and perceived harmonisation of practices. By using a reflexively informed objectivity, this acknowledges the interplay of contexts and researcher-participant positionings and allows for a close analysis of the nuances of another's practice and tacit or explicit inquiry into meanings and intentions within and across these sociocultural contexts. Underlying Bourdieu's view of the world is that it is inherently social, i.e. the range and levels and hierarchies of relationships (e.g. class-based, familial, economic etc.), modes of communication and types of interactions and cultural practices. To come to know or understand persons and their environments is to actively "be" and interact in their worlds, which includes navigating relationships, institutions and literacy practices that make up the multiple, complex social spaces that they inhabit. Claiming that I want to come to know something implies a willingness to listen, learn, communicate and sometimes to immerse oneself – something that cannot be done "objectively". Thus, my "place" as ethnographic researcher cannot be in the margins, for I risk researching and reporting on my participants as "the Other".

This self-study serves as a meta-analysis: a way to revisit previously formed perspectives of three case studies that were conducted in the past 10 years. By taking a reflexive-objective lens, I now place *my researcher Self* under the objective gaze as (an) *Other* participant. My exploration is guided by the following questions: (1) What knowledge and experiences do I bring to the research process? (2) How do my identities position participants? (3) How do my identities position me as participant and the observer? (4) Whose *voice* is re-presented, and in what ways?

Research Design

Using the idea of reflexively informed objectivity through which to enact reflexivity in my research affords me the opportunity to adopt a more critical and objective approach looking at how social norms and collective views, experiences and identities inform my research. Reviewing and reanalysing data were critical to deepening my understanding of the object, i.e. researcher. In this self-study, I revisit data sets from three ethnographic case studies conducted between 2004–2014. Each of the three studies focuses on the literacy and identity practices of adolescent, high school students. I highlight key moments with four female, Caribbean American immigrant, Black adolescents, ages 14–16. In case study #1, I revisit data from Ashley, a recent immigrant to the US; in case study #2, I reflect on my interactions with LeeAnn, a first-generation American high school student; and I also review the case of high school siblings, Kai and Shaana in case study #3.

The four participants were purposefully selected because of their identities as Caribbean immigrants to the USA., the common country of origin, Jamaica, their ages and grade levels. The studies were originally guided by the overarching research question: How do the literacy practices of immigrant youth shape their identities? Exploring this research question required yearlong ethnographies: I participated in and observed multiple aspects of each of these young women's lives – including their homes, communities and schools. Barring the coordination of observation schedules, the total amount of time I spent in the field for each case, and the range of access I had to these participants' homes, communities and schools, was as varied and as particular as the individuals themselves, and was often determined by home/family structures, as well as these adolescents' (and their parents') respective levels of comfort with the research process. Added to this, were the logistical and institutional constraints of time and access to classrooms etc. Thus, in order to gather as much data as possible across these three main contexts (home, school and community) during the course of one academic year, data were collected via observations, interviews, documents/artifacts and researcher field notes.

A Project of Reflexively Informed Objectivity

As part of this project of a reflexively informed objectivity, I looked across pivotal moments or key events previously identified from the three case studies. This analytic approach involved incorporating researcher artifacts (e.g. field notes, journals and memos) with the participants' original data excerpts – this time placing the researcher as active participant and object of study. I then reanalysed these key data sets for evidence of habitus *in action*; i.e. instances where researcher-participant belief systems connected, overlapped and/or mutually shaped each other. This time, these data were analysed using thematic analysis (Fereday and

Muir-Cochrane, 2006) guided by the following research questions: (1) What knowledge and experiences do I bring to the research process? (2) How do my identities position participants? (3) How do my identities position me as participant and the observer? (4) Whose *voice* is re-presented, and in what ways?

After identifying key themes, I composed dialogic narratives that drew heavily on the researcher's artifacts, as well as the participants' interviews and artifacts. The findings were then thematically presented in dialogic narrative vignettes that serve to interrogate the reflexive (1) practices-in-action, (2) the social contexts, and (3) the affordances and constraints of conducting research, analysing data, and interpreting and representing findings with immigrant and minority-group adolescents. To highlight the ways in which reflexivity is embedded into the analysis, I constructed a confessional meta-narrative alongside the supporting empirical data. The meta-narrative – represented in narrative and poetic prose – intertwines my voice as researcher-participant with my four adolescent participants, and acts as a chorus or creative voice-over that is intended to capture my conscious, critical reflections as well as my standpoints and assumptions on the key events and moments. Unlike the original case studies where I made explicit attempts to focus my analyses and write-up on my participants, this time, I joined my voice as I let our words shape each other in a dialogic narrative. In the following section, I present the findings through two thematic metanarratives that tell the story of my researcher Self.

Findings

Prologue

From the depths of my subjective self, I hear the griot. The griot, from my native folk traditions of my African ancestral heritage, embodies the spirit of the oral tradition. The griot is historian, teacher, narrator and documenter of the truths of the experiences of the individual and community. He is the storyteller who calls to the audience in talk, in chant, in poetry, in story and in song. The voice of the griot is rooted in a dialogue so powerful that his story draws you in – engages you, moves you to listen, and to respond, to co-author the texts of the experience and become one with his dialogic voice.

Meta-narrative 1: Home

I feel at home . . . They say home is where the heart is. Perhaps it is because the heart represents life; that the heart is at the core of every being. Home is that warm, protective space that holds your heart – a place where you can just be your Self.

Today, when I rang the doorbell, both mother and daughter come to greet me. First I see Lee Ann's mother as the door opens, and then I see LeeAnn in tow. They're smiling. Once more, I feel totally at ease. The mother comments that I'm right on time. I present them with the gift bag of Caribbean snacks. They thank me. I hand LeeAnn the bumper stickers with "I love my country" in the Jamaican colors. As I do so, I hear LeeAnn's mother express pleasure at the contents of the bag. We all laugh heartily – the snack was a Caribbean favorite.

I get an invitation to go get my slippers and come see the garden. Her mother gives me the grand tour. I smile to myself because the backyard reminds me of my own home in Trinidad. Huge tomatoes ripening and bending toward the rich earth. Spinach. Mint thyme. Yams. Potatoes. Beans. Bell and hot peppers . . . Ashley's father said that he wants a yard, he wants a garden. He wants that feeling of "home". I admitted to her that I also feel the same way. A house is not a home unless there's a back yard or garden, a "porch" or deck. I marveled at how there was so much I could identify with in this family! I got it. It got *them*! The family, the house, the easy rapport, the food and the easy conversation – it just felt like home.

But, sometimes, you just need Home to be that private place where you can protect your Self from the threat of public exposure. A place where you can be yourself and take risks . . . Even if you risk losing a part of oneself . . . That's just how it is.

Ashley: When I'm home, we don't put any barriers on the way we speak. (Referring to her native patois.)

Cheryl: And, when you're in school, out in public . . .?

Ashley: I just don't feel comfortable.

Cheryl: Speaking patois . . . using your accent? Yes?

LeeAnn: Yeah . . . I don't want to feel out of place. I don't want to have my difference hinder me. But, help me if anything.

Ashley: And, I know there are so many Jamaicans at my school. And, they're so proud about it [patois]. Loud about it. And, they've been here for years and years. And, it's still there!

LeeAnn: Back home, it was understood that we were different. And, I liked being different. I liked being Jamaican.

Ashley: And, my relatives – they think I've changed.

LeeAnn: So, when I lost my accent, I was worried that I would lose being Jamaican.

Cheryl: And, now?

LeeAnn: I want to express myself so they can understand me – so, that I can communicate.

Ashley: I'm not the same. That's just how it is. I had to find a way to succeed. I'm not gonna apologise for it.

Meta-Narrative 2: Self and Other

It is Saturday afternoon, and the Shaana and Kai are relaxing at home in the family room. With the television and CD playing in the background, and Kai is on the computer. I sat quietly listening to the two siblings talk about Kai's blog and recall some of their early US secondary school experiences:

Kai [sighs and rolls eyes]: It's like, there's always this curiosity about your race.

Shaana: I mean, it doesn't really matter if you're Black, White, Chinese, Indian. You're still a person.

Kai: I'm kind of to the point where if people ask me about my race, I'm just like, "human race".

Shaana: I like people who are open-minded. I mean, to look beyond just color or looks. Look into somebody's personality as opposed to just judging them by what you see.

Kai: Seriously. Like, I had to fill out this mentoring program paper and you had to write what your race was and I wrote "human race". And, I'm sure that makes them mad.

[Shaana laughs in agreement. She gestured to the computer where I noticed that Kai who had just updated her status on Facebook, was checking out her blog for teens of diverse backgrounds.]

Kai [smiling]: I thought it would be interesting for me to share my opinion . . . I have opinions but, I never really pull through with them I guess. It feels cool to do that.

Shaana [nods]: We're a lot more open-minded.

During the exchange, the young women never stopped to question or explain. Instead, their casual yet sure glances in my direction told me that they believed I could relate. Sure, I wasn't the teen dealing with peer pressure or the high school student trying to navigate school. Still – I got it. Why? Because these stories were in part, my own – I have felt and lived many of these experiences. I understood their successes, as well as their pain, confusion and frustration. I could relate to attempts to be heard, validated for who I am rather than who I am not. Though the contexts, places, spaces and ages may differ, characters may change, and the cultural norms and literacy practices may shift, the stories seem to remain consistent . . .

I remember one of my undergraduate students saying to me, "So, you're from the Caribbean? That makes you Jamaican, right?" This assumption completely negates my native Trinidad and Tobago background and identity, and it disregards the many nations of the Caribbean region. And you may read this and think: potayto, potahto – it's just a word. But, I take this to be yet another powerful reminder that often, words become labels. In assigning such labels and/or assuming them, we become confined to, and are complicit in perpetuating their very definitions. These words then become the texts of how we are perceived and how we perceive ourselves. For in adopting these labels, we all too often adapt to their definitions.

Discussion

The thematic metanarratives reveal that my own identities and the insider knowledge that I bring to my fieldwork when conducting research directly inform the research process and product. While the research problem is typically presented as the focus of research, the understanding of the researcher in that social space can sometimes be sidelined. I illustrate this point by discussing two major themes in this reflexive self-study: (1) Insider power, and (2) Dialogic duelling.

Insider Power

Cultural and symbolic power of socialised norms, dispositions and practices circulates within the social, relational and transactional space of the ethnographic research process, fluidly and simultaneously guiding, structuring and legitimising the interactions, meanings and experiences. In each of the three contexts, the interplay of this cultural and symbolic agency operated along a continuum that served to structure, define and delimit the researcher-participant relationships. By virtue of being identified as member of this specific cultural group (via linguistic and cultural norms and social networks), I was better able to leverage my member status to gain access to my participants and have them share their lives and stories with me. As a cultural "insider" and native, I understood the participants' unspoken assumptions and expectations that I would be able to relate to and understand certain cultural norms and literacy practices. Consequently, the participants made references to material signifiers of their cultural identities (e.g. locations, foods, music etc.) with the expectation that I would not need on-going clarification and background/context. Yet, I recognised that my credibility and authenticity as identity-group member was tested – contingent upon my ongoing ability to prove my status through my active participation.

However, the insider status I held with my participants was not limited to our cultural identities. Because of my social position I was also viewed as knowledgeable "academic insider", i.e. teacher/teacher-educator, who, by virtue of my social position, helped legitimise the social and institutional structures of schooling. These young persons were open and unapologetic in their discussions of the challenges of intersectionality, along with their conformation and/or resistance to dominant social and linguistic competences – all with the tacit belief that I would identify with their experiences.

Granted, it is because I possessed linguistic and cultural competences and subsequently demonstrated symbolic mastery of these practices (i.e., the cultural knowledge and/or dispositions), that I was more adept at navigating multiple social and cultural environments and bringing more complex and culturally responsive analyses than the supposed "outsider" with limited knowledge of these contexts. While in the field, I had "insider" knowledge – and I purposefully exercised its power to serve my academic and professional needs, i.e. conducting research in these specific contexts. My ability to decipher and decode cultural codes marked my cultural and cognitive competence. As Bourdieu (1984a) notes, mastery of linguistic capital allows the individual to move beyond the primary "sensible properties" or ordinary meaning to the secondary or signified meanings. Though, in the original analyses of the cases, I did in fact address issues of power, I had consistently acknowledged the role of power in terms of "access", and in relation to the ethics of adult-minor relationships and interactions. Upon reflection, what was missing from my *practice* of reflexivity was this lens of reflexive-objectivity that now provides a much richer and layered understanding of how power circulated in my relationships with my participants. As researcher, I had strategically leveraged the power of the symbolic capital of my multiple achieved, ascribed and avowed identities as "cultural insider", and even more so as the knowledgeable Other, i.e. educator, literacy expert and adult. It is in this sense, that my "voice" as Caribbean American educator-researcher provided the cultural capital that gave credence to my voice and positioned me as an active participant in the research, and not the initially claimed (and strived for) "objective" observer.

However, just as my participants positioned me as insider because of my symbolic and cultural capital, there came with it specific expectations that I re-present them in an honest and positive light, and in a way that honoured their voice. The insider intuitively understands this unspoken honour code – and to do otherwise would be considered a betrayal and/or signalling oneself as not belonging to the group. It is particularly in the post-fieldwork stage that the researcher-participant relationship marked a clear shift of power toward my participants. Thus, the choices I make in terms of how I represent my participants' voices, how I choose to *word their worlds*, not only reflects the responsibility entrusted me to by my participants to use my work to advocate on their behalf, but also the centrality of our relationship that compelled me to view my research as a platform for their voices. From this perspective, using narrative vignettes allows me to honour participants' voices by using their own words to tell their stories. Just as my participant, Kai, sought out an online forum as virtual space for the voices of diverse and underrepresented youth, so too am I compelled to find a mode of/genre of representation – in this case, narrative – that would honour my participants' voices.

Dialogic Duelling

Applying a reflexively informed objectivity engenders a deeper understanding of and greater accountability in the research process by exposing the tensions of enacting sociocultural identities, the politics of re-presentation and the ethical dilemma of "truth" and voice. I contend that there is value in the individual story and the collective narrative. As an insider to a cultural and racial identity group whose identities, historically, have been silenced and/or operates in the margins, I understood the power of embodiment of identity through the telling one's story. As Ngũgĩ (1993) noted, the voices of the silenced and marginalised have the power to shift the dominant narrative. Through material and immaterial symbols, these young persons' in their various social spaces (home, school and community – physical and virtual) find ways to re-cast dominant narratives of what may have been a single story about them, by representing and re-presenting (them)Selves. I recognise that my researcher Self also deploys my own social and cultural capital to help legitimise my *participants'* cultural capital. For, in so doing, I honour my participants' voices and stories, and I share own experiences and views – not only of the research process, but also my own experiencing of my social and cultural capital embodied in my ascribed identities as Black and immigrant, and achieved identities as learner and educator-researcher.

There is a duality in the ways in which my primary habitus is borne out of my own background and experiences as immigrant, as Caribbean native and Black person/female, connects with that of my participants. In being able to readily identify and empathise with some of the participants' stories and experiences, it immediately/directly shapes my own habitus. While I bring my own experiences to bear on how my participants exist, operate and interact in the world, and the values, cultural beliefs and practices they uphold, these adolescents' own cultural norms, identities and experiences also shape my stance and my relationship with them. My own primary socialisation formative experiences as Caribbean native join in the dynamic fluid movement with my participants' – often working in concert to construct our views, beliefs, feelings, actions and perspectives of events. At the same time, I concede that these narratives do not claim to give *the* "truth" (Cortazzi, 1993); instead, each narrative is presented and re-presented as the *storyteller's/writer's* interpretation and experiencing of an event. My reflexivity (which allows me to step *outside* the research process in order to look *inside*) serves to highlight the access I have as insider, as well as the conflict of the objective-subjective that is inherent in the positioning.

Thus, it is through Bourdieu's work that I confront the "duelling identities" of researcher, academic, minority-group member and storyteller. Within the duelling identities of native ethnographic researcher lies the power struggle between my identities as "native researcher" and "good academic". The intersectionality of my researcher identities – a role that demands some form of "objectivity" and objectification in my analysis and representation of participants – can oftentimes appear to conflict with the ascribed identities of researcher and academic in higher education. For example, just the very act of pursuing literacy and language ethnographies has its inherent tensions particularly when the researcher aspires to conduct research on and with historically linguistically and culturally marginalised peoples, yet do so using a language that historically has been used to marginalise, control and/or silence these very groups. As Street (1997) points out, language use and its meanings vary by context, cultural norms and discourses. In one sense, I have strategically deployed the currency of my social and cultural capital as a Caribbean immigrant in my fieldwork with my participants in order to gain access to their knowledge and resources. In another sense, my conformity to the normative field-specific rules and practices of the academic field serves to define and confine my views of what is "appropriate" and acceptable to the members. Bourdieu (1977b: 21) notes that "the constitutive power which is granted to ordinary language lies not in the language itself but in the group which authorizes it and invests it with authority". Thus, in this case, because specific academic discourse and dominant linguistic codes are valued in academia, they have the power to sanction and legitimise its use. If, as Bakhtin (1981) states, my words come saturated with the meanings of others, then using the mainstream academic language that has historically been used to silence minority/underrepresented groups to tell my participants' stories, then I become complicit in the oppression. Much like the customs and border security checkpoint, I also become a gatekeeper, determining what and whose voice words the world. So, perhaps, there are no "right" words or an acceptable way to objectively represent my dialogic interactions with my participants. And, in choosing to use normative discourses of the academy, it raises some key questions about language and literacy research, such as: Who is conducting this research? Who is telling these stories? Which stories and how are they told? Whose voice is heard?

In Summary

The field of literacy and language ethnographical research in general needs not only to understand *what* knowledge is produced but also *who* is producing it, and how it is framed and presented. It is here that the tensions around issues of identity/voice, of story/storyteller, speaker/listener, insider/outsider and producer/product, bring into focus the power, the politics and the ethics of our various identities and positionalities and the struggles involved in navigating the patterns and normative practices of our sociocultural contexts. Street (1997: 51), in discussing Bakhtin's (1981) concept of the "dialogic", states that "Language, even when employed silently by the single individual is always part of a social interaction, whether imagined others or with the meanings and uses of words that others have employed at other times and places" (p. 51). What Street is suggesting is that as researchers of language and linguistics, we are always consciously and unconsciously engaging with the "contest over meanings, definitions, and boundaries" (Street, 1997: 48) in the framing, interpretations and representations of research. To conduct research that is culturally responsive is to view the individual (voice, literacies etc.) as a part of a collective (identity-groups and normative practices), that is situated within a context; i.e. the environment in which the knowledge is produced and product including its form – i.e. the medium and modes used to express, deliver and present the product.

There is the need to continue to interrogate the power relations of the ethnographic field – not as an add-on or follow-up to our previous research. But perhaps, what the notion of reflexive objectivity does is to push literacy and language researchers to think more closely about the position (pseudo-objectivity) of "truth", even in the specific context – knowing that how one interprets, perceives and receives an event, experience, or word, as well as how one produces a particular written text, are all subject to the social and cultural boundaries, and meanings the writer, reader, speaker and listener assign that language. What is more, conformity without critical reflexivity limits our perspectives, choices and decisions, and in turn, our views on *what* counts and *who* counts.

Central to the social nature of ethnographic research is the question of whose story gets told. Re-visiting and examining the role of the researcher in conducting research leads to deeper and more critical understandings of the ways in which the researcher's habitus, cultural capital and the field, inform the research process and outcomes: data collected, the knowledge formed, generated and disseminated and the experiences produced within that context. By revisiting the research process using Bourdieu's reflexivity, there is evidence that at times, as researcher, my role has been one that "maximizes symbolic capital within the intellectual field at minimal cost" (Maton, 2003: 56). I am therefore complicit in preserving the status quo despite my expressed *intent* to disrupt or critically confront social interests OR as an "instrument of rupture" (Bourdieu, 1988a).

I answer the "So What?" question of the value of adopting a Bourdieusian interpretation of reflexive objectivity (Grenfell, this volume) in ethnographic research by declaring that the traditional, dominant approaches to reflexivity may fall short in their culturally responsibility and far reaching and intuitive to the language and literacy research process/fieldwork. For understanding to take place, meaning making must transcend the false dichotomy of Self as independent/ apart from the Other. The Self displays a particular habitus because of its in/visible relationship and interactions *with* the Other. A researcher's and the field's more conclusive and deeper understanding can only come from a three-pronged approach to reflexivity that incorporates *all* object/subjects of study, the knowledge claims and the modes of representation. "Full reflexivity is collective rather than individualist" (Maton, 2003: 63). It is through the coming together of the social, cultural and material worlds, and our collective *experiencing* of these worlds, that we fully come to know our research in the field.

7

ENACTING REFLEXIVITY IN SECOND LANGUAGE WRITING RESEARCH

A Personal Account of Cultural Production of Authorial Self and Researcher Perception

Lisya Seloni

Introduction

This chapter is about observing myself as a language ethnographer in the process of doing multilingual ethnographic research while revisiting two studies I conducted, and it explores two issues regarding Bourdieu's notion of reflexivity in ethnographic research: (1) the process in which I, as a multilingual scholar, construct a research space through the participants' experiences and (2) the use of reflexivity in the interpretation and representation of ethnographic data. In this reflexive account of two ethnographically oriented studies on second language (L2) writing, I trace how Bourdieu's "reflexive objectivity" is being enacted in ethnographically oriented L2 writing studies while also creating discourses that position the participants. Focusing on the research spaces I inhibit as well as interrogating the intersections within these spaces, I discuss how reflexivity and the extent in which it is included in the reporting of ethnographic data is an embodied performance around texts (Enriquez et al., 2016) and carries important markers of the researcher's identity. After going through the main findings of two studies on academic writing of multilingual students in higher education in two different geolinguistic sites (Central Illinois, US and Istanbul, Turkey), I discuss how the scholarly gaze that is cast upon in academic writing could, at times, prevent one's explicit reflexivity in the writing process. In demystifying the data collection process and investigating my use of reflexivity in academic writing, this self-reflexive account illustrates how a Bourdieusian research stance on reflexivity could bring a higher awareness of theory, intentionality and empathy for practice in language ethnographies that particularly focus on writing experiences of non-native English speaking students.

Reflexivity and the Balancing Role of Multilingual Academics

As an applied linguist whose primary area of research is L2 writing experiences of multilingual students in higher education, *language use* in educational contexts has played a central role in my work. I primarily draw on fields such as educational ethnography, English for specific purposes, writing studies and multilingualism to make sense of the critical moments, complex histories, fears, needs and trajectories of second language (L2) users as well as the institutional constraints and affordances with which they encounter. As a non-native speaker of English myself who went through formal education in a non-English dominant context, my academic identity as a transnational woman scholar has always highly overlapped with my positionality as a researcher conducting language ethnographies. The balancing act of bilingual academics usually leads to a development of contesting identities that are constantly juggled and balanced. As Casanave (2005) states the transition to "the life of a professional bilingual academic does not mean choosing life A or life B; rather it means, recognizing and accepting the heterogeneity of their writing lives" (p. 181). As a multilingual scholar who started her journey as a graduate student in an Anglophone context, this has meant finding a fine balance between staying in the periphery, and also trying to get as close as I can to the center to participate in the scholarly activities of my field while also transitioning into a disciplinary self. While the politics of knowledge production and academic publishing of multilingual scholars have received extensive attention in the field (e.g., Hartley, 2008; Lillis and Curry, 2010; Murray, 2009), we see less attention given to these scholars' use of reflexivity and agency in their own writing and how their reflexivity is recognised and taken up.

Rather than being pre-given through formal education, the use of academic language is an embodied and transmodal performance (Pennycook, 2005). Just as bodies are mobile and in flux in a everyday life, languages and language practices in academic disciplines do not exist in a vacuum and far from cultural repertoires, traditions of disciplines and various epistemologies. When scholarly bodies engage in textual production through navigating disciplinary terrains and practices, they represent various selves and embodied social histories. In this embodied lens of literacy (Enriquez, et al., 2016), "literacies are lived and felt across time and space within discursive communities that value these lived and felt literacies differentially" (pp. 4–5). This embodied performance can be possible through situating the researcher in the research process, which is not free of power struggles and academic gaze cast upon certain bodies. Tracing my reflexivity as a multilingual scholar, the next section will discuss the social organisation of various interdisciplinary paradigms that I draw on in my work. More specifically, I explore how literacy education and writing studies has taken up the issue of *difference* in writing.

Situating Difference in Writing: Overlapping Concepts, Trans-disciplinary Landscapes and the Role of Ethnography

When we look at the body of scholarship around language difference in fields such as composition, applied linguistics and literacy education, we see a diverse range of studies documenting and exploring issues through differing epistemological, methodological and theoretical orientations. The figure below is my attempt to capture the terminology used when it comes to language difference in various settings. While this is not an exhaustive list, it illustrates the diversity of epistemologies, theories and methodological orientations taken across disciplines when we talk about the complex and creative literacy and language practices of multilingual users of English.

It is true that all these orientations to writing treat diversity and the heterogeneity of language as the norm, yet there are differences in terms of each discipline's contexts, demographics, research objectives, theoretical lenses and ideological orientations. Translating concepts such as translanguaging (García, 2009), meterolingualism (Pennycook, 2010) or polylingualism (Gutiérrez, 2008) to classroom practice usually requires writing teachers to create sound pedagogical resources and develop strategies and tools to work with unfamiliar registers,

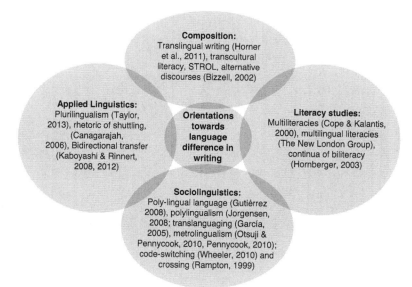

FIGURE 7.1 Language diversity in writing: A trans-disciplinary landscape

conventions and genres. This broadening interest in language diversity encourages us to see the agentive aspect of multilingual writers when they negotiate meaning through the use of their linguistic repertoires. The orientations of language difference in textual production also challenge the static view of language and literacy, valuing the unique contributions and uses of multiple languages as resources. For instance, while translingual writing has recently gained considerable momentum in the US composition studies "which has "established itself as an intellectual movement" (Matsuda, 2014: 478), concepts such as "translanguaging", "pluralingualism" and "third space" have been widely used in the field of applied and educational linguistics to refer to the fluid language practices and uses in real life that go beyond language systems. Over the years, terms such as translingualism and translanguaging[1] have offered practical and, more importantly, empowering pedagogical tools for teachers in contexts where the instructional language is different from the students' home languages. While scholars from different fields make their own allegiances with these terms, I have been interested in crossing disciplinary divides and facilitating conversations among fields such as applied linguistics and composition studies in order to inform my understanding and explorations of the issues L2 writers come across (Tardy, 2017).

Regardless of lexical differences among language-based disciplines, when it comes to explaining the phenomena of linguistic diversity, we see increasing cross-disciplinary uptake and collaborations where scholars productively borrow terms from adjacent fields (hence, the overlap between circles in Figure 7.1) due to the common desire of better serving our diverse students' needs through best pedagogical practices. In this context, I argue that the term *ethnography* serves as a bridge to this ideological versus pragmatic binary reflected in language and literacy-based disciplines when it comes to reflecting on issues related to language difference in writing and addressing issues such as second language development of multilingual writers at different stages of language proficiency. Especially with the social and ethnographic turn in the fields of applied linguistics, composition and literacy studies, there has been a growing interest in and recognition of the use of language ethnographies in understanding complexities of L2 writing (e.g., Lillis, 2008; Lills and Curry, 2010).

One of the most important shifts that this ethnographic turn promoted was to help build the gap between text and context. As Swales and Luebs (1995), put it:

> It is not only texts that we need to understand, but the roles texts have in their environments; the values, congruent and conflictive, placed on them by occupational professional and disciplinary memberships; and the expectations those memberships have of the patternings of the genres they participate in.
>
> (p. 219)

Text-focused approaches to writing, which primarily drew on traditional rhetoric and linguistics, have long dominated academic writing research in the fields such as English for academic purposes. In this orientation, there has been a risk of constructing participants as perpetual foreign language users instead of legitimate users of the second language whose mobile literacy practices allow them to tap on diverse languages, symbols and modalities for communication and negotiation. This monolithic view of non-native writers created a deficit view of language users (be it students studying in the US in different levels or international scholars participating in the global academic discourses) whose struggles primarily come from a lack of language (the language of the dominant group).

The monolithic view of non-native writers was pervasive in earlier SLA research. As a field which has long been under the influence of traditional linguistics with a positivist view of language, the field of applied linguistics has had moments in its history where it treated language as an autonomous object and language learners as deficit communicators. One of the prominent works that shifted this understanding and initiated the social turn (Block, 2003) in the field was Firth and Wagner's (1997) modern language piece in which they made important points about moving away from "an orthodox social psychology hegemony in SLA" (p. 285). Pointing out the methodological biases in SLA studies, this thought-provoking article problematized the positioning of language learners as defective communicators and "subjects" in experimental research settings as opposed to natural ones. In this piece, Firth and Wagner argued for reconceptualization of learners as complex beings who acquire language in social interactions through interactive discourse. More importantly, this view helped the field perceive language learners as "successful multicompetent speakers" rather than "failed native speakers" (Cook, 1999: 204). This social turn in the field recognised that language learning is not only a cognitive phenomenon, but also fundamentally social. Similar to the shift seen in the field of literacy and language ethnographies discussed in Chapter 1, this inseparability of individual and social in language learning also changed the way second language scholars conducted research bringing more pluralistic methodologies and epistemologies.

While language ethnographies with naturalistic data is now a legitimate form of knowledge in educational linguistics (Barton and Hamilton, 1998; Heath, 1983), reflexive writing about such data usually appears in less visible venues such as "forums", sections of academic journals or edited collections (Canagarajah, 2005; Starfield, 2013). Theorising their own lived experiences with English language and English language teaching in a dialogic article published in the forum section of TESOL Quarterly, Lin et. al. (2004) critique the mainstream TESOL theoretical and research cannons with its positivist paradigms:

> Researchers using this paradigm seek to *operationalize* and *quantify* (i.e., define and measure in numerals) human and social phenomena (e.g., language learning and teaching) in terms of *variables* and to *verify*

hypotheses about the relationships (e.g., causal or correlational relationships) among different variables.

(p. 495)

The lack of reflexivity in the field of TESOL was also voiced by Canagarajah (1996) who stated that the field "served to maintain the pretense of objectivity, detachment and neutrality, suppressing the agency of researcher" (p. 323). Despite the non-reflexive research trend that dominated the field, there has been a notable increase recently in the number of published auto-ethnographic accounts and narrative writing on the researchers' lived experiences with various challenges such as gaining credibility in academia as non-native English speakers (e.g., Vandrick, 2009; Casanave, 2005; Casanave and Vandrick, 2003; Kamhi-Stein, 2004; Li, Beckett and Lim, 2005).

It is true that the way we use language and create knowledge through language is shaped by the social structure which "positions social actors in ways that constrain their access to resources and hence their ability to mobilize them" (Heller, 2011: 10). In this context, the power of language ethnographies is in its ability to bring new ways of thinking about language and language research by exploring how agency, personal and social structure work together across time and space. Transcending disciplinary constraints and drawing on broader paradigms of language, what comes next is a critical review of two writing ethnographies that I recently conducted. Revisiting these qualitative inquiries allows me to not only better understand my own positionality as an ethnographer who primarily works with multilingual writers, but also invites me to reflect on some of the changing trends and disciplinary conversations in the field of second language writing.

Two Studies on Multilingual Writers and Academic Writing in Higher Education: Second Language Writing, Language and Ethnography

Acknowledging and negotiating the personal in scholarly activity might feel like an act of rope balancing for many translingual writers who are just like anyone else – ideologically positioned subjects. The question that one encounters is: how does one negotiate the personal in academic writing? While constructing and disseminating scientific knowledge, it is unavoidable to find ourselves in the middle of a cacophony of voices, which leads the researcher to construct certain discourses, positionalities and even writing styles. The type of writing we do as academics is highly complex and ritualised (Pennycook, 2005). As a non-Western researcher writing specifically for a Western audience, I struggle with various aspects of academic writing and representation of self, including how I attempt to erase the traces of my vernacular education, language style, writing persona and simply how I negotiate the transparency of my voice as a transnational woman scholar. The tension I am interested in discussing in the rest of this chapter are related to not only the messy writing process of the research, but also how we construct selves while locating the researcher and the participants in the ethnographic research. In what comes next, I discuss two studies that explore the academic writing experiences of multilingual individuals in higher education. While the first study took place in Central Illinois, the second research was situated in Istanbul, Turkey at a time of great political turmoil in the county.

Study #1: Textographic case study of a Colombian art historian's thesis writing in the US

The primary goal of this study was to illustrate some of the textual practices, negotiation strategies and rhetorical enactments that occurred around one advanced multilingual student's thesis writing experience as he "enact[ed], reproduce[ed] and/or transform[ed] the social activities, the roles and the relations" (Barwarshi, 2003: 45) around a Colombian art historian's thesis writing while negotiating various disciplinary knowledge bases and professional knowledge he brought with him as an art curator. The study took place at a Midwestern university in the United States while I was a tenure-track professor. Even though my own experiences with academic writing was highly intertwined with the focal participant of this study, I wasn't forthcoming about my own positionality as a researcher perhaps due to reasons such as the scope of the study, but more importantly also due to my hesitations in being perceived as too personal as a researcher.

Background: Examining graduate writing and language negotiation beyond texts

In recent years, academic literacy practices of multilingual graduate writers have been studied from a wide range of angles. Both in L1 and L2 writing studies, we see a "beyond text" (Freedman, 1999) movement to better understand the way multilingual writers engage in texts and learn of different genres. While examining literacy practices of multilingual students, most studies in this area adopt a view that learning to write in a second language writing within academic contexts involves students negotiating complex social, cultural and academic tools and resources that are available to them (e.g., Casanave, 2005; Leki, 2007; Tardy, 2009). In fact, my earlier work focused on a cohort of graduate students' academic literacy practices through a micro-ethnographic discourse analysis of their talks around various textual productions in which they were involved (both in and outside of class) as a way to understand key academic literacy practices of their disciplinary discourses as well as literacy events they were involved in new comers to the academic US context. In this line of work, I discussed how disciplinary enculturation does not equate to a unidirectional, unreflective adoption of academic literacy practices in North American graduate schools. Mature writers such as graduate students, especially those whose linguistic experiences are different than the ones who speak and write in privileged varieties of English, strategically negotiate L1 and L2 resources and uptakes as they exercise their agency as multilingual writers.

Drawing on theories of translingualism (e.g., Horner, Lu, Royster and Trimbur, 2011) and cultural-historical activity (Bazerman and Prior, 2004; Prior, 1998), for this particular study, I was interested in asking two questions to understand how my focal participant, Jacob, utilised his cultural and linguistic capital as he was engaged in theory building while composing a high-stake text, namely his MA thesis: (1) What are some of the rhetorical enactments and literacy practices this multilingual writer developed around his thesis writing? (2) What writerly identities are constructed in art oriented, new humanities thesis/ dissertation writing? I employed a *textographic* analysis with an ethnographic perspective to analyse a year-long written, visual and verbal corpus of data. Textography urged me to focus on the situatedness of writing and carefully analyse how textual life histories such as the writers' academic trajectories and identities have an influence on how and what they write. Conducting a close analysis of the texts (spoken, writer and pictorial) that surrounded Jacob's MA thesis and ethnographic interviews allowed me to trace his key literacy practices as a graduate student and provided further insights into the "active discursive processes of construction and interpretation" (Prior et al., 2007: 13) of his academic knowledge. Some of the primary data sources included course papers that Jacob produced in his MA classes, six semi-structured interviews, drafts of his MA thesis chapters and visual texts he produced as pre-thesis writing artefacts such as large posters he created as a way to shed light to the theoretical mapping of his work. The interviews I conducted with Jacob throughout one year were related to the creative and academic work he had done as an art historian before coming to North American higher education and about the new literary activities he was engaged in during the creation of high-stake texts such as his MA thesis. My sense making of the data corpus was not only influenced by my own experiences with academic literate activities, but also influenced by the theories I was reading at that time related to language diversity in writing (Canagarajah, 2006), translingualism (Hornet et al., 2011) and cultural historical activity theory (Prior, 2008). While interpreting Jacob's textual involvement, I encouraged the readers to look at his writing as a "heterogonous social activity that is deeply situated in the act of reading and meaning making, which are in turn heavily situated within multiple linguistic sources" (Seloni, 2014: 90). Most of the texts Jacob produced were multivocal and included hybrid discourses of English and his native language Spanish.

This kind of complexity views writing as connected to many other activity systems, which consist of all the people, texts, tools, rules that work together to achieve a literacy objective. Cultural Historic Activity Theory[2] (CHAT) allowed me to draw my attention to myriad elements of Jacob's textual production[3] and provided me with a deep understanding of the complex set of tools, contexts and activities in which Jacob's texts were created, mediated, consumed and distributed in real life. The application of CHAT very much reminded me of the principles of new and digital literacies (Gee, 2009), coupled with multiliteracies (Cope and Kalantzis, 2000; New London Group, 1996), which move away from the fixed concept of literacy and anchor learning to the individuals' lived experiences and expands the genres, semiotic resources and tools used while making meaning (e.g., Gee, 2015; Schwartz, 2015). As I noted in the article, adopting a cultural, historical activity perspective to understand and further investigate second language writing experiences of international students can enable us to "transcend beyond the instrumental purpose to learning the academic values of the center, and emphasise the importance of multilingual writers' creative attempts to incorporate their local knowledge and vernacular languages into mainstream discourse" (Seloni, 2014, p. 82).

To illustrate this situated and mediated nature of Jacob's academic writing, I focused on a poster that Jacob created as a way to help him make sense of the readings he did for his MA thesis. One day before our scheduled interview, Jacob shared with me a poster, which included a conceptual map of theories where he scribbled many in color-coded notes, in the form of phrases, quotations and interpretations he collected from his theory reading and sense-making process. The text in the poster was both in Spanish and English. It was not only eye opening to see how multifaceted his reading and writing practices were as a visual artist doing academic writing, but it also provided me with a broadened understanding of the rich network of texts that he brought to the writing of his MA thesis. Jacob reported that he had spent two weeks just working on this theory poster, going back and forth between the annotations he had in his books and his class notes. As a discursive practice, the action of map creation was closely connected to his readings.

While writing his thesis, Jacob also stated that he was unsettled because he was in-between a conflicting representation of self as a writer. For instance, in one of our final interviews, he explained how he struggled balancing his artistic and scholarly identities:

> Recently, how I view my writing identity has been changing. Normally I consider myself as an art critic. So, as an art critic I try to make sense of what's out there. Like recently, I am unsure if this is still showing in my writing. One of the current discussions of visual culture scholars is that each time you are writing a narrative sentence, you are in fact translating an image to a text . . . And it has resonated with me because in one sense I am a

scholar, but in another sense, I am an artist. So, I hope I could find a middle point. That is, writing with images. Now in graduate school, I am more a scholar than an artist. I hope that they can live together. By writing about images, I hope to reach to that middle point.

(Jacob, Interview)

In addition to Jacob's use of semiotic resources in dual languages, I also examined the macrostructure of Jacob's MA thesis. I was mainly interested in the writerly identities that he constructed in art-oriented new humanities thesis writing. In thesis writing, the identity of the writer is usually visible through the linguistic resources they choose while engaging in a wide range of argumentative practices such as taking a stance, making a claim or expressing a position. As suggested by Starfield and Ravelli (2006) and Tang and Johns (1999), writers use different kinds of first personal pronouns to represent self in academic writing (I as a guide or architect, methodological I, I as opinion holder and I as originator and reflexive I with a narrative voice). My analysis of Jacob's MA thesis illustrates that Jacob brought a wide range of identities most of which are highly in narrative format which appeared in the form of *Reflexive I*. As Starfield and Ravelli (2006) noted, "the distinctiveness of this reflexive self emerges though a variety of resources which situate the writer at the center of writing and research process" (p. 234). The high occurrence of self-mention as a central rhetorical feature of his writing as an art curator gave him a highly narrative voice. His attempts to bridge the narrative and scholarly voice in his academic writing could be interpreted as a textual reflection of his lived histories as a professional art critic and an emerging scholar or art history.

Reflexion on Knowledge: Putting Personal Back to Writing

While reflexivity seemed to be present in each step of this language ethnography, the act of "reflecting" in writing by locating myself within the research was a rhetorical act influenced by my own disciplinary positionality. In reporting language ethnographies, the degree to which one brings reflexivity can be constrained by existing social practices in academic writing as well as the social position researchers bring to the writing context (e.g., early career tenure-track faculty member at the time of the study). For instance, many of the literacy practices that Jacob was engaged in were closely intertwined with my own as a multilingual scholar myself. During the data collection, Jacob and I fondly discussed how similar processes we go through as multilingual writers and how both of us desire to play with the high-stake genres hoping to move beyond conventions that could help bring our writing identities forward. While sharing my own experiences with academic writing and the identity negotiations during our conversations with Jacob came naturally, it seemed difficult at that time to juxtapose those with his experiences in the reporting of this research. The nature of academic writing somehow encouraged me to divorce my risk-taker self and my narrative voice from the research story I was telling about Jacob. Just like Jacob, I also utilise various semiotic tools such as writing both in Turkish and English while constructing my own ideas during different stages of a research project, and again just like Jacob, I go through a fine balancing act between being creative and sounding authoritative. Yet, in the writing of this manuscript, there was no mention of my own familiarity with Jacob's bilingual literacy practices and negotiations. The role of my own multiliterate and multilingual rhetorical self was strategically hidden from the audience. While one can argue that the purpose of my article was to focus solely on my participant and not the author, the exclusion of the researcher's voice on a topic that is so intertwined with the researcher's own writing identity can be seen as a purposeful attempt to distance oneself from the researcher and the researched.

While revisiting this particular study, I asked myself what Pennycook (2005) pointed out as an important part of being reflexive in the field of applied linguistics: how is then my subject position performed as I wrote this piece? Revisiting this work through the lens of reflexivity showed me that I employed two rhetorical strategies to highlight my *researcher* self while covering my *multi-lingual* self: (a) high inclusion of evidential language in the form of literature review where I included integral and non-integral theories to make my case and (b) foregrounding my arguments on the data itself (specifically, the experiences of Jacob) rather than spending too much time to address the disciplinary tensions.

Establishing a persuasive framework through citing is one of the ways to perform academic identity and writerly voice while writing academic articles. Citation practices that we build on also form our disciplinary allegiances. While reporting on this ethnographic data, I asked myself if I over-relied on others' voices as a way to be persuasive of the importance of moving beyond the borders of disciplines. My goal was to bring to table a trans-disciplinary dialogue that calls for more disciplinary dialogues between composition and second language writing – a conversation that has not been without disciplinary tensions due to varying epistemological and pragmatic differences that each field seems to embrace. Knowing that the inclusion of citations helps establish this persuasive framework and displays the writer's credibility as a researcher (Hyland, 2008), I aligned myself with multiple theories, which helped be gain a deeper understanding of Jacob's literate activities. Yet, it is also important to remember that circulating work and constructing knowledge through drawing on certain frameworks (i.e., citation practices) as a way of displaying researcher's theoretical position in a text is never a neutral act. Citation practices just like other academic literate activities are embodied in political, cultural and historical processes in which writers engage during different stages of textual construction, and it allows to reproduce certain bodies while leaving out others (Ahmed, 2017). Aligning myself with series of language and literacy theories through my uniquely positioned academic identity, my goal was to bring a robust way of sense-making of multilinguals' writing experience and blur the disciplinary boundaries by focusing on diverse bodies across disciplines. Coming back to this project through a Boursieusian framework, I now recognise that negotiating epistemologies that lie behind different theories of writing and literacy provided me with a reflexive space to make sense of my data and gave me the courage to push the boundaries of disciplinary communities.

More specifically, one of the tensions I was responding in the writing processes of this article was the recent debate between both L1 compositionists and L2 compositionists regarding the concept translingualism and what it means in today's diverse composition classrooms. The pedagogical goal of translingual writing has been to blend native English users of English with L2 writers in the hope that L2 writers will engage in translingual strategies such as code-meshing, which would allow them to negotiate multiple languages, linguistic resources and ideological contexts within the US composition classrooms (Horner et al., 2011). Yet, because many second language writers in the field of applied linguistics are "assumed to be pragmatic and interested for the most part in learning how to meet the standards for academic success set by members of the academic discourse community" (Silva and Leki, 2004: 6), there have been some resistance from L2 writing scholars to accept the new terminology due to its disengagement from many important works that has already been done in the L2 writing field (Tardy, 2017). While working on this article, I remember wanting to be cautious in positioning myself in either of these debates not because I did not have a clear position on the issue, but because my goal of understanding Jacob's experiences went beyond the arguments made by each camp. Jacob wanted to achieve academic proficiency as many second language users do, but he also used an abundance of antecedent knowledge, tools and genre hybridity as a thesis writer who had an art curatorship background. His literate activities were complex, and as I stated in my article, what a successful thesis/dissertation entails in his case moved beyond displaying a high level of proficiency within the limits of the dissertation genre. Rather, it included Jacob's engagement with the genre construction, disciplinary contestation and theoretical juxtapositions. In my article, I explained the situatedness of academic writing though cultural-historic activity theory (CHAT), which considered texts as situated in writers' literacy histories and activities and as always intertextual (Prior, 1998). I anchored my second language writing investigation in CHAT as it helped me see academic writing as transcending beyond an instrumental purpose of learning values of the center, and "emphasizes the importance of multilingual writers' creative attempts to incorporate their local knowledge and vernacular languages into the mainstream discourse" (Seloni, 2014: 82).

In addition to the theories with which I aligned myself while making sense of Jacob's academic literacy practices, I took a closer look at the linguistic expressions I used to refer to the writer and the imagined reader of this text through a metadiscourse analysis.[4] Revisiting my study, I realise that my text was consciously structured with a disembodied voice. The use of interactional discourse markers such as self-mentions was not present throughout the manuscript I produced except in the reporting of the data. My reflexive use of first personal pronouns was limited to the reporting instances such as "I argue", "I define" and "I illustrate". While the inclusion of "I" as the architect of the article was used abundantly. More reflexive occurrences of "I" were limited or almost non-existent. Even though the article investigated significant topics in relation to composing high-stake writing in one's second language – in this case, a topic that could allow space for researcher's voice, as I mentioned above, I could not find ways (or was not courageous enough to do so) to reflect my nuanced explorations of these issues as well as my positionality in these issues as a multilingual writer myself.

Several points about researcher positionality and use of reflexivity in writing are worth highlighting here. Part of the problem for not overtly putting the personal in writing could be the field's inclination to focus on the researched and to distinctly separate the text from the subjectivity and lived experiences of the researcher. And, as a junior scholar who wanted to publish in highly-regarded journals, where the self-reflective voice is not always welcomed or perceived as legitimate knowledge, I was hesitant to take risks – at least, this was how I felt at the time of writing this piece. At the end, I was the researcher who was supposed to write her expert opinion on the researched and my purpose was not to provide a "confessional tale". Was this a scholarly gaze cast upon junior scholars? Or, was this simply the way I learned to report on ethnographic data in my field of applied linguistics? Why was there need to demarcate personal voice and the academic voice while reporting of the data? Or, perhaps after all these years of being schooled in a certain way, I was disciplined to keep a disembodied voice while performing academic writing. If we see construction of knowledge though academic writing as a dialogic and social practice, I wonder why we shy away so much from multivocality in academic writing and from "performing the personal" (Pennycook, 2005).

Study # 2: Ethnography of Writing Education. A Close look at Language Teacher Candidates' Experiences with Writing in College[5]

The next study I discuss is on writing instruction and teacher preparedness of English as a Foreign Language (EFL) teacher candidates who were at the time of the study taking first year composition courses in an English-medium university. The study was conducted while I was on sabbatical in Istanbul, the city where I was born and raised, the city where I completed my formal education prior to migrating to the United States for a graduate degree. My interest in genre-based writing instruction in the US context encouraged me to question how English writing instruction takes place in non-Western contexts and what sort of value is assigned to teaching of writing in Turkey, an under-represented research context. Because writing instruction (both L1 or L2) is rarely addressed or addressed in limited ways due to a highly exam-based educational system in secondary curriculum in Turkey, my goal was to explore through ethnographic approaches how foreign language teacher candidates learn writing in their second language during their first year in college. At the beginning of my sabbatical, the guiding research questions were as follows: (1) How do Turkish English as a foreign language (EFL) teacher candidates acquire genre knowledge both in their first and second language and literacies? (2) What training do teacher education programs in Turkey provide to prepare teachers whose native language is other than English, and what's the nature of EFL writing preparation in the Turkish context? My own subjectivity as a transnational scholar who constantly shuttles between Turkey and the US as well as my insider-outsider positionality as an ethnic minority both in Turkey and in the US have had imprints on the reflexive moves I engaged in during data collection.

Second Language Writing Preparedness of Language Teacher Candidates: An Ethnography of a Teacher Education Program's First Year Writing Courses

In the realm of L2 writing scholarship, the role of writing has been mostly investigated through the experiences of various student populations rather than the current or future teachers of these L2 writers. By highlighting the intersections of teacher education and writing instruction, my study explored the complex layers of writing development and genre acquisition of pre-service language teachers, who had no to little exposure to first and second language writing instruction in secondary and high school.[6] My primary goal was to look at both micro and macro discourses around teacher candidate's literacy practices as well as their understanding of second language writing in their first year of college. For this study, I examined three strands of research for which I wanted to look at both micro and macro aspects of writing education in Turkey: (1) Language planning and policy in FL settings: What are the policies related to language education in the local context? How are these policies enacted in the classrooms? How is writing education viewed historically? (2) Research in second language writing in non-English dominant contexts: How is writing thought in EFL settings such as Turkey? What are the institutional and cultural impacts? and finally (3) language teacher education research: how do pre-service language teachers develop teacher literacy on writing and build genre awareness in second language writing? Undertaking an ethnographically oriented teacher literacy research study provided me with a contextual and an in-depth understanding of non-native English speaking teacher candidates' experiences with different modes of literacies, languages and modalities in a highly standardised educational context where writing is not a valued skill to be taught.

My purpose in this section is to unpack two layers of reflexivity while exploring how my evolving interactions with the participants and my ever-changing understanding of the local context have evolved over time: (1) insider-outsider stratification as a glocal researcher in the field and (2) researcher's assumptions on perceptions (Agar, 1996) around pedagogical expectations and socio-cultural realities of the research context. While the insider and outsider stratification are related to how participants viewed me as a researcher (i.e., self-location during data collection), my own assumptions on pedagogical realities and expectations is about the preconceived notions I brought with me about what second language writing pedagogy should look like in an English as a foreign language (EFL) context such as Turkey. Before moving to these two issues of reflexivity, I will briefly introduce the context and provide some of my observations and preliminary findings from the field as the political context in which I landed had an impact on everyday practices and knowledge of the local academic community.

Background: Sabbatical research in time of political turmoil

The year I moved to Istanbul, the city I was born and raised, to spend my sabbatical year marked a politically tremulous time in Turkish history. The day I landed to Istanbul with my spouse and two and a half year old daughter on July 15th 2016, the country witnessed the bloodiest coup attempt in her history. Research was not on my mind on the night of our arrival when we heard F-16's sound bombs over our rooftop while my daughter was sleeping on the next room. I was not even sure if we were going to stay in the country and continue with my research. More than 300 civilians were killed that night when they used their bodies as a shield against tanks and gunshots to protect the regime. Many were left scarred emotionally and physically as the country was faced with a very difficult time. On a life-writing piece where I reflected on what it means to be an accidental immigrant, I described the horrific night of the coup attempt with the following sentiments:

> During all these years I read news about civil wars in the Middle East or lamented over growing authoritarianism in Turkey, I realized how little I actually know about the sheer terror, fear and the hopelessness of the ordinary people who experience political turmoil in their everyday life. This was the reality that my family and I found ourselves during the first few hours we moved back to our beloved homeland, the homeland in which I far longed to live.
>
> (Seloni, 2016: 263)

The months that followed July 15 were long and dark for Turkey in many aspects. The government took strict measures declaring a state of emergency.[7] In fact, my entire sabbatical was spent under the state of emergency particularly impacting the academic life. In the aftermath of the coup attempt, the biggest purge was witnessed in academia. As of today, around 4,800 academics are dismissed from their academic positions with governmental decrees with no outlets to appeal and 15 universities and 600 schools were shut down. Many academics were dismissed through governmental decrees and with no recourse to appeal. For instance, most signatories of the declaration "We will not be a party to this crime", which openly criticised the government's suppression of Kurdish populations and academics who were openly opposed to the government faced purges in addition to those who were linked to the Gulen movement, the alleged organiser of the coup.[8] The purge of academics and other sweeping government decisions left many university departments understaffed even dysfunctional to the extent that some departments had to close down. The picture was bleak for many academics: sadly, several people committed suicide while some went on hunger strike as a response to the government's unjust decisions about their jobs.

Despite all of these turbulences, the classes were in session on October 15, 2016 at the university where I was scheduled to conduct my research. Amid many uncertainties, I found myself in the field getting to know the students, faculty and the university. It would not be wrong to say that one of the things that brought my participants and I together in the initial days of data collection were the common trauma we experienced as a result of the coup attempt and the political aftermaths. Everyone had their unique story to share on the night of July 15, where they were, what they were watching, and how they dealt with the stress or other material consequences of this incident and the aftermaths that had caused to them and their families. The data collection in traumatic times included various struggles, both at the personal and academic level. I could not help but feel privileged as an academic who was not directly affected by the events due to my institutional affiliation. While many Turkish academics in Turkey were being imprisoned or threatened to be fired from their beloved profession, I was about to enter the fieldwork as an academic of Turkish origin, but as someone whose future won't be impacted by the unfair government restrictions.

My fieldwork took place within an English medium public university that attracts the highest scoring students from all over Turkey.[9] The university was established in 1863 during the Ottoman era, and is known as the first American university founded outside the United States. It is located in an affluent neighbourhood in the European side of Istanbul and includes six campuses bordering with the historical Rumeli Hisari castle. The student population is socio-economically and culturally diverse and comes from all over Turkey. I selected 10 focal students with varying degrees of language proficiencies and socio-economic backgrounds, and in the next 10 months the students and I regularly met for three ethnographic interviews. In addition to interacting with focal students, I interviewed five writing instructors in the program on various issues such as their L2 writing pedagogy, the challenges they faced in the writing courses and the learning outcomes of the writing sequence. Three of the five instructors later became my collaborators who co-inquired with me about the ways in which new incoming Turkish students perceived second language literacy and the way in which they developed their academic writing practices. As Kate Pahl also wrote in Chapter 4, the collaborative conceptual understanding of literacy was built within the community through the process of collaborative dialogue in which our literacy ontologies emerged and co-constructed. As Pahl eloquently puts "They are not found independently, by an independent researcher. They are entwined within lives" (p. 72).

Summary of Preliminary Findings

Many of the challenges faced by those who teach foreign language writing in an EFL context seemed to be due to factors such as the sociolinguistic status of English in Turkey, which factors in teacher candidates' motivation and purposes for writing in English, as well as the exam-based environments. In addition to the local realities, my interactions with first year teacher candidates demonstrate that most of them lacked reading and writing experiences both in their L1 and L2 starting due to highly standardised high school curriculum. Most candidates come to college having had little to no experience with writing in either their first or second languages. Ironically, despite their limited engagement with school literacy, the first year writing courses that I observed included linguistically dense and intellectually vigorous readings that required students to do close readings of texts from multiple disciplines. The first year courses are mostly traditionally structured and weeks revolve around academic writing skills through literary and discipline specific texts (e.g., readings from sociology, psychology and philosophy fields). Because many students come from test-based educational backgrounds with limited exposure to reading a wide a range of genres, many teacher candidates reported that they find these readings hard to tackle, which in turn lead to demotivation and demoralisation especially given the students' high achieving backgrounds.

My close reading of course materials with the faculty illustrated over and over again that five-paragraph essays with a focus on argumentation was the preferred writing practice in the writing sequence which teacher candidates were asked to take during their first year. Because a large emphasis is given to guided-composition in the form of five paragraph essays, teacher candidates reported that they found themselves in the cycle of writing-for-exams, which seemed to them an extension of their high school years as well as their English preparatory school experience.[10] A close analysis of student essays also shows teacher candidates exhibit a fixed pattern of writing akin to their preparatory school writing experiences. Because students' language levels were extremely varied, some faculties had hesitations in moving beyond the basic writing five-paragraph essay format. While these were some of my initial observations about how second language literacy was conceptualised and taught in this context, my collaborative work with faculties gave me a layered and a more complex understanding of the everyday knowledge and institutional tensions that were not readily visible to me (Unaldi, Seloni, Yalcin and Yigitoglu, forthcoming).

Reflexivity on the Researcher Assumptions and Perceptions

My primary goal with this second language literacy ethnography was to explore and unpack the patterns of knowledge and literacy experiences of EFL teacher candidates in an English medium university. While gaining a close understanding of their early teacher literacy knowledge, I found myself constantly juggling between emic/etic perspectives, which have been in continuum during my time in the field. The balance betwean en emic (insider's point of view) and etic (outsider's point of view) perspective is something I had to constantly pay attention to during my fieldwork. For instance, what I deemed as important (e.g., the importance of genre-based and situated approaches to writing) as an L2 writing expert who primarily produced scholarship within a Western context was not always relevant or seemed important to my participants (particularly, the faculty). During the sense-making process, my etic perspective needed to be in constant conversation with my local knowledge about and my own lived experiences with the exam-based education system in Turkey.

While my primary goal was to explore what kinds of writing instruction happens in teacher preparation programs, I was also enthusiastic about the possibility of introducing genre-based writing during my workshops and in the teaching of one class in the hopes of broadening teacher candidates' understanding about writing in real world. Even though I never laid this out explicitly, as a researcher I assumed the possibility of transforming teacher candidates' conceptualisation of writing where they could each develop a closer engagement with the process of writing and assume a writer identity. I had ideas about how a successful writing course could be taught in this context and had faith that the concept of genre and genre-based writing instruction could contribute to the seemingly more traditional ways L2 writing was taught to teacher candidates in the Turkish context. Yet, the realities of the local context as well as the teacher candidates' limited language proficiency challenged some of these principles and assumptions I brought with me to the field. At the end, assuming that they all have some sort of relationship with writing let alone writing in multiple genres wasn't quite representative of their realities. Most writing classes in this level were considered as spaces to develop teacher candidates' language proficiency, argumentation and critical thinking skills and even expand their worldview in general. After spending a few months in the field, I had to remind myself that: "the manner in which writing is learned and taught in FL contexts is dependent upon a whole set of material conditions and social practices that do not necessarily coincide with those of SL [second language] contexts" (Manchón, 2009: 202). The test-focused curricula, lack of authentic purposes for L2 writing as well as the focus on grammatical accuracy did not create much urgency in exploring alternative ways to teach writing. Stepping away from my assumptions and agenda, I decided to first document the detailed accounts of how my participants understand their own practices of second language and literacy, what has meaning and significance to them in their local contexts. I was pleasantly surprised to find that many of them in fact engaged in out-of-school literacies such as blog writing and video-gaming. Their L2 literacy practices was more than just a display of certain ways of doing things. They were a set of social and cultural practices and used as a relationship building practice with wider communities (Barton, Hamilton and Ivanic, 2000).

As a result of the felt pedagogical tensions in the field, I came to a better understanding that researchers need to be sensitive to local conditions of teaching and learning and understand some of the broader factors that impact on the choice of writing pedagogy in these settings. Addressing the dilemma between the pedagogical ideals that are usually produced in the West and the constraints of local EFL contexts for writing instruction, Casanave (2009) argues for a need to look into the local circumstances and consider issues related to purposes, attitudes and motivations regarding learning and teaching of L2 writing. If the motivation for writing as communication or creative production is limited, it might be challenging to apply and consider some of the fundamental principles of what we know about good writing instruction. In the second half of my fieldwork, taking an ecological framework invited me to closely look at the institutional and cultural dynamics of EFL teachers' local settings. Through unpacking my perceptions, revisiting my pedagogical knowledge base and the tensions I felt in the local context, I came to better understand that writing instruction in non-English dominant settings are not always directed by best practices as they are practiced in the "center". For many language teacher training programs in non-English dominant contexts, writing courses are rare occurrences, so understanding how writing pedagogies work in local contexts can be more complicated and nuanced than my initial perceptions on what writing instruction should look like in non-English dominant contexts. Systematic ways of watching and carefully observing what was going on became the backbone of my data collection in the second half of my ethnography.

Reflexivity on Observing myself Observing: Insider-Outsider Stratification

Observing oneself observing is a constant work for language and literacy ethnographers. In addition to the research assumption issues I discussed above, locating my personal reflexivity during the time of political conflict in Turkey also involved ongoing reflections. As a researcher who was born and raised in Turkey, I had a good understanding and a heightened consciousness of the educational system including the writing instruction in K-16. Yet, as a long-time outsider to the academic culture in Turkey, certain things were new to me, such as the changing university exam procedures, student population in this particular research context, faculty expectations as well as the history of writing curriculum designed for teacher candidates. Students were curious about my personal and academic experiences in the US (e.g., how I teach writing, what American students are like, how are teacher education programs structured) and some even communicated with me about their desire to study in US based universities. Similarly, writing instructors wanted to explore and understand different ways of looking at writing instruction, yet were limited in time, resources and suspicious of the workability of some of these "new" ways of looking at writing.

As a researcher, I was a Turkish academic speaking and writing in my participants' home language and exhibiting similar cultural practices, but I was an academic living and working in the US and somewhat distant from some of the political, educational and social turbulences that Turkish society was going through as those would not affect my quality of life. In this regard, my scholarly identity positioned me as an outsider. At times, I find it unsettling to speak of issues in my home community to audiences outside to them (my adopted home in the US). As I am still figuring out how my shifting subjectivity as a researcher can be uncovered, I keep in mind Ramanathan's (2005) questions as she writes or speaks in the West about her work in India (e.g., whether she should discuss about her privileged caste positioning while speaking to the Western readers):

> Are we all as situated researchers positioned around a variety of different (ethnic, social, [cross] linguistic, audience-related ideological) stratifications both in our home communities and outside it? When do we speak of issues in our home communities to audiences outside them – something many academics are now doing – which set of dynamics should dominate the researcher's locations and representations in the discursive text?
>
> (p. 296)

As a language ethnographer investigating second language literacy, issues these questions make me mindful of the kinds of effects that my presence and subjectivity might have on the participants, data collection process and the reporting of the ethnographic work. And, while foregrounding the subjectivity of the researcher depends on different dynamics and multiple audiences, experimenting with ways of writing about the researcher's subjectivity can help produce genuine texts where readers do not only read to obtain knowledge to be illuminated, but also experience the "uncertain processes of knowledge making" (Nelson, 2005: 318). With a focus on reflexivity with a Bourdieusian lens, this chapter was my attempt to unpack the messy and embodied processes of knowledge making in two different geo-linguistic sites.

In Summary

This chapter mapped out the theoretical and methodological journeys and tensions I went through in two different ethnographically situated studies on issues related to multilingualism in higher education, specifically focusing on learning and teaching of academic writing. With the first study, I discussed the intersections between one's ever-evolving academic knowledge and the dynamic between their tacit knowledge and personal experiences with the topic. I also focused on the scholarly gaze that is cast in academic writing, which at times prevented my explicit reflexivity during the reporting process of ethnographic data. In the discussion of the second study, I particularly focused on the insider and outsider positioning of the researcher and the tensions one might face when the local realities and pedagogical ideals clash.

Revisiting two language ethnographies and reflecting on my positionality pushed forward my thinking about reflexivity in important ways. I came to understand that while reflexivity can be present in each step of language-based ethnographies, the act of "reflecting" in writing is a rhetorical act that is influenced by the author's positioning and status and can be constrained by existing social practices in academic writing. Focusing on the issue of writer's voice and representation in reporting ethnographic research, I also discussed how reflexivity is an important marker of the writer's voice and is embedded in the language use and rhetorical moves the researchers take in his writing.

While conducting ethnographies, one cannot separate the social and political contexts, actors and the actions involved around the research. As many teacher-scholars conducting language ethnographies do, I also bring multiple conflicting positionalities which are always in-flux, complex and intersectional. In both studies, there were certain values and dispositions, that were central to my understanding of writing and multilingualism, and shaped how I designed and disseminated the studies, interacted with the participants, chose the literature to read and made sense of the literate activities of the participants. Some of these included:

1. Second language literacy is a socially and historically situated activity.
2. Second language writers transfer various linguistic and rhetorical behaviours across languages, and this is an ordinary occurrence of being a multi-competent language user.
3. Multilingual writing is intertextual, multimodal and dynamic.
4. Writing instruction is shaped by the sociolinguistic and educational realities, policies and standardisation processes inscribed by the local context.
5. Second language writers are not conditioned by their language and culture, but they bring their agency and creativity as they strategically "shuttle between discourses to achieve their communicative objectives" (Canagarajah, 2006: 591).

Keeping an open mind on how one's scholarly dispositions can be challenged, revisited and reframed while also productively exploring these dilemmas is at the heart of researcher reflexivity. As I explained in this chapter, reflexivity is a messy and embodied experience, and perhaps as Pennycook (2005) writes "the question becomes not so much how do I write myself into my research, but rather how does my research writing produce a writing subject in a certain way?" (p. 303).

Notes

1 The term translanguaging was first coined by Williams (1994) (later on translated by Baker, 2001), a Welsh linguist who observed in Welsh revitalisation programs that students would read in Welsh, but respond in English in classroom discussions. As Wei (2017) writes translanguaging "is not conceived as an object or a linguistic structural phenomenon to describe and analyse but a practice and a process – a practice that involves dynamic and functionally integrated use of different languages and language varieties, but more importantly a process of knowledge construction that goes beyond language(s)" (p. 15). The term later on was taken up by US based scholar Ofelia García in bilingual education who defined translanguaging as "the act performed by bilinguals of accessing different linguistic features or various modes of what are described as autonomous languages, in order to maximize communicative potential" (García, 2011: 140).

2 Cultural Historical Activity Theory (CHAT) was critical to my interpretation of Jacob's bilingual literate activities. CHAT is derived from actor-network theory and sees an individual literacy activity as:

> situated in concrete interactions that are simultaneously improvised and locally mediated by historically-provided tools and practices which range from machines, made-objects, semiotic means (e.g., languages, genres, iconographies) and institutions to structured environments domesticated animals and plants, and indeed, people themselves.
>
> (Prior et al., 2007: 18.6)

3 CHAT model as applied in the US writing composition contexts provides us with robust ways to investigate people's literacy practices, and is closely aligned with works of new literacy and multiliteracies scholars such as Kris Gutiérrez, Lisa Schwartz, Ibrar Bhratt, David Poveda. All these areas seem to share a common goal of seeing literacy as a social practice and moving beyond the normative genres such as five paragraph essays.

4 Focusing on textual and interpersonal elements within a text, metadiscourse analysis reveals how "writers project themselves into their discourse to signal their attitude towards both the propositional content and the audience of the text" (Hyland, 2004: 156).

5 As opposed to the first study, the reporting of data has only been done in the form of academic presentations. The manuscript explaining this study and findings is still in progress.

6 Refer to Appendix 7.1 to see more information about the study.

7 During the state of emergency (which still continues to date), 300 media channels were shut down, over a hundred of journalists were prisoned, 30 publishing houses were closed, 23 radio channels were removed from air, 15 universities and around 600 schools were closed down. To read more about the events after July 15 and the coup attempt, see the following articles: https://barisicinakademisyenler.net/node/63.

8 For more information about the dismal effect of the purge in academia, see Umut Ozkirilmi's 2017 open-access piece entitled "How to Liquidate a People? Academic Freedom in Turkey and Beyond" in *Globalizations*: http://www.tandfonline.com/doi/full/10.1080/14747731.2017.1325171

9 In the Turkish education system, all high school students take the national university examination in order to be placed into a university for their M.A. degree. This is a high-stakes exam for which students begin getting ready in high school and even earlier. The validity of the Turkish University Entrance test has been debated. More than its significance in determining one's achievement, this event has a social and cultural significance in the Turkish educational landscape.

10 To ensure linguistic preparation for their majors, many English-medium universities in Turkey tests incoming students' language proficiency through a writing exam and places them into intensive English programs called "preparatory schools" if their language proficiency score does not meet the required score of the university.

APPENDIX 7.1 Overview of Study #1 and Study #2

	Language Ethnography 1	*Language Ethnography 2*
Overarching research questions	(i) What are some of the rhetorical enactments and literacy practices this multilingual writer developed around his thesis writing? (ii) What writerly identities are constructed in art oriented, new humanities thesis/dissertation writing?	(i) How do foreign language teacher candidates acquire genre knowledge both in their first and second language? (ii) How can teachers best support and facilitate their L2 students' writing development in different genres?
Context	A public university's MA program in a mid-sized university in the US	A large public research university in a metropolitan area in Turkey
Number of participants	4 graduate students (reporting of the study on one focal participant)	10 undergraduate students (all foreign language teacher candidates)
Data sources	Interviews Field notes Written artifacts such as class papers and MA thesis	Classroom observations Field notes Interviews with students Interviews with writing instructors Writing about writing journals
Disciplinary field	Visual Art Cultural Studies Music	TESOL and Applied Linguistics
Level of education	MA students	First year undergraduate students
Length of research	1 year	1 year
Theoretical framework	Cultural Historical Activity Theory (CHAT) Translingual Writing	Writing pedagogies including genre-based writing Ecological framework towards writing instruction CHAT
Methodology	Textography	Ethnographic case studies
Status of research	Data collection and analysis completed Seloni 2014	Ongoing data analysis

PART III

Reflexivity and Beyond

In Theory and Practice

Introduction

Part III of the book returns us to issues of principle and theory in considering how central reflexivity is to language-based ethnographies. Its rationale therefore is based on the overall structure of the book where in Part I we considered aspects of method and approach and, in Part II we offered examples of reflexivity in practice. Part III seeks to bring these parts together and make more summative statements in taking forward issues for the would-be researcher.

Chapter 8 – Reflecting on Reflections – takes, as its focus, a consideration of the chapters in Part II as a whole. We begin with summarising the key elements in each chapter in turn. They are all very different and we draw out both commonalities and differences in the way the individual researchers articulate their reflexivity over the language-based studies they have undertaken. Such contrasting approaches demonstrate the multidimensional nature of reflexivity as well as the extent to which it can be systematised or liable to *ad hoc* expressions. The chapter distils out a series of salient themes:

- Participant-led literacy ontologies;
- Co-production, collaborative methodologies;
- Time as a significant part of the studies;
- Spatial ontologies as significant within literacy studies;
- Power and agency within literacy studies;
- Affect and emotion within literacy studies.

Each of these themes is taken in turn and discussed in the light both of the other Part II chapters and a range of relevant research literature in order to highlight what comes to the surface about the researcher–research relationship across the projects. As always, issues of language – this time in the ways that reflexivity is expressed – are central to our concerns. The chapter closes with further explorations in synthesising the theory and practice contained in these practical chapters. We see this chapter as a kind of bridge between the early parts of the book and what comes next.

Chapter 9 – Bourdieu, Language-Based Ethnographies and Reflexivity: In Theory and Practice – then returns us explicitly to the work of Pierre Bourdieu. The idea here is to re-express and take forward what reflexivity means for his perspective, both in theory and practice. Here, we first revisit elements of language ethnography and reflexivity in the light of the Part II chapter summaries, and explore *participant objectivation* in practice with respect to the kind of biases that are endemic in research and what a "reflexive view" can do to limit them. A case example is offered by considering Linguistic Ethnography as an academic sub-field. This discussion takes us so far in developing a reflexive stance; however, it is not enough. Next, we consider the whole relationship between language and knowledge itself, and finally the subject and object of research. Here, we make use of Kantian aesthetics and the phenomenology of perception set within a Bourdiesian framework in order to tease out the possibilities of reflexivity within our work. Finally, this amounts to what we term "reflexive objectivity" in which the Self is intimately implicated. Nevertheless, we underline the ways that such needs also to be a collective endeavour. In the last part of the chapter we show how working with Bourdieu itself might be expressed in terms of a series of "levels" towards a greater and greater embracing of what he referred to as a "new gaze" – or *metanoia* – on the world.

This chapter and Part III as a whole lead us towards our final concluding remarks.

8

REFLECTING ON REFLECTIONS

Kate Pahl

Introduction

In this chapter, I begin by providing a summary of the preceding chapters in Part II. The research is then situated in the wider field of language ethnographies. The fields, which emerge and are emergent within these accounts are explored. This is something that Seloni begins to do, when she maps the epistemologies, theories and methodological orientation that come into play when we talk about language diversity in writing (p. 129). Doing this work throws up further questions of how a field is constituted, and raises important questions of how reflexively is enacted in practice. Here, the studies, the texts and the reflexive positionality of the authors are situated within the fields of literacy and language ethnographies. These studies have made it possible to map the fields anew and present a picture of the current state of literacy studies. We will be asking these questions: What it is exactly that constitutes these reflexive accounts as a whole – what do they give us as a field? How can they inform our thinking about language ethnographies as a field of practice? Taken together, they present a fascinating and rich account of what it means to be in literacy and language research, and the attendant complexities of the researcher's relation to the field, as specified in the work presented here.

Part II Chapters

Each chapter in Part II is very different; but all have common characteristics. In all four chapters, the focus is on longitudinal, sustained language and literacy ethnographies, and in particular, the researcher's relation to the field. All four chapters wrestle, sometimes uncomfortably, with what it is to "come to know" in the field. In the chapters there is an element of revisiting, or re-studying the field, and there is also an element of knowing and then re-knowing within the research process. The chapters show how exciting this experience can be in excavating and enacting this process. To summarise the key themes in more detail:

In Chapter 4, ("From Language Ethnographies to Language Ontologies") literacy is introduced as a collaborative concept, through an account of a longitudinal ethnographic project in Rotherham. In this project, the thinking becomes entwined in the relationships in the field, as insights from collaborators begin to seep into analytic categories and ideas. This might be considered in terms of a collapsing of the understandings of how literacy could be defined happens in the field, at the point of relational contact with participants, who themselves become researchers in the process. The studies were carried out over a ten-year period in Rotherham, with a focus on small-scale home and community literacies. They involved participants who co-curated a museum exhibition, wrote stories and poems and became slowly the definers as opposed to the defined in the field of literacy and language research. This repositioning process led to new realisations of what literacy actually was and what it could be, in a way that almost echoes Bourdieu's own journey as described later in chapter nine, to get "beyond words" into a realm of being, knowing and reflecting on that journey. This process only came about because of a sustained commitment to the field, together with an ability to re-visit and to recognise the things that did not go so well, the failures to "see" and to listen first time round. Linguistic ethnography here becomes a kind of failure of seeing. Equally important is the ability to transcend that failure through following through the processes of coming to know. At the core, is the lived life of the researcher, trying to do the work, and failing in a way that then doubles back on itself, and this, then, becomes the project.

In Chapter 5 (Reflexive Layers and Longitudinal Research: What We Might Know Across Time) Compton-Lilly takes the reader on an extraordinary journey. Beginning with a straightforward account of an ethnographic project to explore the literacy lives of ten five-year-old children, the project becomes layered and entwined with the researcher's own life history and story. As the young people in the study grow up, the researcher also grows and changes, and reflexive positionings are caught up in this process. Over time, it becomes clear that the dataset is a live archive that offers Christy, five at the beginning of the study but at the end a young woman, an archive of her life. This is wholly surprising, but also an outcome of the study, and an act of "radical love" within the field. The researcher provides her research subject (Christy) with her own life story so that she can re-create her life archive. It becomes the subject of the chapter rather than the object. Here, the layers are connected to the repositioning of the tale of Christy, as Christy, the subject, comes to the fore and tells her tale, giving new voice and urgency to the concept of reflexive practice. This reflexivity is itself emergent and in a state of "*being* and becoming" (p. 89). This work then makes an understanding of reflexivity much deeper and more profound in a way that Bourdieu would have found hugely insightful.

In Chapter 6 (Insider Identities: Coming to Know the Ethnographic Researcher) the voice of the researcher "comes to know" as a process that is implicated within complex multi-stranded voices that sit across diasporic spaces and are entangled within relationships that themselves shift and grow. Describing a series of studies in which Caribbean American young people's literate identities were the subject of a longitudinal ethnography, the author brings her own self into the mix, so she literally "comes home" with her participants, who in turn, welcome her into their homes. This process of "coming to know" is entwined with ideas of "home" and this space is both the space of the research and a safe space for the researcher. This enormously important work shifts an understanding of reflexivity into something more situated, more personal but also deeply political. As McLean argues, "it immediately/directly shapes my own habitus" (p. 103). As the research is constructed, the habitus of the researcher shifts. This creates a profound attendant shift in the research process in a very Bourdieusian sense. Social, material and cultural worlds collide in a place of coming home, in a collective space of experience and place-making.

Finally, Chapter 7 opens up a space where the researcher, herself a second language learner, learns from second language learners how it is to learn. Seloni's chapter, "Enacting Reflexivity in second language writing research: A personal account of cultural production of authorial self and researcher perception" provides a compelling account of how the reflexive account can be located both within a scholarly gaze but also within the body. In the first study, the academic literacies of a postgraduate student, Jacob, are explored through the lens of both the researcher and the subject of the research being themselves multilingual and the resulting insights were consequently much richer and more layered as a result. Once again, reflexivity is found to be a layered, complex process of "coming to know". The construction of an academic field of study is never neutral, as Seloni eloquently explains. A personal voice comes to the fore and takes up space in order to make sense of the field of study. The second study appears to be a straightforward study of writing instruction and teacher preparedness of EFL teacher candidates in the context of an English medium university in Istanbul in Turkey. However, the study and the research became enmeshed in a wider deeply traumatic event which was a political coup in Istanbul in July 2016 that had far reaching and serious consequences for many academics and resulted in considerable loss of life at the time. The process of sense making was caught up in these events. Reflexivity here is about making sense of events that lie far outside the usual domain of research, but that impact strongly on interpretative and sense making processes. This work continues to resonate long after it has been written about and the writing here is alive with these tensions and processes.

Having summarised the chapters, I now want to discuss further issues emerging from them. This is a process that is not just about the individual accounts, but pertains to the field of literacy and language ethnographies and what these chapters tell us about it. This discussion then provides new directions and thoughts that can be taken forward from the book as a whole about what a focus on reflexivity offers researchers who want to know more about both their field, its genealogies and about how to learn and make sense within that field.

Key Themes Emerging from the Chapters

What emerges from these chapters, when read through the Bourdieusian lens of reflexivity, is a shifting of the field and a movement into certain directions. These are partly connected to where the field is currently, and focus on the situated nature of knowledge and the ways in which knowledge about literacy and language is no longer necessarily attached with the same certainty to "experts" within universities, but is more *distributed* across domains of practice. A process begun as a utopian project by the New Literacy Studies movement (see Chapter 1), in which everyday conceptual frameworks of literacy were understood as being equally "valid" as "school" conceptual frameworks, is now much more widely understood (see Street, 1997). Young people's everyday employment of language can be seen as providing insights through their use and handling, that can inform researchers in the field (see also Rampton, 2010). Time is both a distancing and close concept; lived within the everyday, the unfolding of a coup can happen in 24 hours while a young person grows up over 20 years. Within reflexivity, time both distances and refracts what is known (Samuels and Thompson, 1990). The situatedness of all of the research studies is something that comes to the fore, whether we are in a library in Rotherham, or sitting in a back yard in New Jersey, US, or in Istanbul during a coup. Where we are located is critical for how we research – our lives are intrinsically "in place" (Soja, 2010). Reflexivity within the literary discourse presented here can be seen as borne of conversations, recollections and is about a process of "reciprocal analysis" whereby participants co-construct interpretations with us, within the context of our studies (Campbell and Lassiter, 2010). Our work is then framed and constructed by and with participants, not away from them. We learn "with" not "from" people in the field (Ingold, 2014). Working with Bourdieu subsequently allows us to never forget power and its importance within our studies. Our lens can then be shifted to "hear" what is unheard. McLean's chapter powerfully argues for the need to bring down barriers and to hear again the voices of "home" through an insider lens. Seloni identifies as transnational in her writing and within her research and this powerfully informs how she sees the world. This "fine balance", as she puts it, guides her scholarly work as much as informs her positioning as a scholar within the world.

We have seen that Bourdieu's work derives from that school of ethnography that "feels" and is immersed in an affective relationship to the field. In these studies, the importance of affect, emotion and feeling come to the fore when reflexivity is discussed. Gaze, says Compton-Lilly, is "personal, embodied and enacted". Reflexivity for her involves "declaring baggage" in McLean's words, and this then resonates with a haunted history of migration to America. Knowing comes with feeling. What this then produces is a different kind of literacy and language scholarship, that is located within the body (Enriquez et al., 2016) and produces hidden histories which resonate across each other (Rogers, 2018). A focus on reflexivity with a Bourdieusian lens has produced a different history; one that is often elided within traditional studies. Outlining this learning below *produces the field* differently, and our stance towards it. Below, I shall therefore outline the principal ways in which this difference is located through a series of key themes that provide themselves a lens on the field of literacy and language ethnographies. These include:

- Participant-led literacy ontologies;
- Co-production, collaborative methodologies;
- Time as a significant part of the studies;
- Spatial ontologies as significant within literacy studies;
- Power and agency within literacy studies;
- Affect and emotion within literacy studies.

All of the chapters raise these issues to a lesser or greater extent: Chapter 4 is accented towards participant led ontologies, and co-production; Chapter 5 concerns time; Chapter 6 is about space; and Chapter 7 about power and agency. These themes can also be seen to be key in the wider field of literacy and language ethnographies. Taking them together, they constitute a way forward, a way-marking of the field to come. Here, I outline their key contributions. I shall add a few words on each.

Participant-led Literacy Ontologies

We have identified a shift from looking at *epistemologies* of literacy practices, the researcher's textual practices that then shape understandings of literacy including histories and heritages of practice, to a more *ontological* understanding of where literacy is in the world. Parkin (2016) talks of the switch from earlier socio-linguistics, that "tended towards the 'objective' classification of speech varieties and their social and conceptual correlates" (p. 76), to a movement to a much more fluid understanding of linguistic landscapes that include text, visual, dress, music, that collapse and shift as a response to the lived realities of super-diverse neighbourhoods. Parkin also observes that, "contemporary poly-languaging is an *ontological* act on the part of speakers to empower themselves or to project a desired or appropriate personal image" (p. 77). Participant informed understandings of linguistic realities, rather than reified autonomous understandings, increasingly form the "stuff" of linguistic ethnographies. New Literacy Studies began this turn by considering the ways in which "local practice" could actually be understood as offering epistemological understandings of literacy that were more nuanced, ideological and culturally informed than "autonomous" understandings (Street, 1993). Epistemological understandings of literacy and language that draw on participants' own ontological understandings can provide a much more nuanced and lived account of literacies in action (see Pahl and Rowsell, 2019). Collaborative ethnographies that rely on "reciprocal analysis" (Campbell and Lassiter, 2010) as a form of sense-making produce more ethically responsible texts as well as a form of knowledge that is community owned and understood (Rasool, 2017). In this way, the process of doing ethnography is itself also a process of knowledge creation. Reflexivity highlights this understanding.

Co-production, Collaborative Methodologies

As research practices and processes become more democratic, the ways in which knowing takes place become less clear and are more situated in the everyday. This leads to messy and complex forms of apprehending what is happening. Increasingly, the tools we use are both messy and complex as the insight that methods' practices are incomplete for the world we live in comes to the fore (Law, 2004). In language and literacy ethnographies reflexive objectivity offers a way to see that messiness more clearly, but also to name and articulate its processes and practices. Endemic within this "mess" are workings of power and control, concerns of inequality and systemic racism and sexism that are addressed by post-colonial perspectives and indigenous knowledge production processes. This view enables us to think differently about the work we do, but it also opens it up to new and emergent perspectives. All of the chapters acknowledge that the view that they hold is riven with their own personal stories and that of their participants, and this joint perspective produces the research ideas differently. The settled gaze of the researcher and the settled position of the researched is no longer possible, but instead a kind of dance takes place between the two, as both come to know each other. This is the wider process that all four chapters describe. Part of the reason for that is the length of time spent in the field, and the ability each researcher has to locate herself within the field of study across time and space.

Time as Significant to Studies of Literacy

Many of the chapters describe the importance of time in the revisiting process. The importance of the re-study has been articulated by Crow (Crow and Lyon, 2011) who revisited writing by young people on the Isle of Sheppey collected in the late 1970s by sociologist Ray Pahl. In the "Imagine" project, one of the first projects, involved a revisiting of the Sheppey Study in the form of a film-making project that re-imagined Sheppey in new ways. By revisiting the study, new work was possible. Likewise, in the Rotherham studies, and the studies over an extended period time by Compton-Lilly, revisiting added layers of understanding and comprehension to a field that then became much more than about literacy but became an archive of feelings that then informed literacy studies in a new way. The re-study becomes an essential part of this process. Bourdieu was a master of the re-study – his work exemplifies a revisiting as a mode of inquiry, almost more than any other ethnographer he excelled at this form of engagement.

In these chapters, time loops back, is disrupted, comes back to haunt us. Compton-Lilly's wrestling with the ethics of time provides an illuminating study of what the researcher holds, and why. This study resonates with the work of sociologist Avery Gordon, who writes about the "haunting" of social science by uncomfortable truths:

> At the core of the postmodern field or scene, then, is a crisis in repre-
> sentation, a fracture in the epistemological regime of modernity, a regime
> that rested on a faith in the reality effect of social science. Such a predicament
> has led to, among other consequences, an understanding that the practices
> of writing, analysis and investigation, whether of social or cultural material,
> constitute less a scientifically positive project than a cultural practice that
> organises particular rituals of storytelling told by situated investigators.
>
> (Gordon 2008: 10)

The much-described crises of representation in sociological texts leads to the inevitable understanding of ethnographic texts as "true fictions" (Clifford and Marcus, 1986) and a recognition of how the epistemological and the social are linked in a "double structure of thought" (Gordon, 2008: 12). Gordon's argument is that the social includes a "haunting", an absence, that can be understood as ghostly:

> If we want to study social life well, and if in addition we want to contribute,
> in however small a way, to changing it, we must learn how to identify
> hauntings and reckon with ghosts, must learn how to make contact with
> what is without doubt often painful, difficult and unsettling.
>
> (Gordon 2008: 23)

In these chapters, we seem haunted by Christy, whose life story is held by Compton-Lilly as her researcher turned biographer. We are haunted by the past freedoms in Istanbul, and mourn the loss of freedom of speech. We recognise the haunting of McLean by the spirit of the oral tradition, hearing the voice of the griot, "*rooted in a dialogue so powerful that his story draws you in – engages you, moves you to listen, and to respond, to co-author the texts of the experience and become one with his dialogic voice*".

This view refuses to be separate: it demands that the researcher "becomes one" with the dialogic voice of the other. In my own Rotherham studies, I learned to live with the university as the "Imagined Other" (2017) and instead of occupying a researcher-oriented space, accept how people saw me as shaping the field as it emerged, over time. We learn to live with the self that others see as well as the self we see.

Reflexivity, can then involve a kind of "doubling back", as well as "forward thinking". Doubling back can yield new insights as well as de-centre the lens of the researcher. In these studies, time is used to create a viewpoint that cannot fall within the researcher's grasp. While Compton-Lilly holds Christy's narrative within her data, she also loses her own settled sense of who she is as a teacher and then she needs to re-think her role as researcher as she re-tells Christy's story. As she eloquently says, "Time haunts me professionally".

As described in the opening chapter of this book, Shirley Brice Heath likewise describes her sense of self through the process of doing a re-study (2012). Asking again, and revisiting, can throw up new concerns about interpretations, and validity as things previously assumed are then considered in a different time, in a different light. In this process, the researcher is both archivist, storyteller and myth-maker. "Ways with Words" has created its own myths – Lem's words, hearing the Church Bell, has a mythical quality, as does Hymes' encounter in the *Warm Springs Interlude* (1996). These myths are then re-created within other texts, that become "inventory of traces" that make up the field of literacy and language ethnographies.

Such longitudinal studies create propelling narratives that both destabilise and thicken literacy and language research when tangled up with reflexivity. Under-standings of where young people are at the beginning of a project are refracted over time as their work and lives change in relation to their literacy practices but also in relation to their own identities and ways of knowing. Identities are tangled up in trajectories over time (Nespor, 1997; Wortham, 2006). This then leads to a doubling back in relation to reflexive objectivity. Literacy and language research can become entangled in these trajectories. Future oriented studies are also interesting from this perspective (see Erstadt et al., 2017). Literacy and language ethnographies therefore need to look at time as well as explore in depth the relational nature of identifications within the research. Time itself is a process that folds in on itself in the re-telling and re-imagining of the field.

Spatial Ontologies Within Literacy Studies

The field of literacy has been enhanced by a number of key studies of space (see, for example, Leander and Sheehy, 2004). These have opened up an understanding of how literacy practices both produce space differently but are produced "by" space. The need to account for the specificities of space and time when describing and producing accounts of reflexivity in ethnographic work echoes across a number of ethnographic writings. As Clifford Geertz writes, "No one lives in the world in general. Everybody, even the exiled, the drifting, the diasporic, or the perpetually moving, lives in some confined and limited stretch of it – 'the world around here'" (1996: 262).

McLean (in this volume) observes that, my "place" as ethnographic researcher cannot be in the margins, for I risk researching and reporting on my participants as "the Other". This opens up an opportunity for the researcher to account for the specificities of place. Leander and Sheehy (2004: 3) acknowledged the ways in which discursive practices are not only located in space, but they also produce space, drawing on Lefebvre's idea of space as socially produced (1991). Comber's work has also alerted literacy educators to the fact that, "We cannot simply take places for granted as a backdrop to the real action. Place is constitutive of relations" (2016: 7). Recognising that the literacies of place are produced in social relations leads to a re-theorisation of literacy practices that generates new thinking. As Somerville and Green (2015) observe, place offers a "common language" that can bridge local and global concerns, as well as the real and the representational (p. 175). The active discussions of place in these chapters show that the researcher is "emplaced" within the reflexive triangle as much as the researched. Moving into a place-based account of literacies both accounts for the forming of the reflexive position but disturbs the ontological certainties that come from "other" positions. Returning to McLean, it is dangerous to remain on the margins as it is also dangerous also to place "other" people on margins. Within both spaces, place matters.

In the chapters, we enter libraries, homes, schools, we loiter in the margins of the pages of the texts of our informants and can be caught in their conversations, as well learn again from them and from their texts. Space is both virtual and actual, embodied and felt it is also imagined and re-imagined in language. The process of reflexivity disturbs the ontological certainties of place to produce new accounts of place, that are informed by both the here and now and the "home" that is also "there" not "here", as McLean powerfully describes. Place can limit what is said, as people are restrained where they are, but also it can produce new narratives of loss, displacement and migration (De Fina, 2009). In this process, the literacies of place are intertwined.

Power and Agency within Literacy Studies

New Literacy Studies have always invited discussions of power. McLean asks us to think differently about voice, and about agency in linguistic ethnographic research. Street argued against neutrality as an ethnographic stance:

> The very emphasis on the "neutrality" and "autonomy" of literacy by writers such as Goody, Olson and Ong is itself "ideological" in the sense of disguising this power dimension. Any ethnographic account of literacy will, by implication, attest its significance for power, authority and social differentiation in terms of the author's own interpretation of these concepts. Since all approaches to literacy in practice will involve some such bias, it

is better scholarship to admit to and expose the particular "ideological" framework being employed from the very beginning: it can then be opened to scrutiny, challenged and refined in ways which are more difficult when the ideology remains hidden.

(1993: 7)

One of the questions all of the chapters ask is, "whose side are we on?". They trouble the assumption that the researcher "knows best" and their chapters are imbued with other people's voices, students, teachers, young people, collaborators. The move from the "I" to the "we" is part of the Bourdieusian enterprise. It involves a paradigmatic shift to recognise what a collective reflexivity could be, in a relational sense. The dissolving of the researcher's individual habitus into this broader, more fractured, but also more collective, habitus is described in each of these chapters. The relational nature of the enterprise comes to the fore. As Grenfell (this volume) argues:

> For Bourdieu, researchers need to "disarm" themselves of the power, which leads them into this epistemological "fall". It is a procedure that goes to the heart of the relationship between the researcher and the research and the way that knowledge and understanding of the subterranean feature (generating structures) of data are rendered manifest.

Pahl's study explores what happens when a project takes a collaborative ethnographic approach to the construction of the research questions, and the way in which they are run (Campbell and Lassiter, 2010). This can result in a complex space where research trajectories and purposes are diffuse, layered and positionings are less certain. The layers of reflexivity that occur include individual, person, epistemological, collective and ontological. By seeing the theoretical traditions as layered, as well as the methodological accounts, a more process-driven and emergent conceptual framework for research can be traced that also recognises the "prior ontologies" of literacy that are being constructed in the field (see also Massumi, 2002: 66). Literacy is lived, felt, experienced, woven and articulated in different forms, surfacing indirectly within the project, and captured in many different forms and sensations. The "stickiness" of this is something that Seloni also identified in her study (see also Ahmed, 2004). How can we disentangle ourselves from a field when the field is itself studying us as well? One idea is to move to a more "open" view of literacy as a "meshwork" (Ingold, 2013) that can encompass non-representational as well as representational practice. This opens up literacy to a more emergent frame, articulated here by Ehret, Hollett and Jocius: Language, discourse, culture and, indeed, new media making, are emergent phenomena that are more than locally and transnationally situated: they are materially entangled in the world's becoming (2016: 248).

In this vision, the location of literacy research moves to include "the world" in its emergent forms. This then re-distributes agency into something more diffuse. The ways in which collaborative, emergent and contingent understandings of literacy have been layered up in these studies begins to create a further layering of reflexive understandings of the field, over time, across sites and spaces.

For these studies, the personal must also be political. The threads across the studies are rooted in language ethnographies but spread outwards. Academic literacies intersect with literacies that resonate with affect, with the voices of ancestors, of previous generations as well as a future oriented language that encompasses social change. Activist literacies are imbued with a focus on social change – something all the authors share. The literacies of activism then become imbued with personal as well as collective histories. Citation trails, forms of knowledge production, all are implicated in this process. The process of "coming to know" in McLean's words, is fraught with difficulty – whose words to we use and how do they get used? Whose literacies count? Where? In writing about the field, how do we "know" what we know? And where do people "speak back" against the grain? These are all questions Bourdieu considered, and re-considered over the lifetime of his work.

The Importance of Affect

In the studies featured here, a focus on reflexivity links to work on affect, emotion feeling and life trajectories (Harwood et al., 2017). Literacy studies has now begun to acknowledge the importance of affect in shaping the ways in which knowing is constructed and enacted through the body (see also Enriquez et al., 2016). All of the writers in this book acknowledge the relational and dialogic nature of "coming to know". Many of the insights presented here take an "embodied" form. The research is felt, lived, experienced in complex ways. The concept of embodied literacies (Enriquez et al., 2016) is emergent within the field and its emergent quality haunts the writers as they describe the experience of knowing within the field, and living within that knowing. Ehret (2019) writes that, . . . "writing emerges through an experience of bodies moving and being moved, affecting and being affected, whether or not the feeling of movement is recognized Consciously" (p. 564). Beyond language, affect is a force in the social field that moves writing forward. The process of putting pen to paper, in tracing the line of a linguistic ethnography, involves the body. All of the authors in this book recognise that this is part of the process of tracing reflexivity. In this they echo a turn to the literacies of the body, to recognise that some of this might lie outside language but is about something less to do with representation and more to do with feeling. This then makes a different lens possible for the process of doing literacy research.

Summarising

In this, Part III of the book, we are exploring the implications of the Part II empirical studies in terms of Bourdieu and reflexivity and in terms of the field of literacy and language ethnography. In Part II, layers of reflexivity have been unpeeled. The person who does the research, who analyses the research and then writes up the research experiences time, place, affect, issues of power and inequity in doing this work, while participants become researchers and the research process is itself disrupted by modes of understanding and perception that themselves challenge the research field. Clearly, when researchers go into "the field" they bring an entangled web of practice, reading, thinking, doing and being in the world. In McLean's words, they "confront the duelling identities of researcher, academic, minority-group member and storyteller". Some of this is bodily, and deeply affective. Seloni, for example, attests to the embodied nature of research that is both located in the world, in culture and material objects, and the body. Such research must be seen as being constructed relationally, in interaction with the world. It is also, as Compton-Lilly attests, created across time, and as it moves through time, the view of the researcher changes. The idea of reflexivity is deeply connected to the relationship between the researcher and the research, and subsequently the ways in which knowledge is rendered visible within textual practices. The triangle between researcher, the research field and the production of the text as a result of this encounter is implicated, layered through skeins of reflexivity. These layers of reflexivity incorporate disciplinary as well as personal histories. It is *lived* in the day to day, in a home, in a city, within a school, on the streets around a neighbourhood. The histories of Christy (elementary school student), Shaana (high school student) and Jacob (graduate student) are entwined within these accounts, as they are also implicated in the researchers' histories. As researchers, we have gone through elementary school, high school and graduate school. We have encountered racism, sexism and difficulty along the way. Some of us have obtained tenure, but all of us have been on a journey in which our research is closely bound up with who we are. When we make connections in the field, these are real and our real-ness takes away from "objectivity" as surely as our sense of being part of the lives of others, of their lived realities.

Part of what the authors engage with is how to articulate this bodily interaction with the field and this kind of "living" of the research? What happens could be described in terms of a failure to express, linguistically, what is going on. How can classrooms, lives, neighbourhoods, be "captured" as "data"? As Maggie MacLure (2011) has described, qualitative research has an element of implicit failure within it – as the researcher's attempts pause, stutter, fail and are layered up in a confusion of feelings within a space and a time. Faced with what Seloni observes – that research is bodily, that it sits within the body as well as within language – MacLure might then well argue that a kind of stuttering encapsulates this entanglement of body and language (2011: 1000). We have to give up the idea of language as an autonomous object. Instead, the process of linguistic ethnographic research itself becomes a "giving up", that could be described in terms of failure, enacted within the research.

What does that then do for the field of literacy and language ethnographies? It opens up a space where researchers' linguistic practices, together with the practice of linguistic ethnography, is both unstable and yet more reflexively interrogated. Our use of Bourdieu here becomes a mechanism by which we can both see what is going on here, and "unhinge" it, explore where it doesn't work and where it does work. We can let in, and engage with, new points of theory where our research takes us. Considering the field through the lens of these accounts brings new paradigms to the surface. A Bourdieusian lens is a modernist tool, born from a modernist project, but it opens up a different kind of space, uncertain, open to change, reflexive. The value of Bourdieu's work for us is that it opens out a reflexive space as part of a project that he calls "participant objectivation", around which we have meditated in this book. By making our fields come alive we push the field into a more contingent, alive space, which is layered through our encounters.

Within these studies, we have seen how the moment of literacy and language research sometimes dissolves into a wider picture; of ethics (Compton-Lilly), of identity (McLean), of trauma (Seloni) and of collectivity or contestation (Pahl). This leads to a conundrum with regard to the field of language and literacy ethnographies. Where is the literacy and language in the study when we are looking elsewhere – at different things? When we look at ourselves, where is the field of study? Bourdieu's theory of practice leads us to collapse what we know (the field of literacy and language) with what we do (ethnography) and what we feel (relational). Our work is then located, but it also becomes strange. In this collective "othering", the university, or disciplinary knowledge, can seem to become unseated in the process. The disciplines of language and literacy, the modes of research, ethnography, then look different. We have made the disciplines "strange" in the process, to quote from Agar (1996).

There are a number of implications of this process. The first is the collapse of representational structures as a form to study. Settled notions of literacy and language as fixed and "autonomous" in Brian Street's words (1993) have been critiqued through New Literacy Studies, where all literacy practices are themselves seen as "ideological" and riven with issues of power and cultural and social resonance. The complexity of the relationship between the oral, written and the gestural has also been re-thought in the work of Ruth Finnegan (2015). Also, discrete categorisations of language, such as the concept of "code-switching", have been challenged by more fluid and transient conceptual frameworks, such as trans-languaging (see Blackledge and Creese, 2010). Studying socio-linguistics separately from the people who use language has begun to be seen as problematic and as an ontologically uncertain venture (Parkin, 2016). Instead, everyday concepts of language and literacy are increasingly recognised as being important both as insights about what is going on, but also insights about the field (Escott and Pahl, 2017). We are therefore at a point where representational practices are being questioned; that is the discipline of literacy and language ethnographies is questioned and new theoretical paradigms are being used to understand its processes. Increasingly the boundaries between people and what they study, the objects, humans and other "stuff" in the mix, are shifting, partly as a result of the turn to a "post-human" and new materialist understandings of the world (see Anders et al., 2016). We can no longer sit as comfortably within our ethnographic texts.

In this book, we feature "de-centered selves", "partial knowledge" and "layered accounts" that sit within fractured contexts – of decolonisation, civic war, divided communities, complex stories, the care system. These contexts change how we do research. But, our methods continue the same. As MacLure (2011) has observed:

> But when it comes to analyzing the"data" – interviews, observations, documents, and so on – we often end up, once again, digging up themes or stacking up categories, or finding or enforcing innocence, literal meaning, and uncomplicated goodwill.
>
> (2011: 998)

The writers in this book have wrestled with this paradox, but acknowledge that when they work reflexively, they no longer live within the certainties of "literal meaning and uncomplicated goodwill". Instead, they fall into situations where they feel they know something that is outside the frame of their research; and that knowledge, whether it is of Christy, of home, of another language, makes the research contingent and complex. We might say that the authors in this book live in a world of "*linguistic experimentation* in qualitative research" (MacLure, 2011: 1000), where a kind of dance is conducted between researcher, researched and textual practices. We see these in this book as disturbing that dance by using a Bourdieusian approach in order to ask, "what is going on here?" and "how is this playing out in the field of practice?" – that is, language and literacy ethnographies?

In conclusion, the studies in Part II show the practical consequences of reflexivity on the research process itself; in a way that we believe leads to a much more emancipatory conceptual framework for research and the knowledge production process. This process might be seen finally as even giving rise to what Bourdieu refers to as "radical doubt" (from Descartes) on the part of the researcher themselves. Something of this doubt is indeed captured within these studies, as each of us wrestled with our knowledge production process; and we are very grateful for the honesty shown by the respective authors in opening themselves to a reflexivity that challenges both who they are and of what are they certain. Finally, however, we believe the only way forward for a much more authentically scientific language ethnographic research practice is to begin by grounding the researcher themselves reflexively in the structural relations by which they are created; and, in doing so, to recognise more fully the determinant effects they have on both the way such research is conducted and its findings articulated. But, this approach itself has to be done in a certain way and a certain language in order to remain liable to critical appraisal. This aim can also be read and understood as one that is both highly personal *and* political. In the next chapter, Bourdieu's own understanding of reflexivity is re-visited with greater focus and developed as a way of further exploring what his reflexive approach can mean for language research, in theory and in practice.

9

BOURDIEU, LANGUAGE-BASED ETHNOGRAPHIES AND REFLEXIVITY

In Theory and Practice

Michael Grenfell

Introduction

In this chapter, I want to move towards a summary position if not actually a concluding one *per se*; this because the discussion around language, ethnography and reflexivity and the extent to which Bourdieu furnishes us with new perspectives and practices, is necessarily unfolding and contingent. Nevertheless, in the light of the previous chapters, I think we can say something new and distinct about a position we can occupy in going forward in terms of our research theory and practice around language-based ethnographies and the way that reflexivity may operate within them. I shall begin by revisiting the main themes from Part I of the book in the light of the Part II chapters and the consideration given to the latter in the previous chapter. I shall formally connect aspects of reflexivity emerging in our practical research examples with the kind of practices and insights recommended to us by Bourdieu in his own writing on reflexivity in research activity. However, I then want to probe deeper to tease out what we might understand to be going on in terms of the relationship between language, social science research and ourselves, both individually and as a group in constituting a new form enquiry, the kind of knowledge it gives rise to and how it might be represented equally in the mind of the writer and reader of resultant narrative accounts.

Language, Ethnography and Reflexivity

Part I of our book began by setting out its main themes; in particular, we are interested in language-based ethnographies and the extent to which reflexivity can be said to play a part in their construction and, assuming that it does, what form(s) that might take. Our focus on the work of Pierre Bourdieu arises from our belief that his form of social philosophy offers a particularly original approach both to research practice and what we understand as a reflexive methodology *in situ*. As Chapter 1 made clear, both language and ethnography are distinct academic disciplines with their own provenance and social histories prior to their hybridisation at a particular period of time. Knowing this, first, and considering their distinct histories is, of course, one form of reflexivity as it allows us to set our own endeavours within a chronology of scientific development. It further provides us with the opportunity to realise that these terms – language and ethnography – and the study practices they adopt, are hardly unproblematic, and there is a welter of (theoretical and practical) issues surrounding each of them distinctively before they are employed in tandem. At the core of such are mundane issues of project plan, research questions, data collection and analysis, interpretation and conclusions.

No such activity can take place without a good deal of reflection; indeed, we can hardly get out of bed without calling into being a whole set of cognitive processes in orientating our present moments in relation to the past and the future – what phenomenologists sometimes more grandly refer to as "protension". Actualised in research practice, such reflexivity raises issues of the nature of theory and its relationship to reality and "the truth"; in other words, degrees of confidence over the authenticity of representation, and the means we have to articulate it. We saw the tension in realising that any extraction from reality risks becoming partial truth, at its extreme, no more than reproducing the original relationship that the researcher holds with their object of research, either intellectually and/or empirically. But, we also saw that this danger poses a still greater risk: that, in recognising it, we risk descending into an extreme form of relativism and, understanding that language is by its very nature arbitrary, commit ourselves to a form of ethnography that offers its outcomes as merely the "poetics and politics" of the researcher themselves. Here, the researcher becomes the focus more than the researched. It was partly to offset this danger that we turned to Bourdieu, simply because he developed his own "reflexive method" in opposition to being pulled into such extremes. Features of our account of Bourdieu stressed the way, as is often the case with ethnographers, his own research grew out of personal experience and concerns, and was indeed shaped by them. This realisation again immediately challenges the notion of the "objective researcher" and their privileged "eye". It consequently brings to the fore the whole relationship between the ethnographer and research object, as we have seen in the Part II chapters; both in terms of the biases this can introduce and indeed the insights it might provide. How to discern one from the other? In Chapter 3, we argued that the sort of conceptual tools developed by Bourdieu offered a certain analytic rigor for two principal reasons: first, they were logically necessitated by his own readings of the empirical practical data in which he submerged himself; and second, these acts themselves could be articulated and understood in terms of grounding philosophies identifiable in the neo-Kantian philosophical tradition. Central to that tradition is the whole relationship between subject and object, implying questions of both epistemology and ontology, again as is ably demonstrated by the Part II chapters. Such themes coalesce around the issue of "participant observation"; a term used to describe the common practice of (and thus relationship to) entering ethnographic fields as both participant and observer to see and describe what is occurring there. Unsurprisingly, Bourdieu see "participant *observation*" as a contradiction in terms and in its place posits "participant *objectivation*" where there is an "objectification of the knowing subject", as the researcher turns their tools of analysis on themselves and, in so doing, disarms themselves in order to at least partly escape from the epistemological traps inherent in the act of research. But, what is "participant objectivation" in practice, and does it not actually preserve the subject/object dichotomy the whole enterprise was meant to avoid? It certainly sounds, on the one hand, very close to "objectivity" and "objectification". At the same time, does this acknowledgement of the subjective relativity of the research not return us to the issue of the "impossibility" of interpretation and representation? Can there be a third position somewhat beyond these two: a kind of "reflexivity objectivity", that is neither objective Popperian "knowledge without a knowing subject", nor relative interpretative subjectivity, the sort of nihilistic black hole of *differ-ance* (sic) from which all sense loses its meaning? The rest of this chapter explores and responds to these issues and questions. I do this, first by returning to issues of scholastic biases and what we might do about these, offering exemplary consideration of the case of linguistic ethnography referred to earlier in Chapter 2, and then further in terms of the whole philosophical relation between reflexivity, knowledge and the language we use to represents them, and what it implies for both our relationship to language ethnographic practice and our own empirical selves.

The Research Object, Participant Objectivation and Scholastic Reason

Clearly, there are ways of thinking about any research object – in language-based ethnographies – and this thinking amounts to a construction; by consequence, a reflexive approach is both able to objectify the principles underpinning such a construction and the justification for their deployment. This is why Bourdieu refers to "the construction of the research object" as the "summum of the art" of social science research (1989a: 51). Moreover, it is not something that is operationalized once and for all out the outset of undertaking research, through "a sort of inaugural theoretical act". Rather:

> . . . it is a protracted and exacting task that is accomplished little by little through a whole series of rectifications and amendments . . . that is,

by a set of practical principles that orients choices at once minute and decisive . . .

(ibid.)

We can see this process occurring in the practical reflections in Part II.

If this is a kind of pre-reflexive, and on-going, reflexivity, one of the essential features of it is the pre-given; in other words, how the object of research is normally represented within the academic field or discipline, and here there are issues about language and the assumptions that are made there on the basis of the terms used. As Bourdieu writes, we need to "beware of words" because they present themselves as if they are value-neutral, whereas in effect they are socio-historical constructions, taken-for-granted as expressions of "common sense", but with specialist assumptions about their meanings and imbued with logically practical implications of such meanings. In practice, words are susceptible to a kind of "double historicisation": first, a word is used to represent a certain phe-nomenon at a particular point in time – one which is often constructed and presented in a way which renders as transparent the social and historical aspects of its construction; and second, by not recognising words as such, that de-historicised form is then subject to further historicisation, as the original form is taken as the basis of fact from which further work and elaboration is opera-tionalised. In this way, the most innocent word can carry within it a whole set of un-objectified assumptions, interests and meanings, which confuse the reality of representation with the representation of reality. In other words, at base are un-objectified personal relations and field conventions, which go unchallenged as such because of the interests they bolster. In effect, this is to confuse "substantialist" and "relational" thinking: indeed, it is so easy to (mis)take constructs as things in themselves rather than as sets of relations. To do one rather than the other – without knowing about it, still less acknowledging it – is to accept a whole epistemological matrix which has direct consequences for the way that an object of research is thought about, with the implications this error entails for the methodologies employed to collect and analyse data, and for the conclusions drawn as a consequence. Without a reflexive reconstruction, research therefore risks expressing an unacknowledged pre-existing scholastic orthodoxy (*for itself*) rather than the thing (*in itself*) in praxeological terms.

These issues lay behind the three biases mentioned by Bourdieu and referred to in Chapter 3: the conceptual orthodoxy of their field; their own background and position within it; and the very non-empirical relation that the researcher takes up – *skholè* – *vis-à-vis* the object of investigation (Bourdieu, 2000b: 10). There seem to be two prime ways of doing this. First, there is the need to think conceptually of oneself, both empirically and as researcher, in terms of *habitus*, *field* and *capital*, the very use of which would seem to purge the undertaking of any transcendent, *substantialist* objectivist science (control) in favour of a genuine *relational* one (emancipatory). Second, the need to place oneself in the *field* of knowledge in terms of connections with the *field* of power, connections and relations to the *field* and one's individual personal relationships in terms of *habitus* and its position and proximity to others. Many elements of these areas of relationship and bias are identifiable in the chapters in part although, as is often the case with Bourdieu, not expressed systematically. To sum up these can be expressed as:

Source of Bias

1.   Position in Social Space (*Habitus*/Cognitive Structures).
2.   Orthodoxy of the Field Site (language).
3.   *Skholè* – Scholastic Fantasy (Relations to the world – Substantialist/ Relational).

Reflexive View

1.   Fields in relation to the field of power – my connection/connecting.
2.   My relationship to the doxa in the field; held in institution. What am I connected to? Doxa of the discipline – Aims. Position in field.
3.   My *habitus* and that of other people in the site context. Their *habitus* and mine; personal relationships/networks. My position and proximity.

This *Reflexive View* thus adopts a similar schema to the 3-level method that Bourdieu offers for *field* analysis (see Grenfell, 2012a: Chapter 13), which really covers a range of enquiries set between the individual and society as a whole: the *field* and the *field* of power, the *field* itself and the subjective (dis)positions, *habitus*, of those within the *field* – however, this time deployed in terms of the *field* of the research discipline and the individual researcher rather than the *field* of the research object itself. What might this begin to look like in practice? I want to return to the case of *Linguistic Ethnography* discussed in Chapter 2, so that we can contrast a Bourdieusian approach to reflexivity with that expounded by some of its exponents.

The Case of Linguistic Ethnography

Although, I have chosen to use the example of Linguistic Ethnography in order to exemplify issues of reflexivity and participant objectivation, a similar exercise could be undertaken by any other sub-field of applied linguistics and language-based ethnography itself. What I believe is at stake is the scientific necessity and integrity of this approach to the study of language in terms of its modus operandi. In other words, what does a Bourdieusian approach offer that others do not? What are the extent and the limits of its "science"?

In Chapter 2, we referred to Rampton's argument (2007a) in setting out this "new" field of academic study as an "arena", or "site of encounter" for the study of language *in society*. He writes on behalf of its constituency that it is an academic hybrid of the disciplines of "ethnography" and "language/linguistics", and so is highly pertinent to the themes of this book. As noted above, neither discipline in themselves have existed in isolation and other disciplinary approaches have also developed out of concerns with language within a socio-cultural context: for example, Conversation Analysis, New Literacy Studies and Critical Discourse Analysis. Of course, such a range of approaches relates very closely to the issues discussed above in terms of "the construction of the research object", and there would certainly be value in examining the way socio-cultural issues of language have been approached in the various forms of ethnography – ethnology, anthropology and sociology – raising just the sort of questions about culture and structure addressed previously. How does Linguistic Ethnography shape up within this disciplinary space? Ethnography is intended, Rampton argues, to "open up" linguistics, whilst linguistics "ties down" ethnography (p. 8); and so, offers broader socio-cultural, context features, but with more precise, empirical techniques used in data analysis. By "opening up", linguistic ethnographers intend developing cultural sensitivity, reflexivity and contextual understanding; by "tying down", they intend technical descriptions, systematic analysis and de-limitable processes.

Linguistic Ethnography is, clearly, a "young" academic sub-field, and one primarily inaugurated within a UK-based academic community. It is therefore not possible to comment on the realisation of its agenda up to now: indeed, a special edition of the *Journal of Sociolinguistics* in 2007 was preoccupied almost entirely with issues of definition, with virtually no empirical exemplification. More actual empirical studies have been published since then (for example, Copland and Creese, 2015). However, what might we say about it in terms of its *field* position and those involved in it – *as a reflexive exercise*? In Bourdieusian terms, for example, we might see such processes of definition as involving attempts at establishing *legitimation* in the academic space – to be "recognised" in the *field* of linguistics; and *consecration* – to be acknowledged. This is one strategy to claim objectivity: that is, create one's own critical community. Unsurprising, therefore, that such a field is led and thus dominated by those who created it. But, what justification is there for this? What I want to do in the context of these issues is to draw further on Rampton's defining article, to reflect further on this sub-field as it is constituted and thus make a contribution to the construction of Linguistic Ethnography *as a research object itself*. In a very Bourdieusian way, this turns linguistic ethnography into an object of analysis rather than an unquestioned *instrument* of analysis.

In an informal survey of institutional affiliations of members of the UK-based Linguistic Ethnography Forum (LEF) in 2006, 54 were aligned with education, 53 with language, 17 with culture and area studies, six with anthropology and ten with disciplines such as computing, psychology, medicine and geography.

This statistic highlights the disciplinary *dispositions* of those within the Linguistic Ethnographic grouping: predominantly language and education. The latter are characterised by their multidisciplinary nature. Their position within the academic *field* is therefore often ambiguous, as is the *cultural capital* (symbolic value) that mediates their functions, since they appeal to a multitude of "home" disciplines, all whilst needing to respond to the expectations set them by the *field* of power (basically, politicians' control over curriculum, funding and training). This positioning creates enormous tensions between education and language practitioners in terms of theory and research, and what is valued in terms of each. Such tensions extend to issues of national and international constitution and status. With respect to its hybridity, Rampton points out that the institutional links between linguistics and anthropology have traditionally been weaker in the UK than in the US, which might indeed explain why Linguistic Ethnography began primarily as a UK-based discipline; in other words, there is an academic space that has not been colonised hitherto. UK researchers in education and linguistics have also tended to be older, as entrance into these disciplines generally occurs after individuals have undertaken some years work as a teachers or language specialists – therapists, for example. They consequently emphasise the practical in contrast to the focus on scholarship in the US. Such backgrounds also often result in a more personal investment in the research; indeed, their own experience is frequently a central motivation for research (our Part II chapters attest to the personal involvement and attachment that linguistic ethnographers can hold with the object of their research). This has methodological implications: moving from "inside-outwards", in trying to get analytical distance on what is close-by. So, traditionally, language specialists and teachers begin research by examining their own practical and immediate context in this way. Rampton argues (op. cit.: 5) that this characteristic implies a totally different relation to the object of research when compared to "professional researchers" (in the US) who, by moving "outside-inwards", are attempting to become familiar with the "strange". In the academic *field*, knowledge helps the researcher feel empowered as a professional. The quickest way to acquire it may, therefore, be to address immediate practical interests. Here, there are again issues of theory and practice and the traditional tension between scholarship and practical relevance, which are also at the core of "linguistic ethnography" and Bourdieu's own "theory of practice". These aspects of Linguistic Ethnography demonstrate the importance of the *habitus* of researchers in shaping their methodological approach and preoccupations, as well as the significance of the social conditions that surround them; in this case, the structure of the academic space, its logic of practice and the *capital* that is valued there.

Personal dispositions are therefore tied up with the nature of the academic *field* itself, and the research activity that takes place there. Rampton further points out that academics are generally more fragmented in the UK than in North America – another feature of the national *field*. "Cross-disciplinary" dialogues are therefore easier to establish and maintain in the UK than in the US. This issue involves the strength, or permeability, of discipline boundaries between the countries; it might simply be easier "to hybridise" in the UK than USA. US linguistic anthropologists are also younger, and are therefore less likely to have practical experiences in their respective fields compared to their UK counterparts. Consequently, they are more motivated by theoretical interests than personal experience. Orientations are also distinct: American anthropologists, for example, tend to see cultural differences in classrooms whilst the British sociologists of education come from a tradition that sees class-based social structures in pedagogic systems. These issues go to the heart of the way an individual academic researcher might sense their whole being within the *social space* – as certainty or uncertainty – and the resultant confidence it gives them in terms of how to act and what to think. It follows that Linguistic Ethnography might be seen as a haven for researchers who sense themselves least secure in the academic space where disciplinary purity is often an asset in terms of *cultural capital*. In a way, it is a support and a protection, but it also declares – by its very existence – an inherent disciplinary insecurity; that is, by implicitly declaring that it is for those with interests that do not "fit" in elsewhere. The key point here is that if those involved in Linguistic Ethnography undertook a process of reflexivity – as part of a process of participant objectivation – some of these issues may emerge in a way which might bring to light issues of contingency about their practice: a contingency with epistemological and methodological implications beyond those expressed in the "reflexive accounts" of their research practice.

However, academic *habitus* are not simply constituted of personal background and institutional space. Academic sub-fields are also framed by professional associations. For example, the relationship between the Linguistic Ethnography Forum (LEF) – the main British body for Linguistic Ethnography – and other academic associations is a significant one. Two associations have played important roles in developing LEF: The Sociolinguistics Symposia (SS) and the British Association of Applied Linguistics (BAAL) in the UK. Each has a distinct formative influence. Whilst BAAL is a learned society with large financial resources – Cambridge University Press (CUP) co-sponsors 3–4 specialist seminars each year – the SS take place only every two years and are free-standing events, unsupported by the type of on-going administrative infra-structure provided by BAAL. These relationships themselves need to be understood in Bourdieusian terms as the relations between the commercial world of publishing (CUP) and the academic world of scholarship (SS) (and the tension, therefore, between what Bourdieu terms Scientific and Temporal Power – see Bourdieu 1996a). Such relationships will have an impact on the form that Linguistic Ethnography takes and the direction of scientific knowledge it produces; for example, in terms of what is deemed as marketable and saleable within an (academic) international market. The explosion in the number of academic journals published is evidence of their lucrative nature: a way in which scholarship is sold to commercial publishers for their profit in return for academic *capital* in terms of "internationally peer reviewed" publications – the standard currency for academic promotion. There is therefore an implicit collusion between researchers and publishers; indeed, a new academic area can thus be seen as just another "market opportunity", which benefits both. This may be one reason why, as Rampton argues, the academic constitution of Linguistic Ethnography in the UK by its very nature itself does not provide ideal conditions for the processes of cumulative generalisation of findings – it is just too fragmented: and why there is a lack of unified theory in Linguistic Ethnographic research; although a certain amount of conceptual theoretical language has emerged at a micro-linguistics level: performance, indexicality, entextualisation, metadiscursive framing, etc. It is hard not to see this as partly an outcome of the state of the academic *field* itself set within the *field* of power as a dominated entity within the dominant.

Applied linguistics is, of course, a much larger and broader constituency under which a number of other language-study traditions have grouped, and language-based ethnographies might be seen as one of these, involving academic constituencies outside of both. And, as noted, each particular grouping has adopted particular models of language and linguistics, together with the relevant theories and methodological procedures. Are these traditions compatible and consistent with respect to the issues of theory and practice raised by Bourdieu's approach? In fact, it is impossible not to see these traditions as in some ways competing with each other for what Bourdieu called a "monopoly of truth"; that is, struggling for dominant *field* positions. We are reminded of Bourdieu's view of the *field* of artistic production as a series of generational shifts (1996b/1992: 159) in which, "to impose a new producer, a new product or a new system at any given moment on the market, is to relegate to the past a whole group of producers, products and systems of taste (*or academic perspective*), all hierarchised in relation to their own degree of legitimacy" (ibid. my words in italics). In this respect, the academic *field* behaves just like any other knowledge *field* with generations of activists both displacing and being displaced in a general dynamic for consecration – *connaissance* and *reconnaissance* (what is "known/acknowledged" and what is "recognised") – within the *field*; all this is played out in terms of the relative logics of practice and *capital* configurations at stake there, and with the resultant rewards and penalties (see Grenfell, 1999). Participant Objectivation is intended to raise such issues towards a clearer definition of science and truth.

As I have noted, it is common for researchers to claim "awareness" of what they are doing and why. However, reflexivity for Bourdieu – Participant Objectivation – is more than this, because it involves an "objectification of objectification" itself through an "objectivation of the knowing subject". I have argued that to bring this about, such "objectivation" requires the application of terms such as *habitus, field* and *capital* – and the epistemology underlying them – to both the particular *field* of academic discourse and to those involved actively within it – the researcher and researched. However, it is both an individual and (essentially) a collective undertaking. The products of any language and linguistic analyses need to be understood in terms of their characteristic position within a particular academic space, itself understood in terms of the socio-historical structure of the academic *field* at a particular time. This is what I am encouraging linguistic ethnography to do. This enhanced reflexive awareness permeates Bourdieu's work and makes up the "realist third way" (2004: 200) which he is advocating. Such is logically predicated from the very instant of his epistemological vision, even if it only gained prominence in the last decade of his career. It has to be because his epistemology of practice is too comprehensive to leave the researcher on the outside of it. Indeed, not to include the researcher in it is an act of intellectual bad faith, even if it requires them to vacate the position they have acquired in undertaking the research and *disarming* themselves of the intellectual weapons they have employed to gain it. Why? Because "the truth is that truth is at stake" (Bourdieu, 1990d: 195). Moreover, such is not accomplished without a cost. Indeed, "one must choose to pay a higher price for truth while accepting a lower profit of distinction" (1991a: 34). This can be read as a warning for all of us who adopt a Bourdieusian approach simply because of its own *symbolic capital* – that is, what it can confer in terms of implied distinction within the academic field. Ultimately, therefore, this philosophy is corrosive: both professionally and personally – if taken to its logical conclusion. However, it does put into sharp relief the relationship between the researcher and their research practice and the status of the resultant knowledge, which surely implies issues of integrity and objectivity when set against the danger of subjective bias. We have called it "praxeological" knowledge; although this still raises questions of its nature and the way it might and can be expressed. These questions and issues are uncovered utilising the three biases listed above and what might be done in response to them. However, this is only a beginning, and a reflexive stance can involve a much more rigorous interrogation of the very nature of the subject-object relationship and the language used to express it. Indeed, language per se continues to haunts the discussion since language is very often the basis of thought and, in terms of language-based ethnographies, we are often employing language to refer to language referring to language in distinct socio-cultural contexts. The next section explores these issues of language in a little more depth.

Language, Reflexivity and Knowledge

Throughout this book, we have featured issues of language in conducting language-based ethnographies; in other words, the way that language manifests itself and in turn shapes socio-cultural communities. This focus has led us to enquiry into methodological issues involving the relationships between theory and practice. Moreover, however, we have put the dimension of reflexivity at the centre of our concerns. Here, the questions are: What is it? How far is it possible? Why do it? How to do it? What results? Clearly, reflexivity can be an implicit, unconscious aspect of research practice. But, we have seen that more can be said about it in a very explicit way. Such *objective* manifestations of reflexivity itself necessary involve language, and we have argued that Bourdieu's conceptual terms have a useful role to play here. However, this still raises further questions about the link, indeed overlap, between reflexivity and the language in which it is expressed. What are the limits of reflexivity as expressed in thought and the language, which conveys it? These sections explore these crucial concerns.

Above, I have already noted that, besides his critique of language study, Bourdieu was wary of "words", and indeed warned researchers to "beware of words" (1989a: 54). He then makes the point that sometimes the language of research can become *more real* than the object it aims to represent; this is why there is a need to focus on the language of representation in the constructing of the research object, as it is here that historical *misrecognitions* are hidden. Similarly, the language of reflexivity sometimes risks reproducing another scholastic fantasy – the empirical relationship that the researcher holds with the research object – and the researcher seems to become almost "captured" by their own prosaic. Indeed, language can almost create what it refers to, or might refer to; that is both the form and the content of social phenomena. Bourdieu draws attention to this way that language shapes experience in terms of the phenomenology of the affective life – the topic of a Masters thesis he apparently never completed:

> There is a wisdom that is recorded over millennia, of symptoms which are translated into language (stomach knots, makes me feel sick) . . . or is it that language has produced the symptoms? It was interesting because (in my work in Algeria) there was no language of emotions to do a comparative sociology of affective lives, which would employ language as a means of structuring perceptions and also bodily experiences.
>
> (Bourdieu: 2008b: 352)

Here, language actually structures perception, a little like the Sapir-Whorf hypothesis. This feature somewhat leads us to questions of language, the philosophy of language and ultimately post-modernist issues about the relationship between language in representing the world and/or explaining it.

The play-off between language (conceptual terms) and perceived experience – in research itself – must therefore go to the heart of our epistemological concerns. It is tantamount to saying our thoughts not only shape what we see but in fact almost produce (and indeed limit) what *we can see* and *think*. So, on what are they based? This is not just a question of linguistic relativity with respect to the signified but of actual exegesis and what is claimed in its name. In the same way that, in contemporary physics, if scientists look at electrons as discrete entities, they are discrete entities, and if they look at them as a wave, they (somewhat mysteriously) become a wave, maybe our enquiry into the empirical world requires us to understand the nature of our own *conscious* viewpoint (cognitive relationship) itself and the language we use to express it, in order for us to appreciate the way it shapes what we (can) see.

I believe these perspectives are very close to Bourdieu's view of social space and phenomena as emergent processes. They certainly raise questions about how we conceptualise the social world and ourselves in it – empirically and as science researchers. We do, therefore, need a reflexive understanding of the epistemological status of the concepts we have – *habitus*, *field* and *capital*, etc. – beneath the language used to express them; what they allow us to see – and not see.

The most direct response to this ambition is set out in the *Theory of Practice* itself, and the characteristics of the knowledge outcome intended is made at the beginning of the *Outline of a Theory of Practice* (1977b) where Bourdieu writes of a series of "epistemological breaks": first, from *empirical knowledge* – the naïve state; second, *phenomenological* subjective/sense *knowledge*; and third, from *structuralist* objectivist *knowledge*. There is then, significantly, a final break with theoretical knowledge itself – a *theory of theory* – which is the true characteristic of the *practical rationality* and thus *reflexive objectivity* to which Bourdieu aspires. It is this final element that enshrines principles of reflexivity, which were not fully articulated until later in Bourdieu's intellectual trajectory (see Bourdieu, 1998: Chapter 6, 2000b, 2003, 2004). This place, Bourdieu argues, is achieved by *constructing the generative principles* of research practice; in this case, *in their moment* of its accomplishment. This *science of practices* is thus predicated on *creating* the *conditions of possibility* by its realisation. So, what is this epistemological *generative principle*? And, what are its *conditions of possibility*? And, how do we create them? Such questions imply a need to understand the relationship between the individual, the world, knowledge arising from it and the language used to express this knowledge. Once again, the language we use – the concepts – is clearly crucial in communicating our answers to such questions. Habermas' view on these issues offers a useful point of departure in responding:

> . . . individuals, when they act communicatively, go through the natural (empirical) language, make use of interpretations that are culturally transmitted and make reference to something in the objective world, in the social world, which they share and make, and each one makes reference to something in its own subjective world simultaneously.
>
> (Habermas, 1987a: 499–500)

This points to an inherent transhistorical rationality that is embedded in the very stuff of language for Habermas. Language is humanely communicative and modernist in essence. The task then, Habermas argues, is to abolish systemic "distortions" to communication. The "cooperative principle" of Grice takes a similar line (1975). However, for Bourdieu, such a communicative convergence can never arise from ordinary, empirical language; and there is a danger in Habermas of a transcendentalist illusion in embedding scientific rationalism in the structures of language and consciousness themselves, since conflating them dehistoricises the production of language and the interests is carries. In opposition to Habermas, Bourdieu hence argues that his own concepts are generated out of empirical *practical exegesis* (not theory). Concepts are therefore "logically necessitated" by the observable relationships inherent in the data. This gives them an existential authenticity and offers a "double historicity" of mental structures instantiated in social practice – as phylogenesis (previous *field* structures) and ontogenesis (schemes of perception); all homologous as structuring *and* structured structures. As such, concepts like *habitus*, *field* and *capital* can be seen as providing the foundations for a kind of Bourdieusian "communicative competence" – a "language of association" (linking subjects, the subject and the object and the objects themselves) for those working from this perspective. Here, and through these concepts, the individual is seen as being somewhat "at one" with the collectivity as they all share the same worldview. The "social" world then becomes "objective" – that is, communicable – and thus pertaining to a reality beyond the self (both previously empirical and scientific), although the latter can be accessed through it. At such points, the self and the collectivity become one and the same thing through this practical science; not simply empirically, but in some more "heightened", emancipated realm beyond everyday subjective identification. It follows that the power of such language – the way it is used and the valued outcome of its deployment – carries with it the potential to both change relations to the empirical world and how we act as a result. Epistemological principles underlying these relations are hence critical in ascertaining certain forms of scientific knowledge and their effects.

Returning to Habermas' epistemology, we have already noted three epistemological *modes* are presented by him – *nomothetic, hermeneutic* and *critical* – pertaining to substantive *interests* (see Grenfell, 2014: 151–168 for a Bourdieusian interpretation of such): law-giving, interpretive and emancipatory (Habermas, 1987b). Given the above, however, such modes do not simply represent discrete, implicit epistemological interests – ways of knowing – but also need to be defined and expressed in terms of whole social relations to the world, which have practical, ultimately political, consequences. Bourdieusian science, therefore, implies a different form of relationship to the world and thus with a different *interest*. Such again can be understood in terms of *praxeological knowledge*, which might be seen as a fusion of the three Habermasian modes and sharing each of their corresponding *interests* – interpretative, law-bound (structural) and emancipatory. This is why Bourdieu insists on maintaining *epistemological vigilance*. Keeping these *interests* discrete can never amount to Habermasian *communicative action* or *competence* for him, since each imply a particular scholastic rather than practical understanding of (and thus relation to) the social world. This distinction needs to be objectified in presenting scientific knowledge as part of a reflexive undertaking in its very constitution. Indeed, reflexivity then becomes a principal pre-requisite condition of the possibility of Bourdieusian science as it sets the boundaries between the research subject and the object of research.

The Limits of the Subject-Object Divide

It is again important to stress that Bourdieu's *theory of practice* begins in practice and ends in practice – the first empirical, the second scientific – its generative principle is therefore practice, as are its *conditions of possibility*. So, how do we achieve this reflexive *practical gaze* of practice *in* practice expressed practically? The short answer is by not simply employing these concepts in research but going beyond them and turning them on the research product and researcher as well; and not as some *post hoc* adjunct but as a central part of the entire research process.

Bourdieu clearly saw empirical data through his personal (developing) *habitus* to the objective conditions of their own creation: both needing to be considered as the subject and the object of science. This is partly why he argues that researchers must not feign objectivity as some sort of "disinterested other", and would do better to rely on their own subjective experience in understanding "the objective" (Bourdieu, 2000c). But not, it must be stressed, subjectivity as the empirical – non-reflexive – self, but "scientifically", by thinking in terms of structural relations and developing an "ec-static" language to express a dynamic process. This way of acting is more an ontology than epistemology, as noted in Part II, as it acts both on the object of research and the objectifying subject. Acting from a Bourdieusian perspective, in terms of structural relations instead of positing a disinterested, Archimedean, substantialist viewpoint, therefore needs to be understood as having a causal efficacy on the research object, not simply in terms of a "gaze" (crudely often expressed as "lens"), since it implies practical consequences (and interests) both in terms of its construction and the consequences of analysis. Basically, we already construct the world by what we see and do not see (and why this is the case). There is then a clear distinction between the empirical and scientific *habitus* for Bourdieu – their respective ontologies and epistemologies. The fact that this *theory of practice* is embodied in the concepts – *habitus, field* and *capital* – means that these then need to be regarded as active epistemological matrices capable of affecting ontology and consequent understanding in terms of the phenomeno-logical relationship to the social world – ultimately, both scientifically *and* empirically. Bourdieusian language (concepts) is then epistemologically charged and can provide the *possibility of understanding of* (empirical) practice *as* practice *in* practice, finally to be lived in (emancipatory) practice. To paraphrase Bourdieu: the science of this mode of knowledge finds its foundation in a theory of practice as practice, meaning an activity founded in cognitive operations, which mobilise a mode of knowing, which is not that of theory and concept . . . (but) a sort of ineffable participation in an object known (in practice) (see Bourdieu,

1992: 433 my translation). Language is then both social and personal, and carries meaning from one to the other. The language of his key concepts (carrying an underlying epistemological theory of practice) are partly intended to lay bare the nature of that relationship and, in so doing, change it.

In a very Wittgensteinian sense, Bourdieu argues that language only has meaning in terms of the *situations* within which it is immersed at any one time and place – literally, a game! For him, the schemes of perception which individuals hold, and the language which carries them, are each homologously linked to social structures, which act as both their provenance and social destiny. Just as social agents exist in *network relations*, therefore, words also exist in *networks of semantic relations* to each other – and partly acquire their meaning in terms of difference and similarity *with respect to each other* in specific time and place. Sense and meaning, then, are always determined in the interplay between individual meaning and the social context in which language is being expressed. Such contexts are set within *social space* – often as *fields* – that is, bounded areas of activity: for example, education, culture, politics, etc. Words form a part of such *social space* and *fields* and are ultimately used to represent their *particular way of thinking*. By entering a *field* (implying a semantic network), a word thus takes on meaning *from that field* and defines meaning; which itself differs according to its position within the overall *field* and thus semantic *space*. The attribution of meaning is therefore also a kind of imposition (originating from the *field* context) – what Bourdieu terms a kind of *transformation and transubstantiation* where meaning is changed from one context to another: "the substance signified is the signifying form which is realized" (1991b: 143) in practice. In other words, what is signified and signifying is socially co-terminus for Bourdieu; the meaning necessary to a *field* context is realised in the particular lexical/semantic form. So, words can have one meaning in one context and another elsewhere. It is an imposition because any specific meaning can be projected onto a word – signifying signifier – prior to it being signified as a sign (word).

So, we need to see *habitus* and *field* as outside of this, to a certain extent; that is, not relative to social actualisation but somehow "scientific" – i.e. implying stability of sense and meaning.

We know the world is relational and that language is also relational. The question then becomes what is the relationship between the two; and, in particular, the empirical and scientific world? If they both conform to the same logic, it might therefore be argued that the language of Bourdieu's theory of practice is just as relative as any other. Absolute relativity is, of course, at the base of Post-modern philosophy and draws attention to a certain "nothing" behind words – or, at best, extreme referral. Derrida is a key proponent of this view and criticises any prescribing of meaning by breaking the link between linguistic *signifier* and *signified*. For him meaning is always *differed* – elsewhere (actually nowhere!!). Similarly, it follows that for him the concept is nothing more than a metaphor –

an image to convey what lies beneath reality – with no representational truth. Pushed to an extreme, this argument claims that to do otherwise amounts to nothing more than the philosophical intention to dominate the world through metaphor. Indeed, Bourdieusian concepts are often taken and used in this metaphorical way; with a common view that it is possible to regard data through a Bourdieusian *lens*. Such a metaphoric deployment of these concepts needs to be seen as an attempt to rationalise a data set, to make it contingent and mastered by rationality. Such is completely conducive with Derridean post-modernist philosophy and the arguments he makes for the non-representational deployment of language. Indeed, he argues that nothing surpasses metaphor that is not itself also metaphoric. Metaphor is itself hence dominated by this metaphoric process and would seem to capture Bourdieu's concepts in its turn. However, this is a recipe for again ensnaring thought and language (theory and practice) within a sort of self-referential nihilistic spiral of deflection. All language for Derrida is prone to this, even poetic language (and here we might recall the predilections of such as Marcus and Fischer for employing "poetics" in place of analytic narratives in their ethnographies). But, Derrida argues, such poetics still set out to be both descriptive and objective, that is equally metaphoric and scientific, rational and rigorous – so, hence, solve nothing (all are metaphoric for him). In other words, metaphor cannot master language, thus cannot master a reality beyond words. In sum, language – and the concept – cannot master language – and the concept.

We might as well argue that what is needed is a concept of language which is not language itself, or indeed, a concept of practice which is not itself a practice in understanding practice. Philosophy, as theory of metaphor, will have been first a metaphor of theory. It follows that theory itself can be seen as a metaphor – as an act of seeing. This is why it is so easy to simply *metaphorise* data with descriptive concepts in a Bourdieusian way. If one is to go beyond this, then a rigorous understanding/application of reflexivity both in the actual formation and deployment of concepts at an exegetic level is critical; i.e., in its very act of becoming. How to do this?

Kant and a Theory of Knowledge

I believe that at this point it is worth revisiting Kant on knowledge and understanding as he is a philosopher who attempted to account for experience and how we make sense of it in terms of conceptual thinking.

Kant's philosophy sets out to move away from earlier relativist views of knowledge about the external world, as dependent on sense perceptions and/or beliefs. His attempt to found an "objective knowledge" out of metaphysics was aimed at giving scientific status to what otherwise might be considered individual subjective interpretation (Bourdieu's empirical knowledge). For him, the knowable could only be grasped through the *faculties of the mind*, which made it essentially empiricist (practical by any other word for Bourdieu). These faculties included desire and feeling, but it is the cognitive which is particularly important in this case as it includes *imagination, understanding* and *reason*. He argues that *Imagination* represents a sense object to the mind and *Understanding* classifies and orders the data. *Reason* is then the attempt to understand it in terms of these faculties and is unconditional; ideas of reason exist in and through understanding itself. For Kant, data are then "sensed" by the *imagination*; but *a priori* knowledge is needed for this; for example, concepts of space and time as conditions of existence. Understanding then has the power to form concepts about this experience through *a priori* knowledge: it is in this way that understanding "knows" – that is, through such categories (concepts) as substance, relation, position, etc. Such categories are also shared – they pertain to common assent. What if we add *habitus, field* and *capital* to this list of categories so that we take understanding as represented in the mind through such concepts; formed *a priori*, not as a part of human discourse but as a result of an application of Bourdieusian theory of practice? For Kant, *a priori* categories and the relationship between imagination, knowledge, sense data and understanding amount in essence to what he describes as the "transcendental aesthetic" – literally, sense data experienced in terms of *a priori* knowledge. Objects of thought may come as things themselves or representational objects, or indeed the *conditions of representation*. In fact, I am arguing that these conditions of representation can be understood as Bourdieu's *conditions of possibility* as referred to earlier. In this way, the "knowing subject" for Kant, is replaced by the *functioning of consciousness* for Bourdieu and defines the relation between subject and object. By giving a Bourdieusian twist to this line of argument, I am suggesting that his conceptual tools can offer a quality of knowledge and understanding that is socially constructed and contingent whilst escaping extreme forms of post-modernist relativity; thus, redefining what we mean by subjectivity and objectivity.

Of course, Bourdieu wrote that the divide between objectivity and subjectivity was the most "ruinous" in the social sciences, and also claimed that his intent was to make "a science of the dialectical relations between objective structures . . . and the subjective dispositions, within which these structures are actualised, and which tend to reproduce them" (1977b: 3). And, as we have seen, such structures need to be understood as gradations along a continuum between the ideational and the material. Concepts such as *habitus* and *field* are hence critically important for Bourdieu as a way of mediating the relationship between subject, object and context. Again, this enquiry deserves being pursued so we can understand the nature of the relationship between them, in particular, in terms of the individual and the social.

The subject-object relation itself rests at the base of phenomenology, the view of structure of which Bourdieu so evidently shares. In the *Phenomenology of Perception*, for example, Merleau-Ponty writes:

> This subject-object dialogue, this drawing together, by the subject, of the meaning diffused through the object, and, by the object, of the subject's intentions – a process which is physiognomic perception – arranges round the subject a world which speaks to him of himself, and gives his own thoughts their place in the world.
>
> (1962: 132)

In this way, for Merleau-Ponty, the world as constituting sense is immanent and speaks to us *of ourselves*; it is also an "embodiment" – what Bourdieu would refer to as *hexis* – not simply based in mental activity. In a strange way, "I understand the world and it understands me" (2000c: 408) – an echo of Pascal, quoted by Bourdieu. This is a clearly a very subtle point: Merleau-Ponty does not intend that the world is sentient, as human. It is subject consciousness that "sees" the world; but this world still "calls" on the subject to know what it already knows, to be conscious of what it is already "conscious" of.

Such leads us to a consideration of the nature of consciousness itself as an expression of this relation. To this extent, subject-object exists as a single "flesh"; for Merleau-Ponty and Bourdieu in his turn, they are intimately connected, and one only leaves off where another begins and vice versa. This is not to say that the visible blends into us, or we to it; rather, "the seer and the visible reciprocate one another and we no longer know which sees and which is seen" (Merleau-Ponty 1968: 139). The flesh then appears as an element – like water, air, fire and earth, rather than an actual thing: spiritual/material, mind/matter, idea of thing.

To return to Kant, when sense data as an object is intuited by imagination, there is a point of intuitive resonance that lies beyond the individual judgement – of right and wrong, for example – and represents the power to form judgments itself: that is, a sense of understanding that is literally "beyond knowing", an empathy or identification but of universal assent. How does this come about? (Kant, 1956/1788, 1961/1781, 1987/1790 – see Grenfell and Hardy, 2007: 36–39 for a summary).

If we take artistic aesthetics as an example, the distinction between *sensation* and the *beautiful* is useful here, where the faculty of feeling replaces structure derived from concepts. The beautiful – a sub-set of sense data – is again presented to understanding (in time and space) by imagination, but is not converted via conceptual categorisations because non-cognitive feeling accompanies intuition: in other words, non-cognitive feelings replace concepts. Since there is no conceptual categorisation to provide form, what is presented is *the power to form concepts itself*. A consciousness without anything to be conscious of – it is "disinterested" – that is contemplative rather than cognitive (conceptual/theoretical). In Kant's philosophy of art, this is *transcendental aesthetics – the disinterested pure gaze* – that lies beyond sensation. However, the key point here, for Bourdieu, is that this is not a universal of pure aesthetics, but the reflection of a certain – bourgeois – relationship to the world (see 1984a): superior, detached, masterful, but empty – a kind of absence because it reflects its own position in the social world (neither one thing or another) – a kind of *nothingness*.

The ambition for "objective knowledge" in science might be seen as also sharing the same sense of "disinterestedness": "what Bourdieu would call the aspiration of "*knowledge without a knowing subject*" – Popperian World 3. In this case, it is less that data are presented by imagination to understanding without concepts, but that pre-existing – *a priori* – concepts provide the power to form. But, here, it is "concepts" with a particular social provenance and relation to the world, and thus interest – positivist. In effect, it is the cognitive effect of the aesthetic side of the bourgeois power to transcend – but, this time through objective knowledge – by asserting not so much *the truth* but a certain *truth* which carries with it its own undisclosed interest and thus legitimacy and consecration; this time legitimated in the name of reason. We might even say that *knowledge without a knowing subject* is akin to the pure aesthetic gaze in its claim to a transcendent objectivity, when it is nothing other than the transcendental sense of the bourgeois intellingentia, and its relative structural position in society: what Bourdieu once described as "thoughtless power and powerless thought". The outcome is an – un-reflexive – interest in asserting this knowing and misrecognising its inherent relative relationship to the world.

Bourdieu wants to replace such *objective knowledge* with *reflexive objectivity* – *practical rationality* and *praxeological knowledge*. Terms like *habitus, field* and *capital* therefore need to be embodied and actualised as intense *epistemological matrices*. Another way of expressing the same argument would be in terms of "semantic density" (see Maton, 2014); in other words, they are not just conceptual terms or descriptive metaphors but contain a kind of epistemological "genome" through which sense data are apprehended and understood. In a sense, the ultimate source behind such concepts is not the bourgeois nothingness alluded to above with respect to that certain relationship to society but emancipatory (critical) knowledge, which again represents a different relationship to society and its knowledge structure. Here, *habitus, field* and *capital* might even be seen as acting as a *kind of epistemological mordant* between subject and object (the empirical and scientific subject): an *a priori* epistemological understanding which conveys the principle of practice instantiated in the present – as they speak *to* us and *of* us: to see oneself as *habitus, field* and *capital* at the point of seeing and of what is seen. These terms hence carry the notion of contingent understanding, but not one of tentativeness or conjecture. Rather, they lead to a form of *radical doubt* (Bourdieu, 1992: 235) on the part of the researcher; a kind of Rortyan *final vocabulary* (Rorty, 1980) as a pragmatic expression of the best we can do at any one particular time. They further stabilise knowledge in a way, which shares many of the features of Popperian theory – predictability, generalisability, open to articulation, useful and simple. Such amounts to an ambition to form a theory of practice that aims to be distinct from both objectivist abstraction, and the intoxicating subjective familiarity of common sense interpretation apprehended in its everyday obviousness.

The difficulty is when *the subject makes for themselves an object – in their own image* – and thus with all the implied assumptions of view. This is inevitable to a certain extent. However, if that making is carried out in terms of Bourdieusian concepts – praxeologically validated – then, as I have argued, terms such as *habitus*, *field* and *capital*, etc. can mediate between subject and object in a way that constitutes a *different interest*: an interest with a different ethical, value-based generative principle. Basically, this offers, and indeed allows, a different – emancipatory – view of the world. Consequently, instead of a subject objectifiying an object *as an object*, the subject sees itself literally in it: but not as a subjective mirror of individual empirical identity but at an epistemological moment grounded in the same generative principles as their scientific practice. In this way, as Bourdieu states it in *The Weight of the World* (1999: 609), it is less about seeing oneself in another than as being "able to take up all possible points of view", recognising that, faced with the same conditions, one would likely *be* and *do* the same. This is not to be every man/woman, and for everyone to be the same, but to see the structural relations and principles in exegesis – immanent – that manifest themselves in *this way at this particular time and place and individual*, knowing that given the same conditions *we may well act and be the same*. One acknowledges and sees oneself in others and others in oneself as the outcome of particular formative conditions; not as a separate object-other. Bourdieu calls this knowledge a "spiritual exercise" (ibid.: 612) and a sort of "intellectual love" (ibid. possibly borrowed from Spinoza) – a "non-violent" method since it offers no imposition of meaning, *no symbolic violence*. There is here no authority, nor the faculty to "think things independently".

It is also a kind of love because it is based on mutual recognition and regard; a high form of attention. It is the product of Being reflecting on Being in a state of collective social identity. At this point, Bourdieu's epistemology does indeed become an ontology. We might call this Objective Subjectivity or Subjective Objectivity, which amount to and are the same. To articulate this level of understanding and knowledge is always *a posteriori*. But, mostly, in reality it is realised at a point of instantiation. It is also a case of the past and the future literally *being* in the present, which is, really, the only place they can exist. This is a consciousness or reflexive refraction through Bourdieusian theory of practice and concepts such as *habitus*, *field* and *capital*. The empirical *habitus* is scientific and the scientific *habitus* is empirical. The transcendental sense beyond the power to form concepts then becomes less the bourgeois sense of nothingness – the pure objective or aesthetic gaze – but *the logical essence of practice itself*, which is nothing other than the past (a sociological history) instantiating itself in the present (a historical sociology) – a kind of sociological *karma*. This power *to be* present – this process – is "grasped" at the point *of* and *in* becoming rather than in the thing itself formed.

We might conclude that reflexivity is less concerned with "how *to do* it" than "how *to be* it". The researcher is implicated in his theorising; the gaze is necessarily "personal" but with the potential for praxeological science. It might be seen as a theory that is a gaze and a gaze that is expressed in theoretical terms, but one that also furnishes us with a theory that can generate the gaze in practice – if understood in terms beyond the concepts to their generation – in and through practice. The gaze is then subject to the gaze which is subject to the gaze which is subject to the gaze as a kind of internal recurrence, but is not eternally recurrent in a nihilistic post-modernist way as it is bounded by reflexive concepts of practice in practice. Basically, we always return to the same principles of practice. Time is the deciding factor here.

The Reflexive Self

It might seem that reflexivity is not explicitly apparent in the early and mid-period Bourdieu's work. And, some even find the personal "revelations" – summed up as "le Rosebud de Pierre Bourdieu" in *Le Nouvel Observateur* at the time of his death – or his final lecture at the *Collège de France*, published later in the *Sketch for a Self-Analysis* (2007/2004) to be a somewhat *post hoc* formulation of how "he would wish to be read" (for example, see Lamont, 2012). They do not see the empirical studies carried out in the Béarn, or Algeria and indeed in Education, as necessarily reflexive. Even *Homo Academicus* can be read as Bourdieu reflecting on his own professional field *in retrospect*. At the same time, reflexivity was clearly an inherent part of Bourdieu's initial research endeavours in the way he brought his own *habitus* – both professional and personal – to the objects of his studies. Moreover, as noted, the original French version of *Outline* had a chapter on "the observer observed" (pp. 225–234) and, from the *leçons* given in Paris from the mid-1980s, we see an explicit awareness of the need for a "sociology of sociology" as a way of breaking out of the box in which contemporary sociologists have shut themselves (Bourdieu, 2016a: 1116). By the last decade of his career, of course, reflexivity was clearly central to Bourdieu's concerns (see Bourdieu, 1990d, 1992, 2007). Finally, he extended the reflexive element of his work as an attempt *to objectify the social forces that acted upon him* (Bourdieu, 2007/2004; see also Eakin, 2001); offering the method as of use equally to a general and academic public (for example, Bourdieu, 2000c). At base of such reflexivity is an epistemological epiphany described above. The outcome of this vision can itself be expressed as the ontological *separation* he made between his own *empirical subject* and *scientific subject*:

> The scientific habitus can be independent in relation to the habitus. Basically, there are two subjects. There is the empirical subject. Myself, when I go to a meeting, I am like everyone. I am nervous. I am angry. I say, "this guy is an idiot, why does he say that? I agree with the other one".

> Like everyone. When I analyse that, it is not the same subject. It is a subject that objectifies that, who understands why Bourdieu is angry. It is another subject, which is very difficult to maintain in life. In everyday life, one becomes an empirical subject once again . . . but it is possible to create a kind of torn out subject . . . and the more it is collective and reflexive, the more it is separate from the empirical subject . . . I have learnt with age and experience that the knowing subject can change the naïve subject a little. There are things that one understands better and suffers from less.
>
> (1995, op. cit.: 38–39)

So, a reflexive approach cannot ultimately be only an individual enterprise but necessitates a collective commitment; others have pointed out the necessity of a collective response (see Deer, 2014/2008), what Shirato and Webb (2003) refer to as a field "meta-literacy". There is a paradox because Bourdieu was so scathing about other forms of reflexivity – with their illusion of being able to "transcend thought by the power of thought itself". Rather, for him, it is a question of transcending both empirical and conventional scholastic thinking by the power of his theory of practice and the epistemological vision it makes available. No wonder he referred to it as a *metanoia*.

At the end of Arthur Miller's biography *Time Bends* (1987/1995) he writes about looking out at the field behind his house from the writing desk on which he had created so much work. He comments that he looked at the trees, the ones he had seen through so many seasons. And, at one point, a sort of chiasmic reversal takes place as he realises that it is the trees that are looking at him.

The notion, therefore, of developing an individual reflexive attention is one way of developing the strength of reflexive objectivity in our work as language ethnographers. Indeed, all that is really objective depends on the quality and the extent of our attention to reflexivity in the way here described. So, this is necessary on an individual researcher level. In one sense, it is a division of attention: partly within, partly without, and partly among those working in this way. This is not just an individual condition, but one developed within, for and by the associated collectivity of researchers working in this way. Developing such a reflexive practice more fully collectively is even qualitatively something more. Something like: rather than us holding the collective epistemology in the presence of our individual reflexivity, the collective holding us. The cultivation of this two-way reflexive relationship is critical: in other words, collective reflexivity, while simultaneously practicing individual reflexive capacity. This condition can be understood as a singular reflexive attention, but a singular on quite a different collective level.

This collective-singular condition that lies at the heart of Bourdieu's reflexivity: a singular subjectivity that does not make of itself an object; a subject that instead sees itself in the object, and the object as an expression of the subject – but this time not empirical and un-reflexive but as a "scientific" presence within a self-acknowledged collectivity. In this way, Bourdieu calls on all of us to see ourselves in society but also society in ourselves; not as two separated events but as co-terminus – thus, the individual and the community. God and Man: he reminds us at the end of *Pascalian Meditations* that "society is God" (2000b: 245), meaning that such is not simply an academic or intellectual activity, but an expression of truth – a consciousness/attention that is a higher form of love – identification of sameness and difference as one and the same thing. We then see the social forces of what is potential, impossible and necessary – even what is good and evil in the world – since it allows a view which is able to observe the very point where the empirical self enters between subject and object to allow misrecognition in terms of judgement and the expression of self/group interests, turning away from and at the expense of a potential liberatorial reflexive scientific view. To grasp this ethical dimension of Bourdieu, if only for an instant, is certainly beyond the words we use but can guide what we do as a result.

Conclusion

In is clear from the discussion in this chapter that in order to understand reflexivity, and work reflexively, we need to tease out not only the relationship between the subject and object, but also how it is articulated and the language used to express it. Heidegger once referred to language as the "house of being" and we have seen the extent to which epistemology and ontology are collapsed within a Bourdieusian paradigm. So much so that out theory and practice, our method and analysis, our narrative accounts are all part of one reflexive epistemological vision: however, it is not a "transcendent vision", but a practically lived one. We have a theory of practice from Bourdieu, which furnishes us not only with a language of association, but an association in itself. To this extent, it is not fanciful to think of individual researchers working in this way as a "community of practice". If such requires a reflexive attitude on the part of those active in the researcher field, it also asks for a reflexive reading of the emergent texts on the part of their audience. It is a disservice to the ambitions being attempted in this project if accounts of research conducted in this way are treated "outside of the method field", as just another research tract liable to be "fair game". In this way, Bourdieu is indeed challenging not only our everyday understandings of the world but our academic ones as well.

In dealing with "language-based ethnographies", it seems that we have spent a lot of time attempting to get "beyond words" themselves, or at least using them from a *praxeological attitude* to lead us to the nature and use of reflexivity within them. Finally, as with Bourdieu, it is worth stressing that this is an unfolding journey – both practically and philosophically. Indeed, we might even see using Bourdieu as characteristic of certain "levels" of understanding and application:

- Level 1: Use of Key Concepts – for example, *habitus, field, capital* – to animate a narrative.
- Level 2: Planning a Research Project systematically from a Bourdieusian theory of practice. A common focus here begins with the biographical and qualitative analysis (*habitus*) and works up.
- Level 3: More Critical Approach to Research Object Construction – a sustained attempt to map the *field* and *fields* within fields, with greater use of quantitative methods. The focus here often begins with the *field* and its relationship within *fields* and works down to *habitus*.
- Level 4: A greater consolidation of the three phases and the three levels described earlier in this chapter with a more sustained reflexive relationship – participant objectivation – to the research.
- Level 5: Developing a fully formed praxeological attitude – metanoia – to all aspects of research activity.
- Level 6: Internalising the theory of practice at an indivdual subjective level: the epsistemology becomes an individual ontology. The empirical *habitus* is increasingly superceded by the scientific *habitus*: at this point, the carriers of the epsietomology – the key concepts – begin to fade.
- Level 7: Emergence of Reflexive Objectivity as a singular and group consciousness.
- Level 8: . . .

It goes without saying that these should not be read as linear or hierarchical but as *potentia* – and can be realised temporarally at any one instant in conducting research.

CONCLUSION

This book began with an enquiry into the way language-based ethnographies have a wide and multifarious history and, in the Introduction, we described how each of its principal themes needed to be seen as a complex interweaving of ideas and practice. Part of our intent has been to unpick these strands and somewhat reassemble them in a conscious manner in both assessing past and suggesting a steer to future practice.

Our *point de départ* was ethnography itself and its roots in classical anthropology. The history of studying cultures is a lengthy one and, invariably, language has been included in much of it. However, it is only in comparatively recent times that the focus has been on language itself; in other words, the anthropological causation and effects of language within a culture. If such is true generally, there has a been a particular enthusiasm in educational research to look at the ways language manifests itself in pedagogic processes, partly in terms of social differentiation. We know that so-called objective standards of functional literacy have been somewhat eclipsed by a more nuanced view of language events as socio-culturally conditioned. New Literacy Studies announced this direction and has, in turn, given birth to a much wider view of literacy as a prescribed norm in all sorts of social activities: the arts and creativity, gender and nationality, private and public life. How these are expressed in language and also shaped by language form the foundational concerns of language-focused ethnography. But, reflexivity is another thing.

Human beings are by their nature "reflexive" and both our conscious and unconscious minds are in a state of continual reflexive flux– implicitly and explicitly. Anthropology has also always been a reflexive enterprise since it involves one observing another, which must necessitate questions about the status of observer and the observed. But, finally, outcomes of such are both formulated and expressed in language, which itself can be scrutinised in terms of the provenance and social constructions buried within it. Part I of our book tracked these relationships and alighted on the nature of reflexivity itself. We saw a range of interpretations and uses of reflexivity. We contrasted *reflexivity* with *reflectivity*. On the one hand, reflection may be no more than a little semi-conscious self-awareness or *post hoc* dwelling on the effectiveness of a particular practical activity. Yet, on the other hand, we raised issues of reflexivity within the contemporary philosophy, which challenge our understanding of both what it is to be human, and indeed the language we have at our disposal to express ourselves. Invariably, such enquiries involve research activity – what we do and why? – and the status of its outcomes. In the final analysis, these questions pertain to the very nature of our individual subjectivities and our attempts to make stable objective statements about the world. Why Bourdieu?

Bourdieu is known perhaps primarily as a sociologist but, as we have noted, his is a sociology that is heavily imbibed with both philosophy and anthropology. Moreover, issues about language are central to his oeuvre. We offered something of his own personal and professional trajectory in Part I and showed how, based on ethnographic field-work, he developed a theory of practice which can be defined in terms of its reflexive nature. How that is done, and with what conceptual tools, are central to his research method. It is in that spirit that we took Bourdieu into the practical case accounts in Part II. In each case, we offered the opportunity to researchers who had conducted language-based ethnographies, and had once recourse to Bourdieu in doing so, to reflect on their activities with the passage of time, again deploying thinking about reflexivity derived from a Bourdieusian perspective. What emerged was often messy and personal, but touching on issues that are real and totally relevant to any discussion about the conduct of language ethnography and its outcomes. Inviting in the personal we in no way detach ourselves from the socially authentic – quite the opposite.

It is out of these accounts that we were able to distill out key aspects and dimensions of reflexivity exhibited by our researchers. We felt it was important to take these for what they are in the first instance; in other words, without imposing too overtly a developed theoretical interpretation. Nevertheless, we also wanted to also approach these accounts with a more formal statement of what we know about language and reflexivity, and even develop a more speculative thinking in going beyond it. Part III of this book, therefore, included both the immediately authentic and further theoretical explorations. What this has amounted to for the book as a whole, in effect, is a span, which includes the most mundane and utilitarian and the furthest reaches of theoretical expression. These positions are represented in the minutiae of everyday lived experience and the best we can achieve in theoretical abstraction. Yet, in terms of theory and practice we see them as one and the same thing, and each sharing epistemological and ontological conditions. In this light, to be "practical" *is* saturated with theoretical assumptions, implied or otherwise, whereas to "theorise" *is* a practical activity. As such, it is an issue of context relationship.

The whole book was described as a "journey" at the outset, and it has been one that has constructed a kind of three-part sandwich for us, with practical research being placed between contextual issues of theory and reflections on outcomes, which take forward our thinking about the place of reflexivity in language-based research. We would make the following summary points.

First, central to our scholarly practice in language-based ethnographies has been the very "construction of the research object" since it is at this initial stage that three principle elements of the research are defined: the relationship to the object in relation to the personal perspectives of the researcher and their position in the academic field; the language used to represent it; and therefore the degree of convergence or divergence instantiated in any one particular stance. Research fields are invariably conservative in preserving their own particular orthodoxies because of the interests such hold up. Therefore, to conform to or break from such *doxa* is a seminal epistemological act with "political" consequences. Bourdieu's is a radical and critical theoretical perspective, and encourages such a "rupture" or "break" from the conventionalities of academic discourse in seeking to found the praxeological gaze he is advocating.

Second, "construction of the research object" was stated at one of the three defining aspects of Bourdieusian research: the other two being *field analysis* and *participant objectivation*. We have stressed the necessity of invoking the full scope of these three, and not just as a single act, but co-terminus in the research inter-vention. Research object construction is, in a way, a "pre-reflexive reflexivity" but must involve the practical plan for *field* analysis and *participant objectivation*. In other words, the three aspects need to be active throughout the research project and build on each other. Similarly, we have drawn attention to the "levels" of *field* analysis: the *field* and the *field* of power; the *field* itself; and the *habitus* of those involved in the *field* and the positions they occupy within it. Again, without wishing to prescribe methodological rules, we have suggested that all three need to be taken into consideration and related to each other in data collection and analysis, as our researchers did in their discussion in Part II.

Third, is language itself. We have gone to some lengths to address both the multifarious forms of language and their respective effects; and there have been examples of the abstract and mundane, the concrete and the hypothetical, the practical and the theoretical. Language is often used in a very everyday, semi-automatic way in the ethnographic studies reported upon in Part II, but then these are sorted and discussed in principled ways, which include the theoretical. Language is then again used to reflect on the research where all sorts of issues emerge; including time, contingency, affect and gender. As a whole, such con-stitute dynamics of power and identity, played out both within the ethnographies and the researchers relationship to them, which are similarly expressed in language.

"Beware of words", we have quoted Bourdieu as warning – or at least, "be aware" of them for the power they carry and instill. That power can be libertorial but it can also be ensnaring as it conditions not just what we think, but what we *can* think – which has serious consequences for the outcomes of our research activities. In a way, it is easy to be captured by language, or at least key terms of phrases which seduce us by appealing to our most undisclosed elective affinities, those most deeply rooted in our empirical selves and constituent of our upbringing. Bourdieu's theory of practice – practically derived, theoretically expressed and empirically exemplified – is intended as the means to escape such misrecognitions and move towards a genuinely "enlightened" science.

Fourth, is this issue of links between philosophy and anthropology within which Bourdieu's method situates itself – somewhat precariously. Besides the practical insistence of epistemological vigilance – itself involving ontological challenges for the researcher – is the whole "science of language" as it now exists: from the most functionally empirical to the most post-modernist relative. During the twentieth century, the philosophy of man became to the philosophy of language, but did so at a time when the whole stability of language was being undermined by post-modernist thinking. The end results were sometimes for researchers to become almost diffident in expressing anything, as language could not be relied on to provide objective accounts. If research findings gravitated to "poetics and politics", researcher reflexivity similarly spiralled into a nihilistic black hole of supreme relativity. In this world, everything is contingent, equal and, ultimately, meaningless – literally. Bourdieu theory and the conceptual tools he provides, somewhat takes us to the edge of this abyss; so, whereas he insists of the power and contingency of language, the tools are intended to "stabilise" the discourse sufficiently to be able to say something useful about the object of research, in its praxeological manifestation, albeit couched in what he terms "radical doubt". But, such doubt, although contingent, is not timorous but offers its findings in the light of "the best we can presently do" and our "final vocabulary", which is of course never final – but ongoing, unfolding. Such a research undertaking somewhat necessitates the revisiting of analyses and projects exemplified in our Part II case examples.

Fifth, and by extension, is the whole parallel between the subject and object (indeed subjectivity and objectivity), and the signifier and the signified in language. The crux of the matter is that anyone alighting in one *or* the other somewhat necessarily excludes the other. Describing them in this bipolar way leads to an inescapable trap, or vicious circle, which spirals back into a kind of intellectual feedback loop. Such is the nature of the conscious mind. Any alternative requires a different way of thinking – dialectical or divided thinking – which seeks to appre-hend explanation and understanding in the very act of explanation and under-standing: always in flux and of the moment – even if subsequently literary conventions require a stable version for be offered. In this book, we have argued that such a praxeological attitude is incumbent on the researcher to develop, as it is on the reader. Un-reflexive reading is just as damaging as un-reflexive writing.

Sixth, therefore, is reflexivity itself, which resides, we have seen, not in the subject or the object – not in the chosen sign or the signifier – but in the exact relationship between the two – the synapse of understanding. At this point, the subect (researcher) does not make of itself an object (research) but sees itself as one and the same. In the biased view, this is simply to reassert and empirical *habitus*, however socio-culturally derived. Yet, what Bourdieu's epistemology suggests is that it is possible to create another "scientific" (knowledge-based) *habitus*, which is somehow "torn out" of the pre-set constructions of social origins; and this is done through language and the epistemology it carries.

Seventh, two profound implications follow from this position. First, it is not something that is accomplished overnight. In our final chapter, we expressed the "levels" that researchers have to go through in their thinking and practice – and this scheme was partly derived from empirical observations and personal experience. The intention here is not to assert precedence or superiority but to see a developmental form of thinking and practice that emerges in the course of prolonged engagement with a Bourdieusian perspective in a range of research projects, including those focusing on language. Second, this "gaze" – what Bourdieu describes as *metanoia* – only occurs when this epistemological way of seeing the world is imbied to such an extent that the scientific *habitus* somewhat displaces the empirical one. Curiously, at this point, the conceptual terms – expressed in language – seem to fade away as one sees the social world in exegesis in terms of the generating structures of social discourse where interests and power are played out in *field* contexts between individuals endowed with differential forms and quantity of symbolic power. At this point, there is almost no need to name them, in the same way that there is no need to name all the notes in appreciating a Beethoven sonata. If his seems like somewhat of a personal epiphany – indeed where epistemology becomes ontology – we have also stressed that it can only sustain itself if it is a shared experience. Initially, Bourdieusian terms allow a "language of association" within a "community of practice". However, such necessitates reflexivity on/in its own differentiated structures with varying activity and apprehensions. Ultimately, we move towards a position where the individual gaze and the group gaze are one and the same. At this point, to think as an individual is to think the group; and, perhaps more importantly, group thinking becomes that of the individual.

Finally, eighth, we have called the outcomes "reflexive objectivity"; since we believe it is the best term to describe the nature and status of the resultant knowledge and how it was derived. As we have seen, it is a reflexivity that is rigorous and epistemologically charged, and an objectivity that is stable but dynamic.

We live in a world that seems to be becoming increasingly precarious; and language and its effects is a central cause for concern in explaining that precariousness. Besides the effects of postmodernism and the fragmentation of sense that it results in, there has been the whole rise of social media and the way the world has become language-information driven. But, again, in so becoming, language is incriminated in the very dissolution of once accepted modernist aspirations. We see democracy challenged, inequality justified and continual war accepted – all in the use of language that is called into being and made use of by individuals and groups with their own particular *interests*. Besides postmodernism, we now refer to post-human – indeed, post-truth, post-theory, post-feminist and the like. We are certainly not wishing to dismiss any of these. It is clear that we live in a world that is awash with language and literacy in its various forms, visual and otherwise. To this extent, we feel the arguments presented in this book extend beyond the concerns of language ethnographers and their particular methods, as the writers show up for us the realities of life and what we might said about them – and indeed how. The kind of perspectives we have managed to distill out from their experience and readings warrant closer examination for the light they shed on a range of issues at the centre of which is just what is the relationship between ourselves and the other – whatever and whoever that might be – and the language which we call upon to both express and sustain it.

ABOUT THE AUTHORS

Michael Grenfell

Michael Grenfell has held Chair positions in in Ireland, Scotland and England, including 1905 Chair of Education in Trinity College Dublin, Research Director at the University of Southampton, and Adjunct Professor at the University of Canberra, Australia. He has an extensive background of research on Bourdieu, with whom he worked on various projects including three periods as visiting scholar at the *École des Hautes Études*, Paris. His publications include: *Bourdieu: Agent Provocateur* (2004), *Arts Rules: Bourdieu and the Visual Arts* (2007, with C. Hardy), *Bourdieu, Language and Linguistics* (2007), *Bourdieu: Key Concepts* (Routledge, 2012), *Language, Ethnography and Education* (Routledge, 2012), *Pierre Bourdieu* (Bloomsbury, 2014) and *Bourdieu and Data Analysis* (Lang, 2014).

Kate Pahl

Kate Pahl is a Professor of Arts and Literacy at Manchester Metropolitan University and Head of the Education and Social Research Institute there. Her work is concerned with literacy and language in communities with a focus on arts methodologies and co-production. Her publications include Campbell, Pahl, Pente and Rasool (Eds) *Re-Imagining Contested Communities* (Policy, 2018), together with *Materializing Literacies in Communities* (Bloomsbury, 2014). Her research is concerned with young people, voice, identity and civic engagement. For many years she has conducted longitudinal ethnographic work in Rotherham, UK with a focus on literacy and language.

Cheryl A. McLean

Cheryl McLean is an Associate Professor of Literacy and English Education at the Graduate School of Education, Rutgers University. Her research on adolescent literacy focuses on and explores the intersection of practices (language, texts and communicative tools), social contexts (environments, communities, local-global, digital and multimodal), culture and identity and pedagogical instruction.

Catherine Compton-Lilly

Catherine Compton-Lilly is the John C. Hungerpiller Professor at the University of South Carolina. As a professor in the College of Education, Dr. Compton-Lilly teaches courses in literacy studies and works with local educators. In her work, she follows eight of her former first grade students through high school. In a current study, now in its tenth year, she is exploring the longitudinal school experiences of children from immigrant families. Dr. Compton-Lilly has authored several books and many articles in major educational literacy journals including the *Reading Research Quarterly*, *Research in the Teaching of English*, *Written Communication* and the *Journal of Literacy Research*.

Lisya Seloni

Lisya Seloni is an Associate Professor of TESOL and Applied Linguistics in the Department of English at Illinois State University, where she teaches courses on, second language writing, TESOL methods and materials and cross-cultural issues in teaching English as an international language Her research explores ethnographic approaches to second language writing, academic socialisation and issues related to sociopolitical context of English language teaching and linguistic landscape in the city. She is specifically interested in the ways translingual writers construct knowledge and text in various writing environments across the disciplines. She is the co-author of *Ethnolinguistic Diversity and Literacy Education*. Her most recent publications have appeared in the *Journal of Second Language Writing*, *English for Specific Purposes*, *Language Policy* and the *Journal of Language and Politics*.

BIBLIOGRAPHY

Adorno, T. (1990/1966). *Negative Dialectics*. London: Routledge.

Agar, M. (1996). *The Professional Stranger: An Informal Introduction to Ethnography*. 2nd edition. New York: Academic Press.

Ahmed, S. (2004). *The Cultural Politics of Emotion*. Edinburgh: Edinburgh University Press.

Ahmed, S. (2017). *Living a Feminist Life*. Durham, NC: Duke University Press.

Anders, P. L., Yaden, Jr. D. B., Iddings, A. C., Da Silva, K. L., and Rogers, T. (2016). Editorial. *Journal of Literacy Research*, *48*, 3, 255–257.

Arnaut, K., Blommaert, J., Rampton, B., and Spotti, M. (Eds.) (2016). *Language and Superdiversity*. London: Routledge.

Bakhtin, M. M. (1981). *The Dialogic Imagination: Four Essays by M. M. Bakhtin*. (C. E. M. Holquist, Trans.). Austin, TX: University of Texas Press.

Bakhtin, M. M. (1986). *Speech Genres and Other Late Essays* (M. Holquist and C. Emerson, Eds.). Austin, TX: University of Texas Press.

Barad, K. (2007). *Meeting the Universe Half Way: Quantum Physics and the Entanglement of Matter*. Durham, NC: Duke University Press.

Barrett, E. and Bolt B. (2007). *Practice as Research*. Chippenham, UK: I.B. Tauris.

Barton, D. and Hamilton, M. (1998). *Local Literacies: Reading and Writing in One Community*. London and New York: Routledge.

Barton, D., Hamilton, M., and Ivanic, R. (Eds.) (2000). *Situated Literacies: Reading and Writing in Context*. London: Routledge.

Barwarshi, A. (2003). *Genre and the Invention of the Writer: Reconsidering the Place of Invention in Composition*. Logan, UT: Utah State University Press.

Baynham, M. and Prinsloo, M. (Eds.) (2009). *The Future of Literacy Studies*. Basingstoke, UK: Palgrave Macmillan.

Bazerman, C. and Prior, P. (2004). *What Writing Does and How It Does It: An Introduction to Analysis of Texts and Textual Practices*. Mahwah, NJ: Lawrence Erlbaum.

Blackburn, M. and Clark, C. (2007). *Literacy Research for Political Action and Social Change*. New York: Peter Lang.

Blackledge, A. and Creese, A. (2010). *Multilingualism*. London: Continuum Press.

Blommaert, J. (2008). *Grassroots Literacy: Writing, Identity and Voice in Central Africa*. London: Routledge.

Bloome, D. and Carter, S. (2004). *Discourse Analysis and the Study of Classroom Language and Literacy Events: A Microethnographic Perspective*. New York: Routledge.

Bloome, D., Beierle, M., Grigorenko, M., and Goldman, S. (2009). Learning over time: Uses of intercontextuality, collective memories, and classroom chronotopes in the construction of learning opportunities in a ninth-grade language arts classroom. *Language and Education, 23*, 4, 313–334.

Block, D. (2003). *The Social Turn in Second Language Acquisition*. Washington, D.C: Georgetown University Press.

Bourdieu, P. (1958). *Sociologie de l'Algérie*. (New Revised and Corrected Edition, 1961). Paris: Que Sais-je.

Bourdieu, P. (1961). Révolution dans la révolution. *Esprit*, Jan., 27–40.

Bourdieu, P. (1962a). *The Algerians* (A. C. M. Ross, Trans.). Boston, MA: Beacon Press.

Bourdieu, P. (1962b). Célibat et condition paysanne. *Études rurales*, 5–6, 32–136.

Bourdieu, P. (1962c). De la guerre révolutionnaire à la révolution. In F. Perroux (Ed.) *L'Algérie de demain*. Paris: PUF.

Bourdieu, P. (with Darbel, A., Rivet, J. P., and Seibel, C.) (1963). *Travail et travailleurs en Algérie*. Paris and The Hague: Mouton.

Bourdieu, P. (with Sayad, A.) (1964a). *Le Déracinement, la crise de l'agriculture tradionelle en Algérie*. Paris: Les Editions de Minuit.

Bourdieu, P. (with Passeron, J.-C.) (1964b). *Les étudiants et leurs études*. Paris and The Hague: Mouton, Cahiers du Centre de Sociologie Européenne.

Bourdieu, P. (1966). L'idéologie dominante. *Démocratie et liberté*, Paper given at *La Semaine de la Pensée Marxist* (5–15 mars), in *Démocratie et liberté*, Paris, Édition sociales, 167–173.

Bourdieu, P. (1971/1966). Intellectual field and creative project. In M. F. D. Young (Ed.) *Knowledge and Control: New Directions for the Sociology of Education*. London: Macmillan.
— *Champ intellectuel et projet créateur. Les Temps Modernes*, November, 865–906.

Bourdieu, P. (1972). Les stratégies matromoniales dans le système de reproduction. *Annales*, 4–5, 1105–1127.

Bourdieu, P. (with Passeron, J.-C.) (1977a/70). *Reproduction in Education, Society and Culture* (R. Nice, Trans.). London: Sage.
— *La Reproduction: Eléments pour une théorie du système d'enseignement*. Paris: Les Editions de Minuit.

Bourdieu, P. (1977b/1972). *Outline of a Theory of Practice* (R. Nice, Trans.). Cambridge: Cambridge University Press.
— *Esquisse d'une théorie de la pratique. Précédé de trois études d'ethnologie kabyle*. Geneva, Switzerland: Droz.

Bourdieu, P. (1979a/1977c). *Algeria 1960* (R. Nice, Trans.). Cambridge: Cambridge University Press.
— *Algérie 60 structures économiques et structures temporelles*. Paris: Les Editions de Minuit.

Bourdieu, P. (with Passeron, J.-C.) (1979b/1964). *The Inheritors, French Students and their Relation to Culture* (R. Nice, Trans.). Chicago, IL: The University of Chicago Press.
— *Les héritiers, les étudiants et la culture*. Paris: Les Editions de Minuit.

Bourdieu, P. (1984a/1979). *Distinction* (R. Nice, Trans.). Oxford: Polity.
— *La Distinction. Critique sociale du jugement*. Paris: Les Editions de Minuit.

Bourdieu, P. (1988). On interest and the relative autonomy of symbolic power. *Working Papers and Proceedings of the Center for Psychological Studies*, 20.

— *L'ontologie politique de Martin Heidegger, nouvelle edition, Actes de la recherché en sciences sociales*, 5–6 November, 109–156

Bourdieu, P. (1988/1984b). *Homo Academicus*. (P. Collier, Trans.). Oxford: Polity.

— *Homo Academicus*. Paris: Les Editions de Minuit.

Bourdieu, P. (with Wacquant, L.) (1989a). Towards a reflexive sociology: A workshop with Pierre Bourdieu. *Sociological Theory*, 7, 1, 26–63.

Bourdieu, P. (1989b). Reproduction interdite. La dimension symbolique de la domination économique. *Études Rurales, janvier 15–36*, 113–114.

Bourdieu, P. (1990). The scholastic point of view. *Cultural Anthropology*, 5, 380–391.

Bourdieu, P. (with Boltanski, L., Castel, R., and Chamboredon, J.-C.) (1990a/1965). *Photography. A Middle-brow Art* (S. Whiteside, Trans.). Oxford: Polity.

— *Un Art moyen, essai sur les usages sociaux de la photographie*. Paris: Les Editions de Minuit.

Bourdieu, P. (with Darbel, A. and Schnapper, D.) (1990b/1966). *The Love of Art. European Art Museums and their Public* (C. Beattie and N. Merriman, Trans.). Oxford: Polity Press.

— *L'Amour de l'art, les musées d'art et leur public*. Paris: Les Editions de Minuit.

Bourdieu, P. (1990c/1980). *The Logic of Practice* (R. Nice, Trans.). Oxford: Polity.

— *Le sens pratique*. Paris: Les Editions de Minuit.

Bourdieu, P. (1990d/1987). *In Other Words: Essays Towards a Reflexive Sociology* (M. Adamson, Trans.). Oxford: Polity.

— *Choses dites*. Paris: Les Editions de Minuit.

Bourdieu, P. (1991a/1982). *Language and Symbolic Power* (G. Raymond and M. Adamson, Trans). Oxford: Polity Press.

Bourdieu, P. (1991b/1988). *The Political Ontology of Martin Heidegger* (P. Collier, Trans.). Oxford: Polity Press.

Bourdieu, P. (with Chamboredon, J.-C. and Passeron, J.-C.) (1991c/1968). *The Craft of Sociology* (R. Nice, Trans.). New York: Walter de Gruyter.

— *Le Métier de sociologue*. Paris: Mouton-Bordas.

Bourdieu, P. (with Wacquant, L.) (1992). *An Invitation to Reflexive Sociology* (L. Wacquant, Trans.). Oxford: Polity Press.

— *Réponses. Pour une anthropologie réflexive*. Paris: Seuil.

Bourdieu, P. (1993/1980). *Sociology in Question* (R. Nice, Trans.). London: Sage.

— *Questions de sociologie*. Paris: Les Editions de Minuit.

Bourdieu, P. (with Grenfell, M.) (1995). *Entretiens*. CLE Papers 37: University of Southampton.

Bourdieu, P. (1996a/1989). *The State Nobility. Elite Schools in the Field of Power* (L. C. Clough, Trans.). Oxford: Polity Press.

— *La noblesse d'état. Grandes écoles et esprit de corps*. Paris: Les Editions de Minuit.

Bourdieu, P. (1996b/1992). *The Rules of Art* (S. Emanuel, Trans.). Oxford: Polity Press.

— *Les règles de l'art. Genèse et structure du champ littéraire*. Paris: Seuil.

Bourdieu, P. (1998/1994). *Practical Reason*. Oxford: Polity Press.

— *Raisons pratiques*. Paris: Les Editions de Seuil.

Bourdieu, P. (1999/1993). *The Weight of the World. Social Suffering in Contemporary Society* (P. Parkhurst Ferguson, S. Emanuel, J. Johnson, and S. T. Waryn, Trans.). Oxford: Polity Press.

— *La Misère du monde*. Paris: Seuil.

Bourdieu, P. (2000a). Making the economic habitus. Algerian workers revisited (R. Nice and L. Wacquant, Trans.). *Ethnography*, 1, 1, 17–41.

Bourdieu, P. (2000b/1997). *Pascalian Meditations* (R. Nice, Trans.). Oxford: Polity Press.
— *Méditations pascaliennes*. Paris: Seuil.

Bourdieu, P. (2000c). Participant Objectivation. Address given in receipt of the Aldous Huxley Medal for Anthropology, University of London, 12th November, *Mimeograph*, p. 12.

Bourdieu, P. (2003). Participant Objectivation. *The Journal of the Royal Anthropological Institute*, *9*, 2, (June 2003), 281–294.

Bourdieu, P. (2004/2001). *Science of Science and Reflexivity*. Cambridge: Polity Press.
— *Science de la science et réflexivité*. Paris: Raisons d'Agir.

Bourdieu, P. (2007/2004). *Sketch for a Self-Analysis*. Oxford: Polity Press.
— *Esquisse pour une auto-analyse*. Paris: Raisons d'Agir.

Bourdieu, P. (2008a/2002). *Bachelors' Ball*. Oxford: Polity Press.
— *Le bal des célibataires. Crise de la société en Béarn*. Paris: Seuil.

Bourdieu, P. (2008b). *Esquisses Algériennes*. Paris: Seuil.

Bourdieu, P. (2012/2003). *Picturing Algeria*. New York: Columbia University Press.
— *Images d'Algérie*. Paris: Actes Sud.

Bourdieu, P. (2013). *Manet: Une revolution symbolique*. Paris: Raisons d'agir/ Seuil.

Bourdieu, P. (2016a). *Sociologie générale. Cours au Collège de France 1983–1986 (Vol. 1)*. Paris: Raisons d'Agir.

Bourdieu, P. (2016b). *Sociologie Générale : Cours au Collège de France 1983–1986 (Vol. 2)*. Paris: Raisons d'Agir Seuil.

Braidotti, R. (2013). *The Posthuman*. Cambridge: Cambridge University Press.

Brandt, D. and Clinton, K. (2002). The limits of the local: Expanding perspectives of literacy as a social practice. *Journal of Literacy Research*, *34*, 3, 337–356.

Bright, G. (2012). A practice of concrete utopia? Informal youth support and the possibility of 'redemptive remembering' in a UK coal-mining area. *Power and Education*, *4*, 3, 314–326.

Burgess, R. (1984). *In the Field*. London: Allen and Unwin.

Burnett, C., Merchant, G., Pahl, K., and Rowsell, J. (2014). The (im)materiality of literacy: the significance of subjectivity to new literacies research. *Discourse: Studies in the Cultural Politics of Education*, *35*, 1, 90–103.

Campbell, E. and Lassiter L. E. (2010). From collaborative ethnography to collaborative pedagogy: Reflections on the other side of Middletown Project and community-university research partnerships. *Anthropology and Education Quarterly*, *41*, 4, 370–385.

Campbell, E. and Lassiter, L. E. (2015). *Doing Ethnography Today: Theoretical Issues and Pragmatic Concerns*. Oxford: Wiley-Blackwell.

Campbell, E., Pahl, K., Pente, E., and Rasool, Z. (Eds.) (2018). *Re-imagining Contested Communities: Connecting Rotherham through Research*. Bristol, UK: Policy Press.

Canagarajah, A. S. (1996). From critical research practice to critical research reporting. *TESOL Quarterly*, *30*, 2, 321–330.

Canagarajah, A. S. (2005). Rhetoricizing reflexivity. *Journal of Language, Identity and Education*, *4*, 4, 309–315.

Canagarajah, A. S. (2006). Toward a writing pedagogy of shuttling between languages: Learning from multilingual writers. *College English*, *68*, 6, 589–604.

Candlin, C. and Hyland, K. (Eds.) (1999). *Writing: Texts, Processes and Practices*. Harlow, UK: Addison Wesley Longman.

Casanave, C. P. (1998). Transitions: The balancing act of bilingual academics. *Journal of Second Language Writing*, *7*, 2, 175–203.

Casanave, C. P. (2005). Uses of narrative in L2 writing research. In P. K. Matsuda and T. Silva (Eds.) *Second Language Writing Research: Perspectives on the Process of Knowledge Construction* (pp. 17–32). Mahwah, NJ: Lawrence Erlbaum Associates.

Casanave, C. P. (2009). Training for writing or training for reality? Challenges facing EFL writing teachers and students in language teacher education programs. In R. Manchón (Ed.) *Writing in Foreign Language Contexts: Learning, Teaching, and Research* (pp. 256–277). Bristol, UK: Multilingual Matters.

Casanave, C. and Vandrick, S. (2003). *Writing for Scholarly Publication: Behind the Scenes in Language Education.* Mahwah, NJ: Lawrence Erlbaum Associates.

Charlesworth, S. J. (2000). *A Phenomenology of Working Class Experience.* Cambridge: Cambridge University Press.

Chomsky, N. (1965). *Aspects of Theory of Syntax.* Cambridge, MA: MIT Press.

Clay, M. M. (2001). *Change Over Time in Children's Literacy Development.* Portsmouth, NH: Heinemann.

Clifford, J. and Marcus, G. E. (1986). *Writing Culture: The Poetics and Politics of Ethnography.* London: University of California Press.

Coessens, K., Crispin, D., and Douglas, A. (2009). *The Artistic Turn: A Manifesto.* Ghent, Belgium: The Orpheus Institute.

Comber, B. (2016). *Literacy, Place and Pedagogies of Possibility.* London: Routledge

Compton-Lilly, C. (2007/2003). *Reading Families: The Literate Lives of Urban Children.* New York: Teachers College Press.

Compton-Lilly, C. (2011). Time and reading: Negotiations and affiliations of a reader, grades one through eight. *Research in the Teaching of English, 45,* 3, 224–252.

Compton-Lilly, C. (2012). *Reading Time: The Literate Lives of Urban Secondary Students and their Families.* New York: Teachers College Press.

Compton-Lilly, C. (2013). Literacy and identity construction across time and space: The case of Jermaine. *Journal of Adolescent and Adult Literacy, 56,* 5, 400–408.

Compton-Lilly, C. (2014a). The development of writing habitus: A ten-year case study of a young writer. *Written Communication,* 31, 371–403.

Compton-Lilly, C. (2014b). Temporal Discourse Analysis. In P. Albers, T. Holbrook, and A. Flint (Eds.) *New Methods in Literacy Research,* 40–55. New York: Routledge.

Compton-Lilly, C. (2015). Revisiting children and families: Temporal Discourse Analysis and the longitudinal construction of meaning. In J. Sefton-Green and J. Rowsell (Eds.) *Learning and Literacy over Time: Longitudinal Perspectives* (pp. 61–78). New York: Routledge.

Compton-Lilly, C. (2016). *Reading Students' Lives: Literacy Learning Across Time.* New York: Routledge.

Cook, V. (1992). Evidence for multicompetence. *Language Learning, 42,* 4, 557–591.

Cook, V. (1999). Going beyond the native speaker in language teaching. *TESOL Quarterly, 33,* 2, 185–209.

Cope, B. and Kalantzis, M. (Eds.) (2000). *Multiliteracies: Literacy learning and the design of social futures.* Psychology Press.

Cope, B. and Kalantzis, M. (2009). Multiliteracies: New literacies, new learning. *Journal of Pedagogies: An International Journal, 4,* 3, 164–195.

Copland, F. and Creese, A. (with Rock, F. and Shaw, S.) (2015). *Linguistic Ethnography: Collecting, Analysing and Presenting Data.* London: Sage.

Cortazzi, M. (1993). *Narrative Analysis.* London: Falmer Press.

Creese, A. (2015). Case study one: Reflexivity, voice and representation in linguistic ethnography. In F. Copland and A. Creese (with F. Rock and S. Shaw) (Eds.) *Linguistic Ethnography: Collecting, Analysing and Presenting Data* (pp. 61–88). London: Sage.

Crow, G. and Lyon, D. (2011). Turning points in work and family lives in the imagined futures of young people on Sheppey in 1978. In M. Winterton, G. Crow and B. Morgan Brett (Eds.) *Young Lives and Imagined Futures: Insights from Archived Data Timescapes Working Paper 6*, available at: www.timescapes.leeds.ac.uk/events-dissemination/publications.php.

Curry, M. J. and Lillis, T. (2013). *A Scholar's Guide to Getting Published in English*. Bristol, UK: Multilingual Matters.

Casanave, C. P. (2005). *Writing games: Multicultural case studies of academic literacy practices in higher education*. Routledge.

Deer, C. (2008). Reflexivity. In M. Grenfell (Ed.) *Pierre Bourdieu: Key Concepts* (pp. 199–212). Durham, UK: Acumen.

De Fina, A. (2009). From Space to Spatialization in Narrative Studies. In J. Collins, S. Slembrouck, and M. Baynham (Eds.) *Globalisation and Language in Contact: Scale, Migration and Communicative Practices* (pp. 109–129). London: Continuum.

Dicks, B., Flewitt, R. B., Lancaster, L., and Pahl, K. (2011). Introduction to special issue on Multimodality and ethnography: Working at the intersection. *Qualitative Research*, 11, 1–16.

Duranti, A. and Goodwin, C. (1992). *Rethinking context: Language as an interactive phenomenon*. Cambridge: Cambridge University Press.

Eakin, E (2001). 'Social status tends to seal one's fate , says France's master thinker', *New York Times*. 6th January.

Ehret, C. (2019). Propositions from Affect Theory for Feeling Literacy through the Event Theoretical Models and Practices of Reading. In D. E. Alvermann, N. J. Unrau, and M. Sailors (Eds.) *Theoretical Models and Processes of Literacy*. 7th edition. New York, NY: Routledge.

Ehret, C. Hollett, T., and Jocius, R. (2016). The matter of new media making: An intra-action analysis of adolescents making a digital book trailer. *Journal of Literacy Research*, 48, 3, 346–377.

Enriquez, G., Johnson, E., Kontovourki, S., and Mallozzi, A. (Eds.) (2016). *Literacies, Learning and the Body: Putting Theory and Research into Pedagogical Practice*. London: Routledge.

Erstad, O., Gilje, O., Sefton-Green, J., and Arnseth, H. C. (2016). *Learning Identities, Education and Community: Young Lives in the Cosmopolitan City*. Cambridge: Cambridge University Press.

Erstad, O. and Sefton-Green, J. (Eds.) (2013). *Identity, Community and Learning Lives in the Digital Age*. Cambridge: CUP

Escott, H. and Pahl, K. (2017). Learning from Ninjas: Young people's films as a lens for an expanded view of literacy and language. *Discourse: Studies in the Cultural Politics of Education*. doi/full/10.1080/01596306.2017.1405911

Facer, K. and Pahl, K. (Eds.) (2017). *Valuing Collaborative Interdisciplinary Research: Beyond Impact*. Bristol: Policy Press.

Fereday, J. and Muir-Cochrane, E. (2006). Demonstrating rigor using thematic analysis: A hybrid approach of inductive and deductive coding and theme development. *International Journal of Qualitative Methods*, 5, 1, 80–91.

Finnegan, R. (2007). *The 'Oral' and Beyond: Doing Things with Words in Africa*. Oxford and Chicago, IL: James Currey/University of Chicago Press.

Finnegan, R. (2015). *Where is Language? An Anthropologist's Questions on Language, Literature and Performance*. London: Bloomsbury Academic.

Firth, A. and Wagner, J. (1997). On discourse, communication, and (some) fundamental concepts in SLA research. *The Modern Language Journal, 81*, 3, 285–300.

Flewitt, R. (2008). Multimodal literacies. In J. Marsh and E. Hallet (Eds.) *Desirable Literacies: Approaches to Language and Literacy in the Early Years* (pp. 122–139). London: Sage.

Freedman, A. (1999). Beyond the text: Towards understanding the teaching and learning of genres. *TESOL Quarterly*, 33, 764–768.

García, O. (2009). Education, multilingualism and translanguaging in the 21st century. In T. Skutnabb-Kangas, R. Phillipson and A. K. Mohanty (Eds.) *Social Justice Through Multilingual Education* (pp. 140–158). Bristol, UK: Multilingual Matters.

García, O. (2011). *Bilingual Education in the 21st Century: A Global Perspective*. Oxford: John Wiley and Sons.

Gee, J. P. (1991). What is Literacy? In C. Mitchell and K. Weiler (Eds.) *Rewriting Literacy: Culture and the Discourse of the Other* (pp. 3–12). New York: Bergin and Gravey.

Gee, J. P. (1996). *Social Linguistics and Literacies: Ideology in Discourses*. 2nd edition. London: Taylor & Francis.

Gee, J. P. (2009). *New Digital Media and Learning as an Emerging Area and 'Worked Examples' as One Way Forward*. Cambridge, MA: MIT Press.

Gee, J. P. (2014). *An Introduction to Discourse Analysis: Theory and Method*. 4th edition. New York: Routledge.

Gee, J. P. (2015). *Social Linguistics and Literacies: Ideology in Discourses*. London: Routledge.

Geertz, C. (1993/1973). *The Interpretation of Cultures*. London: Fontana.

Geertz, C. (1996). Afterword. In S. Feld and K. H. Basso (Eds.) *Sense of Place* (pp. 259–262). Santa Fe, NM: School of American Research Press.

Giroux, H. A. (1988). *Teachers as Intellectuals: Toward a Critical Pedagogy of Learning*. New York: Greenwood Publishing Group.

Gordon, A. (2008). *Ghostly Matters: Haunting and the Sociological Imagination*. Minneapolis, MN: University of Minnesota Press.

Gouldner, A. (1971). *The Coming Crisis in Western Sociology*. London: Heinemann.

Gregory, E. and Williams, A. (2000). *City Literacies: Learning to Read across Generations and Cultures*. London: Routledge.

Grenfell, M. (1999). Language: Construction of an object of research. In M. Grenfell and M. Kelly (Eds.) *Pierre Bourdieu: Language, Culture and Education* (pp. 27–40). Bern, Switzerland: Peter Lang.

Grenfell, M. (2004). *Pierre Bourdieu: Agent Provocateur*. London: Continuum.

Grenfell, M. (2007). *Pierre Bourdieu: Education and Training*. London: Continuum.

Grenfell, M. (2008). Postscript: Methodological principles. In M. Grenfell (Ed.) *Pierre Bourdieu: Key Concepts* (pp. 219–228). New York: Routledge.

Grenfell, M. (2011). Towards a study of language and linguistic study. In M. Grenfell *Bourdieu, Language, and Linguistics* (pp. 197–225). New York: Continuum Press.

Grenfell, M. (Ed.) (2012a). *Pierre Bourdieu: Key Concepts*. 2nd edition. Stocksfield, UK: Acumen.

Grenfell, M. (2012b). A future synthesis: Bourdieu, ethnography, and new literacy studies. In M. Grenfell, D. Bloome, C. Hardy, K. Pahl, J. Rowsell, and B. V. Street (Eds.) *Language, Ethnography, and Education: Bridging New Literacy Studies and Bourdieu* (pp. 174–196). New York: Routledge.

Grenfell, M. (Ed.) (2014). *Pierre Bourdieu: Key Concepts*. 2nd edition. London: Routledge.

Grenfell, M., Bloome, D., Hardy, C., Pahl, K., Rowsell, J., and Street, B. V. (2012). *Language, Ethnography, and Education: Bridging New Literacy Studies and Bourdieu*. London: Routledge.

Grenfell, M. and Hardy, C. (2007). *Art Rules: Pierre Bourdieu and the Visual Arts*. Oxford: Berg.

Grenfell, M. and Lebaron, F. (2014). *Bourdieu and Data Analysis: Methodological Principles and Practice*. Bern, Switzerland: Peter Lang.

Grice, H. P. (1975). Logic and conversation. In P. Cole and J. Morgan (Eds.) *Studies in Syntax and Semantics III: Speech Acts* (pp. 183–198). New York: Academic Press.

Gumperz, J. (1982). *Discourse Strategies*. Cambridge: Cambridge University Press.

Gutiérrez, K. D. (2008). Developing a sociocritical literacy in the third space. *Reading Research Quarterly*, *43*, 2, 148–164.

Habermas, J. (1987a). *Knowledge and Human Interests* (J. J. Shapiro, Trans.). Cambridge: Polity Press.

Habermas, J. (1987b). *Theory of Communicative Action (Volume I)*. Oxford: Polity Press.

Hall, S. (2007). Richard Hoggart: The uses of literacy and the cultural turn. *International Journal of Cultural Studies*, *10*, 1, 39–49.

Halliday, M. A. K. (1978). *Language as Social Semiotic*. London: Routledge.

Hamilton, M. (2015). The everyday and faraway: Revisiting local literacies. In J. Sefton-Green and J. Rowsell (Eds.) *Learning and Literacy Over Time: Longitudinal Perspectives* (pp. 98–115). London: Routledge.

Hammersley, M. and Atkinson, P. (1983). *Ethnography: Principles in Practice*. London: Routledge.

Hartley, J. (2008). *Academic Writing and Publishing: A Practical Handbook*. London: Routledge.

Harwood, V., Hickey-Moody, A., McMahon, S., and O'Shea, S. (2017). *The Politics of Widening Participation and University Access for Young People: Making Educational Futures*. London: Routledge.

Heath, S. B. (1982). What no bedtime story means: Narrative skills at home and school. *Language in Society*, *11*, 2, 49–76.

Heath, S. B. (1983). *Ways with Words: Language, Life and Work in Communities and Classrooms*. Cambridge: Cambridge University Press.

Heath, S. B. (2012). *Words at Work and Play: Three Decades in Family and Community Life*. Cambridge: Cambridge University Press.

Heller, M. (2011). *Paths to Postnationalism: A Critical Ethnography of Language and Identity*. Oxford: Oxford University Press.

Hirst, P. (1966). Educational theory. In J. W. Tibble (Ed.) *The Study of Education* (pp. 29–58). London: Routledge and Kegan Paul.

Hornberger, N. H. (Ed.) (2003). *Continua of Biliteracy: An Ecological Framework for Educational Policy, Research, and Practice in Multilingual Settings (Vol. 41)*. Bristol, UK: Multilingual Matters.

Horner, B., Lu, M., Royster, J., and Timbur, J. (2011). Language difference in writing: Toward a translingual approach. *College English*, *73*, 3, 303–321.

Hyland, K. (2008). Genre and academic writing in the disciplines. *Language Teaching*, *41*, 4, 543–562.

Hyland, K. and Tse, P. (2004). Metadiscourse in academic writing: A reappraisal. *Applied linguistics*, *25*, 2, 156–177.

Hymes, D. (Ed.) (1996). *Ethnography, Linguistics, Narrative Inequality: Towards an Understanding of Voice*. London: Routledge.

Ingold, T. (2013). *Making: Anthropology, Archaeology, Art and Architecture*. London: Routledge.

Ingold, T. (2014). That's enough about ethnography. *HAU: Journal of Ethnographic Theory*, 4, 1, 383–395.

Jay, A. (2014). Independent Inquiry into Child Sexual Exploitation in Rotherham 1997–2013 available at: www.rotherham.gov.uk/downloads/file/1407/independent_inquiry_cse_in_rotherham (accessed 12. 6. 2017).

Jenkins, R. (2002). *Pierre Bourdieu*. New York: Routledge.

Jewitt, C. and Kress, G. (Eds) (2003). *Multimodal Literacy*. New York: Peter Lang.

Jørgensen, J. N. (2008). Polylingual languaging around and among children and adolescents. *International Journal of Multilingualism*, 5, 3, 161–176.

Kaboyashi, M. and Rinnert, C. (2012). Understanding L2 writing development from a multicompetence perspective: Dynamic repertoires of knowledge and text construction. In R. Manchón (Ed.) *L2 Writing Development: Multiple Perspectives* (pp. 101–134). Berlin, Germany: De Gruyter.

Kamhi-Stein, L. D. (2004). *Learning and Teaching from Experience*. Ann Arbor, MI: University of Michigan Press.

Kant, I. (1956/1788). *Critique of Practical Reason*. New York: Liberal Arts Press.

Kant, I. (1961/1781). *Critique of Pure Reason*. London: Macmillan.

Kant, I. (1987/1790). *Critique of Pure Judgment*. Cambridge: Hacket.

Kell, C. (2006). Crossing the margins: Literacy, semiotics and the recontextualisation of meanings. In K. Pahl and J. Rowsell (Eds.5) *Travel Notes from the New Literacy Studies: Instances of Practice* (pp. 147–172). Bristol, UK: Multilingual Matters.

Kinloch, V. (2010). *Harlem on Our Minds: Place, Race and the Literacies of Urban Youth*. New York: Teachers College Press.

Kress, G. (1997). *Before Writing: Rethinking Paths to Literacy*. London: Routledge.

Kress, G. (2003). *Literacy in the New Media Age*. London: Routledge.

Kuby, C. R., Gutshall Rucker, T., and Kirchhofer, J. M. (2015). 'Go be a writer!': Intra-activity with materials, time and space in literacy learning. *Journal of Early Childhood Literacy*, 15, 3, 394–419.

Kuby, C. R. and Rowsell, J. (2017). Early literacy and the posthuman: Pedagogies and methodologies. Editorial to Special Issue. *Journal of Early Children Literacy*, 17, 3, 285–296.

Kuhn, T. (1970/1962). *The Structure of Scientific Revolutions*. 2nd edition. Chicago, IL: Chicago University Press.

Lamont, M. (2012). How has Bourdieu been good to think with? The case of the United States. *Sociological Forum*, 1, 228–237.

Lareau, A. and Schultz, J. (Eds.) (1996). *Journeys Through Ethnography: Realistic Accounts of Fieldwork*. Boulder, CO: Westview Press.

Lassiter, L. E. (2005). *The Chicago Guide to Collaborative Ethnography*. Chicago, IL: Chicago University Press.

Latour, B. (1986). The politics of explanation: An alternative. In S. Woolgar (Ed.) *Knowledge and Reflexivity: New Frontiers in the Sociology of Knowledge* (pp. 155–176). London: Sage.

Latour, B. (1987). *Science in Action*. Cambridge, MA: Harvard University Press.

Law, J. (2004). *After Method: Mess in Social Science Research*. London: Routledge.

Leander, K. and Sheehy, M. (Eds.) (2004). *Spatialising Literacy Research and Practice*. New York: Peter Lang.

Leander, K. and Boldt, G. (2013). Rereading 'A Pedagogy of Multiliteracies': Bodies, texts and emergence. *The Journal of Literacy Research*, *45*, 1, 22–46, March.

Lee, H. (1960/2002). *To Kill a Mockingbird (1962)*. New York: Harper Perennial Modern Classics.

Lefebvre, H., (1991). *The Production of Space*. Cambridge, MA: Blackwell.

Leki, I. (2007). *Undergraduates in a Second Language: Challenges and Complexities of Academic Literacy Development*. Mahwah, NH: Lawrence Erlbaum Associates.

Lemke, J. (2000). Across the scales of time: Artifacts, activities, and meanings in ecosocial systems. *Mind, Culture, and Activity*, *7*, 4, 273–290.

Lemke, J. (2005). Place, pace and meaning: Multimedia chronotopes. In S. Norris and R. Jones (Eds.) *Discourse in Action: Introducing Mediated Discourse Analysis* (pp. 110–122). New York: Routledge.Li, G. and Beckett, G. (Eds.) (2005). *'Strangers' of the Academy: Asian Women Scholars in Higher Education*. Herndon, VA: Stylus Publishing.

Lillis, T. M. (2008). Ethnography as method, methodology, and "deep theorizing": Closing the gap between text and context in academic writing research. *Written Communication*, *25*, 3, 353–388.

Lillis, T. M. and Curry, M. J. (2010). *Academic Writing in a Global Context: The Politics and Practices of Publishing in English*. London: Routledge.

Lillis, T. M. and Curry, M. J. (2006). Professional academic writing by multilingual scholars: Interactions with literacy brokers in the production of English-medium texts. *Written Communication*, *23*, 1, 3–35.

Lin, A., Grant, R., Kubota, R., Motha, S., Sachs, G. T., Vandrick, S., and Wong, S. (2004). Women faculty of color in TESOL: Theorizing our lived experiences. *TESOL Quarterly*, *38*, 3, 487–504.

Luke, A. and Freebody, P. (1997). Shaping the social practices of reading. In S. Muspratt, A. Luke, and P. Freebody (Eds.) *Constructing Critical Literacies: Teaching and Learning Textual Practices* (pp. 227–242). Cresskill, NJ: Hampton Press.

Lyon, D. and Carabelli, G. (2015). Researching young people's orientations to the future: The methodological challenges of using arts practice. *Qualitative Research* [Online]: 1–16. Available at: http://dx.doi.org/10.1177/1468794115587393.

Lyotard, J.-F. (1979). *La condition post-moderne*. Paris: Les Éditions de Minuit.

MacLure, M. (2011). Qualitative inquiry: Where are the ruins? *Qualitative Inquiry*, *17*, 10, 997–1005.

Mahuika, R. (2008). Kaupapa Maori Theory is critical and anti-colonial. *MAI-Review*, *3*, 4, 1–16.

Manchón, R. (Ed.) (2009). *Writing in Foreign Language Contexts: Learning, Teaching, and Research (Vol. 43)*. Bristol, UK: Multilingual Matters.

Marcus, G. E. and Fischer, M. M. J. (1986). *Anthropology as Cultural Critique*. Chicago: University of Chicago Press.

Martin-Jones, M. and Jones K. (Eds.) (2000). *Multilingual Literacies: Reading and Writing Different Worlds*. Amsterdam, Netherlands: John Benjamins.

Massumi, B. (2002). *Parables for the Virtual: Movement, Affect, Sensation*. Durham, NC: Duke University Press.

Maton, K. (2003). Pierre Bourdieu and the epistemic conditions of social scientific knowledge. *Space and Culture*, *6*, 1, 52–65.

Maton, K. (2014). *Knowledge and Knowers: Towards a Realist Sociology of Education*. London: Routledge.

Matsuda, P. (2014). The lure of translingual writing. *PMLA*, *129*, 3, 478–483.

Maybin, J. (2000). The New Literacy Studies: Context, intertextuality and discourse. In D. Barton, M. Hamilton, and R. Ivanic (Eds.) *Situated Literacies: Reading and Writing in Context* (pp. 197–209). London: Routledge.

Maybin, J. (2006). *Children's Voices: Talk, Knowledge and Identity*. Basingstoke, UK: Palgrave Macmillan.

Maybin, J. (2013). Working towards a more complex sociolinguistics. *Journal of Sociolinguistics*, *17*, 4, 547–555.

Merleau-Ponty, M. (1962/1945). *Phenomenology of Perception*. London: Routledge and Kegan Paul.

— *La Phénoménologie de la perception*. Paris: Gallimard.

Merleau-Ponty, M. (1968/1964). *The Visible and Invisible*. Evanston, IL: Northwestern University Press.

— *Le Visible et l'invisible, suivi de notes de travail*. Paris: Gallimard.

Miller, A. (1995/1987). *Time Bends: A Life*. London: Bloomsbury.

Morrell, E. (2008). *Critical Literacy and Urban Youth: Pedagogies of Access, Dissent and Liberation*. London and New York: Routledge.

Mouffe, C. (2004). *The Democratic Paradox*. London: Verso.

Murray, R. (2009). *Writing for Academic Journals*. Berkshire, UK: McGraw Hill/Open University Press.

National Reading Panel (2000). *National reading panel: Teaching children to read: An evidence-based assessment of the scientific research literature on reading and its implications for reading instruction: Reports of the subgroups*. Washington, DC: U.S. Department of Health and Human Services, Public Health Service, National Institutes of Health, National Institute of Child Health and Human Development.

Nelson, C. D. (2005). Crafting researcher subjectivity in ways that enact theory. *Journal of Language, Identity, and Education*, *4*, 4, 315-320.

Nespor, J. (1997). *Tangled Up in School: Politics, Space, Bodies, and Signs in the Educational Process*. Mahwah, NJ: Lawrence Erlbaum Associates.

Neuman, S. B. and Celano, D. (2001). Access to print in low-income and middle-income communities: An ecological study of four neighbourhoods. *Reading Research Quarterly*, *36*, 1, 8–26.

Neuman, S. B. and Celano, D. (2006). The knowledge gap: Implications of levelling the playing field for low-income and middle-income children. *Reading Research Quarterly*, *41*, 2, 176–201.

Neuman, S. B. and Celano, D. (2012). *Giving Our Children a Fighting Chance: Poverty, Literacy and the Development of Information Capital*. New York: Teachers College Press.

New London Group (1996). A pedagogy of multiliteracies: Designing social futures. *Harvard Educational Review*, *66*, 1, 60–92.

Ngũgĩ, W. (1993). *Moving the Centre: The Struggle for Cultural Freedoms*. Oxford: James Currey.

No Child Left Behind Act (NCLB) (2001). www.ed.gov/nclb/landing.jhtml (accessed January 27, 2016).

O'Connor, D. J. (1958). An introduction to the philosophy of education. *The Journal of Philosophy*, *56*, 19, 766–770.

Otsuji, E. and Pennycook, A. (2010). Metrolingualism: Fixity, fluidity and language in flux. *International Journal of Multilingualism, 7,* 3, 240–254.

Pahl, K. (2002). Ephemera, Mess and Miscellaneous Piles: Texts and Practices in Families. *Journal of Early Childhood Literacy, 2,* 2, 145–166.

Pahl, K. (2012). Time and space as a resource for meaning-making by children and young people in home and community settings. *Global Studies of Childhood, 2,* 3, pp. 201–216.

Pahl, K. (2014a). *Materializing Literacies in Communities: The Uses of Literacy Revisited.* London: Bloomsbury Academic.

Pahl, K. (2014b). The Aesthetics of Everyday Literacies: Home Writing Practices in a British Asian household. *Anthropology and Education Quarterly, 45,* 3, 293–311.

Pahl, K. (2017). The University as the Imagined Other: Making Sense of Community Co-produced Literacy Research. *Collaborative Anthropologies, 4,* February, 129–148.

Pahl, K. and Allan C. (2011). 'I don't know what literacy is': Uncovering hidden literacies in a community library using ecological and participatory methodologies with children, *Journal of Early Childhood Literacy, 11,* 2, 190–213.

Pahl, K. and Escott, H. (2015). Materialising literacies. In J. Rowsell and K. Pahl (Eds.) *The Routledge Handbook of Literacy Studies* (pp. 289–503). London: Routledge.

Pahl, K. and Khan, A. (2015). Artifacts of resilience: Enduring narratives, texts, practices across three generations. In J. Sefton-Green and J. Rowsell (Eds.) *Learning and Literacy Over Time: Longitudinal Perspectives* (pp. 116–133). London: Routledge.

Pahl, K. and Pollard, A. (2008). 'Bling – the Asians introduced that to the country': Gold and its value within a group of families of South Asian origin in Yorkshire. *Visual Communication, 7,* 2, 170–182.

Pahl, K. and Pollard, A. (2010). The case of the disappearing object: Narratives and artifacts in homes and a museum exhibition from Pakistani heritage families in South Yorkshire. *Museum and Society, 8,* 1, 1–17.

Pahl, K. (with Pollard, A. and Rafiq, Z.) (2009). Changing identities, Changing spaces: The Ferham Families Exhibition in Rotherham. *Moving Worlds, 9,* 2, 80–103.

Pahl, K. and Rowsell, J. (2010). *Artifactual Literacies: Every Object Tells a Story.* New York: Teachers College Press.

Pahl, K. and Rowsell, J. (2019). *Living Literacies.* Cambridge, Mass: MIT Press.

Park, B. (1988). *The Kid in the Red Jacket.* New York: Yearling.

Parkin, D. (2016). From multilingual classification to translingual ontology: A turning point. In K. Arnaut, J. Blommaert, B. Rampton, and M. Spotti (Eds.) *Language and Superdiversity* (pp. 71–88). London: Routledge.

Pennycook, A. (2005). Performing the personal. *Journal of Language, Identity and Education, 4,* 4, 297–304.

Pennycook, A. (2010). *Language as a Local Practice.* London: Routledge.

Pinnell, G. S. and Fountas, I. (1996). *Guided Reading: Good First Teaching for All Children.* Portsmouth, NH: Heinemann.

Popper, K. R. (1967). *The Logic of Scientific Discovery.* London: Hutchinson.

Preissle, J. and Grant, L. (2004). Fieldwork traditions: Ethnography and participant observation. In K. B. deMarrais and S. D. Lapan (Eds.) *Foundations for Research: Methods of Inquiry in Education and the Social Sciences* (pp. 161–180). Mahwah, NJ: Lawrence Erlbaum Associates.

Prior, P. (1998). *Writing/Disciplinarity: A Sociohistoric Account of Literate Activity in the Academy.* (The Rhetoric, Knowledge and Society Series, Charles Bazerman, Series Editor). Mahwah, NJ: Lawrence Erlbaum Associates.

Prior, P. (2008). Flat CHAT? Reassembling literate activity. *An Invited paper presented at the Writing Research Across Borders Conference*, February 2008. Santa Barbara, CA.

Prior, P., Solberg, J., Berry, P., Bellwoar, H., Chewning, B., Lunsford, K., Rohan, L., Roozen, K., Sheridan-Rabideau, M., Shipka, J., Van Ittersum, D., and Walker, J. (2007). Re-situating and re-mediating the canons: A cultural-historical remapping of rhetorical activity. A collaborative core text. *Kairos, 11*, 3, 1–29.

Rabinow, P. (1977). *Reflections on Fieldwork in Morocco*. Berkeley, CA: University of California Press.

Ramanathan, V. (2005). Some impossibilities around researcher location: Tensions around divergent audiences, languages, social stratification. *Journal of Language, Identity and Education, 4*, 4, 293–297.

Rampton, B. (1995). Language crossing and the problematisation of ethnicity and socialisation. *Pragmatics: Quarterly Publication of the International Pragmatics Association (IPrA), 5*, 4, 485–513.

Rampton, B. (2007a). *Language in Late Modernity: Interaction in an Urban School*. Cambridge: Cambridge University Press.

Rampton, B. (2007b). Neo-Hymesian linguistic ethnography in the United Kingdom. *Journal of Sociolinguistics, 11*, 5: 584–607. Web version: www3.interscience.wiley.com/cgi-bin/fulltext/117980211

Rampton, B. (2010). An everyday poetics of class and ethnicity in stylization and crossing. *Working Papers in Urban Language and Literacies*, 59. www.kcl.ac.uk/sspp/departments/education/research/Research-Centres/ldc/publications/workingpapers/abstracts/WP059-An-everyday-poetics-of-class-and-ethnicity-in-stylization-and-crossing.aspx

Rasool, Z. (2017). Collaborative working practices: Imagining better research partnerships. *Research for All, 1*, 2, 310–322.

Ravetz, J. and Ravetz, A. (2016). Seeing the wood from the trees: Social Science 3.0 and the role of visual thinking. *Innovation: The European Journal of Social Science*, 30, 104–120.

Reading First (2002). www2.ed.gov/programs/readingfirst/index.html (accessed January 27, 2016).

Richardson, E. (2006). *Hiphop Literacies*. London: Routledge.

Rogers, R. (2018). *Reclaiming Powerful Literacy Practices: New Horizons for Critical Discourse Analysis*. London: Routledge.

Rogers, R., Mosley, M., Kramer, M. A., and Literacy for Social Justice Teacher Research Group (2009). *Designing Socially Just Learning Communities*. London: Routledge.

Rorty, R. (1980). *Philosophy and the Mirror of Nature*. Oxford: Blackwell.

Rowsell, J. (2013). *Working with Multimodality: Rethinking Literacy in a Digital Age*. London: Routledge.

Rowsell, J., Burke, A., Flewitt, R., Liao, H.-T., Lin, A., Marsh, J., Mills, K., Prinsloo, M., Rowe, D., and Wohlwend, K. (2016). Humanizing digital literacies: A road trip in search of wisdom and insight. Digital Literacy Column. *The Reading Teacher, 70*, 1, 121–129.

Rowsell, J. and Pahl, K. (2007). Sedimented identities in texts: Instances of practice. *Reading Research Quarterly, 42*, 3, 388–401.

Rowsell, J. and Pahl, K. (Eds.) (2015). *The Routledge Handbook of Literacy Studies*. London: Routledge.

Saldaña, J. (2003). *Longitudinal Research: Analyzing Change Through Time*. Walnut Creek, CA: Altamira Press.

Samuels, R. and Thompson, P. (1990). *The Myths We Live By*. London: Routledge.

Sanjek, R. (Ed.) (1990). *Fieldnotes: The Makings of Anthropology*. New York: Cornell University Press.

de Saussure, F. (1966/1916). *Course in General Linguistics* (W. Baskin, Trans.). New York: McGraw-Hill.

Schroeder, C. L., Fox, H., and Bizzell, P. (Eds.) (2002). *ALT DIS: Alternative Discourses and the Academy*. Boston, MA: Heinemann.

Schwartz, L. H. (2015). A fund of knowledge approach to the appropriation of new media in a high school writing classroom. *Interactive Learning Environments*, *23*, 5, 595–612.

Sefton-Green, J. and Rowsell, J. (Eds.) (2015). *Learning and Literacy Over Time: Longitudinal Perspectives*. London: Routledge.

Seloni, L. (2012). Academic literacy socialization of first year doctoral students in the US: A micro-ethnographic perspective, *Journal of English for Specific Purposes*, *31*, 1, 47–59.

Seloni, L. (2014). "I'm an artist and a scholar who is trying to find a middle point": A textographic analysis of a Colombian art historian's thesis writing. *Journal of Second Language Writing*, *25*, 1, 79–99.

Seloni, L. (2016). In search of an identity: An accidental immigrant's story of belonging and migration. In R. Bali (Eds.) *"This is my new homeland" Life stories of Turkish Jewish immigrants*. Istanbul: Libra Books.

Shirato, T. and Webb, J. (2003). Bourdieu's concept of reflexivity as metaliteracy. *Cultural Studies*, *17*, 3–4, 539–552.

Silva, T. and Leki, I. (2004). Family matters: The influence of applied linguistics and composition studies on second language writing studies – Past, present, and future. *The Modern Language Journal*, *88*, 1, 1–13.

Smith, L. T. (1999). *Decolonizing Methodologies: Research and Indigenous Peoples*. London: Zed Books.

Snell, J. (2013). Dialect, interaction and class positioning at school: From deficit to difference to repertoire, *Language and Education*, 7, 2, 110–128.

Soja, E. (2010). *Seeking Spatial Justice*. Minneapolis, MN: University of Minnesota Press.

Somerville, M. and Green, M. (2015). *Children, Place and Sustainability*. Basingstoke, UK: Palgrave Macmillan.

Starfield, S. (2013). Researcher reflexivity. In C. Chappell (Ed.) *The Encyclopedia of Applied Linguistics*. Oxford: Wiley-Blackwell.

Starfield, S. and Ravelli, L. J. (2006). 'The writing of this thesis was a process that I could not explore with the positivistic detachment of the classical sociologist': Self and structure in new humanities research theses. *Journal of English for Academic Purposes*, *5*, 3, 222–243.

Stein, P. (2003). The Olifantsvlei Fresh Stories Project: Multimodality, creativity and fixing in the semiotic chain. In C. Jewitt, and G. Kress (Eds.) *Multimodal Literacy* (pp. 123–139). London: Peter Lang.

Strauss, A., and Corbin, J. (1990). *The Basics of Qualitative Research: Grounded Theory Procedures and Techniques*. Newbury Park, CA: Sage Publications.

Street, B. V. (1984). *Literacy in Theory and Practice*. Cambridge: Cambridge University Press.

Street, B. V. (Ed.) (1993). *Cross-Cultural Approaches to Literacy*. Cambridge: Cambridge University Press.

Street, B. V. (1995). *Social literacies: Critical approaches to literacy in development, ethnography and education*. London: Longman.

Street, B. V. (1997). The implications of 'New Literacy Studies' for literacy education, *English in Education, 31*, 3, 26–39.

Street, B. V. (2000). Literacy events and literacy practices: Theory and practice in the new literacy studies. In M. Martin-Jones and K. Jones (Eds.) *Multilingual Literacies: Reading and Writing Different Worlds* (pp. 17–29). Amsterdam/Philadelphia, PA: John Benjamins.

Street, B. V. (Ed.) (2005). *Literacies Across Educational Contexts: Mediating Learning and Teaching.* Philadelphia, PA: Caslon Press.

Street, J. C. and Street, B. V. (1991). The schooling of literacy. In D. Barton and R. Ivanic (Eds.) *Writing in the Community* (pp. 11–31). London: Sage.

Swales, J. M., & Luebs, M. (1995). Towards textography. In B.-L. Gunnarson and I. Backlund (Eds.) *Writing in academic contexts* (pp. 12–29). Uppsala: Unit for Advanced Studies in Modern Swedish (FUMS), Upsala University.

Swartz, D. (1997). *Culture and Power: The Sociology of Pierre Bourdieu.* Chicago, IL: Chicago University Press.

Tang, R. and Johns, S. (1999). The 'I' in identity: Exploring writer identity in student academic writing through the first person. *English for Specific Purposes, 18*, S23–S39.

Tardy, C. M. (2009). *Building Genre Knowledge.* West Lafayette, IN: Parlor Press.

Tardy, C. M. (2016). *Beyond Convention: Genre Innovation in Academic Writing.* Ann Arbor, MI: University of Michigan Press.

Tardy, C. M. (2017). Crossing, or creating divides? A plea for transdisciplinary scholarship. In B. Horner and L. Tetrault (Eds.) *Crossing Divides: Exploring Translingual Writing Pedagogies and Programs* (pp. 181–188). Logan, UT: Utah State University Press.

Taylor, C. and Hughes, C. (Eds.) (2016). *Posthuman Research Practices in Education.* Basingstoke, UK: Palgrave Macmillan.

Taylor, S. K. and Snoddon, K. (2013). Plurilingualism in TESOL: Promising controversies. *TESOL Quarterly, 47*, 3, 439–445.

Thomas, W. I. and Thomas, D. S (1928). *The Child in America: Behaviour Problems and Programs* (pp. 571–572) New York: Knopf.

Tusting, K. (2000). The new literacy studies and time: An exploration. In D. Barton, M. Hamilton, and R. Ivanic (Eds.) *Situated Literacies: Reading and Writing in Context* (pp. 35–53). London: Routledge.

Tyler, S. A. (1986). Post-modern ethnography: from document of the occult to occult document. In J. Clifford, and G. Marcus (eds.) *Writing Culture* (pp. 122–140). Berkley: University of California Press.

Unaldi, A., Seloni, L., Yalcin, S. and Yigitoglu, N. (forthcoming). The role of writing in EFL teacher preparation programs in Turkey: Institutional demands, pedagogical practices and student needs. In L. Seloni & S. Henderson-Lee *Second Language Writing Instruction in Global Contexts: English Language Teacher Preparation and Development.* Multilingual Matters.

Vandrick, S. (2009). *Interrogating Privilege: Reflections of a Second Language Educator.* Ann Arbor: University of Michigan Press.

Wacquant, J. D. (1992). Toward a social praxeology: The structure and logic of Bourdieu's sociology. In P. Bourdieu and J. D. Wacquant *An Invitation to Reflexive Sociology* (pp. 1–59). Chicago, IL: University of Chicago Press.

Wei, L. (2017). Translanguaging as a practical theory of language. *Applied Linguistics 2018, 39*, 1, 9–30.

Wheeler, R. S. (2009). "Taylor cat is black": Code-switch to add Standard English to students' linguistic repertoires. In J. C. Scott, D. Y. Straker, and L. Katz (Eds.) *Affirming students' right to their own language: Bridging language policies and pedagogical practices* (pp. 176–191). Routledge.

Williams, C. (1994). 'Arfarniad o Ddulliau Dysgu ac Addysgu yng Nghyd-destun Addysg Uwchradd Ddwyieithog, [An evaluation of teaching and learning methods in the context of bilingual secondary education]', Unpublished doctoral thesis, University of Wales, Bangor.

Williams, R. (1965/1961). *The Long Revolution*. London: Pelican.

Williams, R. (1989/1958). *Resources of Hope: Culture, Democracy, Socialism*. London: Verso.

Woolgar, S. (1988a). Reflexivity is the ethnographer of the text. In S. Woolgar (Ed.) *Knowledge and Reflexivity: New Frontiers in the Sociology of Knowledge* (pp. 14–34). London: Sage.

Woolgar, S. (1988b). *Knowledge and Reflexivity: New Frontiers in the Sociology of Knowledge*. London: Sage.

Wortham, S. (2006). *Learning Identity: The Joint Emergence of Social Identification and Academic Learning*. New York: Cambridge University Press.

Wortham, S. and Reyes, A. (2015). *Discourse Analysis Beyond the Speech Event*. London: Routledge.

INDEX

Note: The Index uses UK spelling. Page numbers in **bold** refer to Tables.

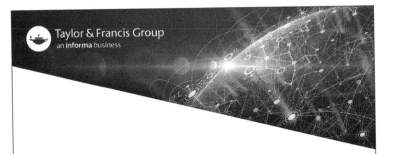

Taylor & Francis Group
an **informa** business

Taylor & Francis eBooks

www.taylorfrancis.com

A single destination for eBooks from Taylor & Francis
with increased functionality and an improved user
experience to meet the needs of our customers.

90,000+ eBooks of award-winning academic content in
Humanities, Social Science, Science, Technology, Engineering,
and Medical written by a global network of editors and authors.

TAYLOR & FRANCIS EBOOKS OFFERS:

A streamlined
experience for
our library
customers

A single point
of discovery
for all of our
eBook content

Improved
search and
discovery of
content at both
book and
chapter level

REQUEST A FREE TRIAL
support@taylorfrancis.com

 Routledge
Taylor & Francis Group

 CRC Press
Taylor & Francis Group